T5-AGO-055

811.3
Low

159219

Lowell.
Uncollected poems.

Learning Resources Center
Nazareth College of Rochester, N. Y.

Uncollected Poems of

JAMES RUSSELL LOWELL

EDITED BY THELMA M. SMITH

GREENWOOD PRESS, PUBLISHERS
WESTPORT, CONNECTICUT

DISCARDED

LEARNI...

NAZARETH COLLEGE

Library of Congress Cataloging in Publication Data

Lowell, James Russell, 1819-1891.
    Uncollected poems of James Russell Lowell.

    Reprint of the ed. published by University of
Pennsylvania Press, Philadelphia.
    Bibliography: p.
    Includes indexes.
[PS2305.A18 1976]   811'.3   76-15583
ISBN 0-8371-8852-0

Copyright 1950

UNIVERSITY OF PENNSYLVANIA PRESS

All rights reserved

Originally published in 1950 by University of Pennsylvania
Press, Philadelphia

Reprinted with the permission of Pennsylvania Press

Reprinted in 1976 by Greenwood Press,
a division of Williamhouse-Regency Inc.

Library of Congress Catalog Card Number 76-15583

ISBN 0-8371-8852-0

Printed in the United States of America

811.3
Low

TABLE OF CONTENTS

ILLUSTRATIONS

To my Mother

Preface

This volume is an annotated edition of the printed poems of James Russell Lowell not collected in the standard Elmwood edition. The poems Lowell himself rejected from his early volumes are not included; but the editor has attempted to collect all other poems, from periodicals and similar publications, for the present edition. Fred L. Pattee wrote in the Introduction to *Conversations on Some of the Old Poets* (1901): "The final edition of his works, arranged and edited by his own hand during his maturest years, contains a surprisingly small portion of his entire literary product. . . . We cannot understand a writer in any full sense of the word unless we have his complete work and can study it in chronological order. We must be able to see the forces that moulded him, . . . and what in the case of Lowell is more important, perhaps, we must estimate his influence at every step upon his contemporaries and his age." It is hoped that the present edition will contribute to such a study of Lowell.

It is a particular pleasure to acknowledge my indebtedness to my friend and preceptor Professor Sculley Bradley who first called to my attention the need for such a study and who has generously given counsel and criticism.

It is a privilege to acknowledge my obligations to Professors Arthur Hobson Quinn, Roy F. Nichols, Richard H. Shryock and William C. McDermott. Mr. Ferris Greenslet generously shared his special knowledge of the Lowell family. Professor Leon Howard, who is preparing a study of Lowell's earlier years, has given me valuable advice, and Professor Harry Hayden Clark generously permitted me to read, before publication, his Introduction to *Representative Selections from James Russell Lowell*.

I wish to thank the staff of the University of Pennsylvania library, especially the former members Mr. Eliot Morse and Mr. Charles Mish. The Harvard University library gave me access to the Lowell manuscripts, and I am indebted to Mr. Charles Jackson and Miss Carolyn E. Jakeman of the Houghton library and to Miss Bella da Costa Greene, then of the Pierpont Morgan library.

Finally I wish to express my thanks to the members of the Lowell family, particularly Dr. Francis Burnett and Mrs. Lois Cunningham.

THELMA M. SMITH

Dickinson College
February, 1950

Introduction

"When I my commentators have (who serve dead authors brave
As Turks do bodies that are sworn to stir within the grave,—
Unbury, make minced-meat of them, and bury them again),
They'll find deep meanings underneath each sputter of my pen,
Which I, a blissful shade (perhaps in teapoy pent, by process
Of these new moves in furniture, this wooden metempsychosis),
Accept for mine, unquestioning, as prudent Göthe choused
The critics out of all the thoughts they found for him in Faust."
                                                    "Our Own."

The present commentator has failed to find any very "deep meanings,"
in Lowell's sense of the word, in the sputters of his pen contained in this
edition of his uncollected verse. His deepest meanings, his best poems,
are still to be found among those selected by the poet for his collected
works. Yet many of the poems in the present edition are fraught with
ideas of real interest for the student of Lowell and the American life of
the nineteenth century.

Among the poems in this edition are several varieties of verse that
Lowell practiced consistently: the sonnet, the nature lyric and the reflec-
tive lyric, the song, the ballad, the patriotic poem, the simple narrative,
the epigram, the satiric and humorous poem, and social verse. There are,
of course, certain personal and prevailing characteristics of Lowell which
permeate all categories of this verse: his light and humorous touch, his
lambent wit, and his vigorous satire against all that challenged his great
concept of human freedom in a chaste democracy. Most pervasive is his
love for mankind and nature.

The youthful poems in this volume which represent subjective treat-
ments of personal love, like the earlier love lyrics preserved in the
Collected Edition, are excessively sentimental and often simply literary
exercises. By contrast, however, the later poems here, including several
addressed to various women whom he much admired, represent intellec-
tual love on a level of artistic integrity and sincerity. From the very
beginning, the more "intellectual" poems—epigrams, satires, humanitarian
poems on reform, the nature lyrics and the tributes to other authors—
show a characteristic excellence.

It is interesting, in reading the poems in this edition in their order of
composition, to note the rapid strengthening of the poet's art and the
emergence of his mature personality. As might be expected by the reader
familiar with Lowell, a number of these poems are sonnets. Those he
rejected from his *Collected Edition* were, in the main, wisely omitted.
But several of the earlier uncollected sonnets, such as "To Keats," "I love

those poets," and "Where are the terrors that escort King Death," have emotional veracity. The later sonnets, as "In a Volume of Sir Thomas Browne," equal many in his final collected works.

The vigorous "Hymn" ("One house, our God, we give to thee"), also the rousing patriotic lyrics, "Ye Yankees of the Bay State" and "A Rallying-Cry for New-England, against the Annexation of Texas," show the youthful Lowell at his best. "New Year's Eve, 1844" is a successful reflective lyric. The ballad "Gloomily the river floweth" is a striking imitation of the folk-ballad of the supernatural. Not so genuine are "The Mystical Ballad" and "Ballad of the Stranger," the later a folk-ballad in six-stressed couplets. Lowell's first attempts at simple narrative verse are not very satisfactory. Understandably, the story of *"Homer's neu Helden-gedicht,"* the first of his published poems, is merely told with clumsy undergraduate attempts at humor. Later tales are somewhat better, such as "The Poet and Apollo" or "The Burial of Theobald," a Keatsian romance. There is no narrative in this volume, however, to compare with "The Vision of Sir Launfal"; and indeed Lowell never excelled in the romantic narrative or descriptive poem.

From the beginning, as has been said, those poems were his best which afforded scope for his powerful intellect. His addresses to women in his mature life have already been mentioned. Allied in spirit is "Agatha," which, though hardly a love poem, catches with fine discrimination the admirable qualities in an older woman friend. The parody, "Verses" ("O, share these flowers"), is a good imitation of the eighteenth-century formal love lyric. The translation from Voltaire, "To Madame du Chatelet," presents, with propriety, the high comedy of love in old age. These two poems suggest that Lowell might well have lent his talents more frequently to the writing of social verse. Even the frankly didactic was often made entertaining by the luminous mind of its author, as in the case of *The Power of Sound,* an extraordinary rhymed lecture. The present collection also contains a number of brilliant epigrams—"Reform," "An Epigram on Certain Conservatives," "His greatness not so much in genius lies," and "Voltaire," who was willing to "scoff at God for an antithesis."

Lowell's humor was not restricted to his social verse and epigrams. The best poems in this volume manifest the wit and corrective humor which so deeply marked Lowell as a man. It was so persistent a characteristic that his friends observed it even during his periods of deep sorrow, as after the death of his wife, Maria White. The poet consciously employed wit and humor* both for artistic effects and as a weapon. In a review of Browning he wrote, "Wit makes other men laugh, and that only once. It may be repeated indefinitely to new audiences and produce the same

* See his "Humor, Wit, Fun, and Satire," *Century,* XXV, n. s. (November, 1893), 125.

result. Humor makes the humorist himself laugh. He is part of his humor, and it can never be repeated without loss."*

From the awkward undergraduate humor of "To Mount Washington" to the great humor in *The Biglow Papers* less than a decade later is an incredible advance, but the poet accomplished it in long, rapid strides, as a chronological examination of the poems in this volume will show. Indeed, even in undergraduate days he was capable of happy effects of humor from time to time, as in the "Skillygoliana" of the present collection. The poet frequently devoted his humorous talent to sheer amusement, as in the vernacular ballad "Without and Within" of the present volume, a companion piece to a poem of the same name in the *Collected Edition.* Many of the poems written in letters to friends are also good examples of this talent. (See "Poseidon Fields," p. 154.) In the same spirit he wrote the children's poems in this volume: "Lady Bird" and "Hob Gobbling's Song." This humorous gift, however, was to reach its greatest usefulness in Lowell's satires on the political corruptions of his time, and in his poems on humanitarian reforms, especially abolition. Such poems are by all standards the finest work represented in this text and will be more fully treated in a later passage.

First there are a number of questions of a more general nature which should be considered. It is pertinent to inquire whether Lowell's failure to include these poems in his collected works has any critical significance. It seems clear that Lowell did not neglect these poems for solely aesthetic reasons. Many of the poems dropped from successive volumes of his poems were rejected obviously because of their insufficient merit, but these periodical poems were not necessarily subjected to such scrutiny. A number of them are diffuse or sentimental, as has been pointed out, but many of them are excellent. Sometimes it is demonstrable that Lowell, in the pressure of a busy life, simply forgot a magazine poem and lost track of it. Certain of the earlier poems in this collection may have been discarded because the poet recognized their indebtedness to other poets— particularly Keats, Wordsworth, Burns, Emerson, Poe, and Tennyson. Other poems deal with subjects resembling those of poems retained in the *Collected Edition.* "Without and Within, II: The Restaurant" closely parallels the situation of "Without and Within" in the *Collected Edition;* similarly, "Indoors and Out" resembles "Forlorn." A number of poems written in the heat of political controversy were so vitriolic that the poet may well have hesitated to give them the authority of collected poems at any time during his life. His anonymous satire upon Jim Fisk, for example, tempted him a great deal, and he was about to put it into his volume, when he was warned by his lawyer that its publication might make him subject to legal action. Regretfully he laid it aside, with the remark, "It

* Horace E. Scudder, *James Russell Lowell* (Boston, 1901), I, 29.

will keep."° For many reasons, therefore, it is not to be supposed that any given poem was regarded by Lowell as inferior only because he did not collect it.

The poems in this volume represent a cross-section of Lowell's career from 1837 to 1891. The bulk of this work, like the larger volume of his poetry in general, was published before the Civil War. Poems were published in a number of magazines, newspapers, and gift books or annuals, whose variety suggests the range of Lowell's popularity and literary associations. The earliest of these magazines was *Harvardiana,* the college literary magazine whose life at Harvard exactly corresponds to the four years of Lowell's residence as an undergraduate there. He was one of the five editors in 1837-38, during which his first sixteen poems and his earliest prose appeared in the magazine, to which, by definition of his editorial functions, he was supposed to furnish poetry and general entertainment. Rufus King, later a prominent Ohio attorney, and Walter Lippit were to furnish the long serious articles; Charles W. Scates, another lifelong friend of Lowell, was designated official literary critic; while Nathan Hale, Jr. could be presumed to have inherited editorial ability and to be useful in all capacities.† The five editors contributed more than half the contents of the magazine and bore all the financial risk.

Many other magazines are represented in the publication of subsequent poems in this volume. One appeared in 1840 in the *Southern Literary Messenger* over the pseudonym "Hugh Perceval." In 1841 and 1842, the *Dial,* organ of the Transcendentalists, printed three, and *Arcturus* published four in 1842. In the same year Nathan Hale, Jr., Lowell's college friend of the *Harvardiana* days, inaugurated *The Boston Miscellany of Literature and Fashion,* which ran only a year, and printed seven of these uncollected poems. In 1843 Lowell founded his own magazine, *The Pioneer,* in collaboration with Robert Carter. This promising venture survived for only three months, partly because Lowell became ill, but eight of the poems in this volume have been recovered from its pages. Lowell had begun to contribute to *Graham's Magazine* early in his career, and by 1844 he could boast that Graham was paying him $30 for each poem. Ten of the poems in the present volume appeared in *Graham's* between 1841 and 1850. In 1844 and 1845 he contributed one of this group of poems to *The Present,* one to the *American Review,* and two to the *Broadway Journal.* In 1849 one appeared in *Holden's Dollar Magazine.* *Putnam's Monthly* published four of these poems from 1853 to 1855. In 1857, when the *Atlantic Monthly* was founded, Lowell became

---

° See Note on "An Epitaph," pp. 270-71.
† Edward Everett Hale, *James Russell Lowell and His Friends* (Boston, 1899), pp. 25-30.

its first editor. To its pages he contributed a succession of poems, nine of which, published over the half-century from 1858 to 1907, have never before been collected, and appear in the present edition. Apparently the only magazine edited by Lowell to which he did not contribute a good bit of his own verse was the *North American Review*. After the Civil War he became a frequent contributor to the *Nation,* and ten of the uncollected poems in the present volume are from its files from 1866 to 1890.

In the early period particularly, Lowell published a number of these poems over a series of pen-names: "Hugh Perceval," "H. Perceval," "Hugh Peters," "H. P.," and "F. De T." An appreciable number are entirely anonymous, especially the more vehement political satires.

As was suggested, a few of the poems in this volume were found either in newspapers, annuals, or gift books. More of them appeared in the *National Anti-Slavery Standard* than in any other newspaper—eight in the decade from 1841 to 1851. This was to be expected, since during part of this time Lowell was retained by the *Standard* as a regular contributor and a member of the staff. The *Boston Morning Post,* the *Boston Courier,* and the *New York Ledger* each printed one of the poems of this collection. *The Token* for 1842 contained "The Ballad of the Stranger," Lowell's first contribution to an annual or a gift book. Two other annuals are represented in this collection, *The Liberty Bell* and *Victoria Regia.*

It was pointed out earlier in this discussion that Lowell's witty and satiric poems, in which he fought the battle of "good against evil in the life of his times," constitute the best work in the present collection. One is reminded of an early conception of the poet's function which Lowell expressed in "L'Envoi."

> But, if the poet's duty be to tell
> His fellow-men their beauty and their strength,
> And show them the deep meaning of their souls,
> He also is ordained to higher things;
> He must reflect his race's struggling heart,
> And shape the crude conceptions of his age.*

He understood that poetry could mirror the life of the time, and more than that, it could be a vital force in elevating the moral spirit of mankind. Lowell's own poetry exerted an enormous influence upon his age. His writings show him molding political thought and quickening the social conscience of America. Lowell's weapons—humor and biting satire —carried his message. (It should not be thought that this role of the poet was one entirely settled with Lowell—see, for example, "The Poet" and "Flowers" in *A Year's Life.*—As in his account of himself in *A Fable*

* *Poems* (1844), pp. 273-74.

for Critics, the conflict between the goals of social reform and aesthetics remained with him.)

Lowell's first published reaction to public affairs occurred in college days when, in the amusing "Skillygoliana, No. III," he asks:

> Has Texas, freed by Samuel the great,
> Entered the Union as another state?
> No, still she trades in slaves as free as air,
> And Sam still fills the Presidential chair,
> Rules o'er the realm, the freeman's proudest hope,
> In dread of naught but bailiffs and a rope.

A year later the vigorous challenge to "Ye Yankees of the Bay State" makes clear the poet's own strong feelings that Massachusetts, cradle of liberty, should brook no infringement of American rights by red-coated British in 1839 any more than she did in 1776. Again in "A Rallying-Cry for New-England, against the Annexation of Texas," and in "Another Rallying Cry," patriotic fervor is clear and true, and the poet pleads with his fellow citizens to arm and, if need be, to fight, against what to him is clearly a moral wrong.

In a letter to Edmund Quincy, Feb. 25, 1854, Lowell makes evident his belief that all citizens interested in the welfare of their country should speak out against political wrong-doing. He tells Quincy he hopes to find time to do a letter from Mr. Sawin on the Kansas-Nebraska difficulties.

> I do long to have my shot, too, at those Nebraska swindlers. I think every man who feels like a gentleman ought to speak out, nay, every man who hasn't passed his Master's degree in blackguardism. Was there ever anything so dirty? Texas is as white as an angel to it, and Tyler a Hyperion to Pierce. Wasn't it good that Sam Houston should speak against this bill? The prince of darkness is a gentleman and can't stand *that.**

Continually in the poems in this edition, as in the *Biglow Papers* and in the vigorous political essays which poured forth from his pen, we find opinions on the political issues of the day. "A Worthy Ditty" is a clear picture of Lowell's disgust at the Reconstruction disorders in the South. He was pleading at the same time in the *North American Review* for legislation which would bring the Southern states back to a just pride in the Union and would utilize the best qualities of the South. Throughout Charles Sumner's long career as a senator from Massachusetts, Lowell showed a wise comprehension of the duties of a citizen to his elected representative, and there are a number of letters preserved in the Harvard library from Lowell to Sumner, generally praising him for support of a policy with which Lowell agreed, but occasionally suggesting possible action or firmly indicating dissent.

---

* M. A. DeWolfe Howe, ed., *New Letters of James Russell Lowell* (New York, 1932), p. 47.

The election of 1876 marks the culmination of Lowell's interest in politics. He recognized the low position to which the national conscience had sunk during the Grant administration; and with vitriolic pen he wrote "An Epitaph," "The World's Fair, 1876," "A Dialogue," and "Campaign Epigrams," all to be found in the present volume. Godkin, editor of the *Nation*, and a friend of Lowell, had been attracting favorable attention from those political leaders who recognized the dangers of corrupt government. Lowell wrote frequently to Godkin expressing his appreciation of the good fight, often suggesting editorials.* As far back as 1871 (December 20) he had written: "Give Schenck another shot. Also say something on the queer notion of the Republican Party that they can get along without their brains. 'Time was that when the brains were out the man would *die*' but *nous avons changé tout cela.*" Godkin printed in the *Nation* the poems just named, which were bitterly satiric in their denunciation of "boss rule." These poems concerning the Hayes-Tilden election of 1876 are the more interesting because they mark a turning point in Lowell's public life. He was extremely active in politics at this time. He was a delegate to the Republican convention which nominated Hayes and made speeches supporting his campaign. Yet he had the courage, as these poems show, to oppose local Massachusetts Republicans whose dishonor had reflected discredit upon the party— men like General Butler, who was implicated in the scandalous "Sanborn contracts." Lowell was appointed an elector and cast his vote for Hayes. Hayes had been an admirer of the *Biglow Papers,* but the assistance of Lowell in the election must have been a potent factor in deciding the President to recommend him for the post of Minister to Spain in 1877. It seems evident that no record of American history from 1840 to 1890 can represent accurately the current of political opinion and events without considering the unassuming but steady and really powerful influence which Lowell wielded.

Lowell was interested not only in national politics, but according to the testimony of a Cambridge politician, Frank L. Chapman, he was willing to devote time and thought to local political issues. "I have often seen Mr. Lowell at the caucus," said Chapman when interviewed by a reporter from the *Cambridge Tribune* in February, 1892.† "He was quite regular in attending the republican caucus before the mugwump movement set in, and he was quite interested in the proceedings, though he never put himself forward at all. I remember once when he wanted some particular thing done, and instead of making the necessary motion himself he got me to offer it. . . . Before he went abroad the last time he generally showed an interest in all local matters of a political nature.

* MS correspondence, Harvard library.
† "Mr. Lowell in Politics," *Cambridge Tribune,* February 20, 1892, p. 1.

He was more frequently seen in the local political meetings than others of the scholarly class, and probably was better posted on the current of sentiment than they could possibly be."

Lowell was a Whig, an Abolitionist, a Republican, and a Democrat as each of these groups moved forward toward a goal which seemed to him good. Never did he support any party simply as a partisan. Lowell's friend Charles Briggs characterized him, said Curtis, as a natural politician but one "like Milton—a man . . . with an instinctive grasp of the higher politics, of the duties and relations of the citizen to his country, and of those moral principles . . . essential to the welfare of States."*

As has been indicated, the true poet, in Lowell's estimation, was he who invoked the aid of the Muse in the cause of oppression and suffering. And to this ideal Lowell remained true from the early college verse with its thrust at Texas and Sam Houston's "trading in slaves" (February, 1838); from his interest in and sympathy for the neglected American Indian, which runs through all the college verse and is very marked in the *Class Poem;* to the mature reflection in the "Postscript, 1887" to "An Epistle to George William Curtis," which shows the poet picking up again after long silence the reed of the Muse—

> And, as its stops my curious touch retries,
> The stir of earlier instincts I surprise,—
> Instincts, if less imperious, yet more strong,
> And happy in the toil that ends with song.

The early poems, both in this volume and in the *Collected Edition,* are full of a generalized humanitarian impulse which came to Lowell from the very New England air he breathed. His youth was the period of desire to free all men from bonds—bonds of actual slavery, bonds of degrading poverty, bonds of ignorance, bonds of a political forging. "Thank God," wrote Lowell,

> That I have sorrows now to make me ken
> My strength and weakness, and my right to be
> Brother to those, the outcast and the poor,
> Driven back to darkness from the world's proud door!†

He believed in the destiny of America and in the ultimate triumph of democracy as a way of life which would remove those bonds and give freedom to the individual man. Even in his youth Lowell was aware of the failures of America, and wrote concerning them. His later satires—"The World's Fair" and "Tempora Mutantur"—which gave rise to so much criticism of Lowell as a traitor to the fundamental belief in

---

* George W. Curtis, *James Russell Lowell* (New York, 1892), p. 20.
† See Sonnet XXXV, *Poems* (1844), p. 265. Also "Fourth of July Ode," *A Year's Life,* pp. 138-39.

democracy, show no more clear awareness of evils than the indictment
written thirty years earlier in the portion of "A Chippewa Legend" which
he rejected from his *Collected Edition.* "And thou, my country," the poet
wrote:

> To whom God granted it in charge to be
> Freedom's apostle to a trampled world, . . .
> Art little better than a sneer and mock,
> And tyrants smile to see thee holding up
> Freedom's broad Aegis o'er three million slaves!*

But just as in later life Lowell's criticism of America as "the land of
Broken Promises" was not a rejection of his belief in democracy and
the democratic way of life, so his faith shines clear in the last passage
of the quoted poem which addresses America:

> Thou yet shalt do thy holy errand; yet,
> That little Mayflower, convoyed by the winds
> And the rude waters to our rocky shore,
> Shall scatter Freedom's seed throughout the world,
> And all the nations of the earth shall come,
> Singing, to share the harvest-home of Truth.†

Although Lowell had not thrown in his lot with the abolitionists when
he wrote his *Class Poem* in the spring and summer of 1838, even in that
will be found a keen sense of man's duty to those less fortunate than he.
The abolitionists are playfully accused of talking too much and doing
too little. But Lowell was already beginning to throw off the conservatism
of the Harvard youth. His notebook for 1838-39 is full of passages about
slavery. In November of 1838 he wrote to his friend George B. Loring,
"I am fast becoming ultra-democratic. . . . The abolitionists are the only
ones with whom I sympathize of the present extant parties."‡ By the
autumn of 1840 Lowell was a wholehearted abolitionist. Probably about
that time he wrote on the cover of his *Class Poem:*

> Behold the baby-arrows of that wit
> Wherewith I dared assail the woundless Truth:
> Love has refilled the quiver and with it
> The man may win forgiveness for the youth:—
> And yet from whom? for well, ere this, I know
> That Truth hath no resentments: she returns
> A kiss in full atonement for the blow:
> Let who hath felt it say how deep it burns.§

---

* *Poems* (1844), p. 225.
† *Ibid.,* p. 227.
‡ Ferris Greenslet, *James Russell Lowell* (Boston, 1905), p. 32.
§ MS in the possession of Mrs. Stanley Cunningham. This is a copy on a single
sheet, in ink, with a pencil annotation, probably added later: "Written in 1840 on
a copy of my Class Poem."

By 1842 Lowell was not only an ardent convert to the cause of abolition, but he wrote in the sonnet "Thou art a woman" his support of feminism and his desire that women too should do their part "For Him and for his blessed cause of Truth." Strong evidence of Lowell's position concerning the evils of slavery is given in "A Rallying-Cry for New-England, against the Annexation of Texas." A year later, in 1845, for the *Liberty Bell*, the poet wrote "The Happy Martyrdom," a vigorous satire against the church for supporting institutions rather than the fundamental good. He accuses the church of supporting slavery, of using the Bible "To keep thy light from bursting in," of brooking with patience "For the rich sinner's sake, the sin." "King Retro," written in 1849, is a neat summary and satire of the arguments being used at that time by the South for the extension of slavery and for a new fugitive slave law. "King Backward" probably refers to "King Cotton" as a symbol of the South and implies quite obviously that the South was not willing to recognize that slavery had been made an anachronism by industrial improvements. There are several other good examples in this volume of Lowell's crusading verse; for example, the satire on the compromises of the North, "The Northern Sancho Panza and His Vicarious Cork Tree," and the satire on Webster, "A Dream I Had."

Although in the ardor of youth Lowell had twice in this volume seemed to advocate force, once against England in the poem "Ye Yankees of the Bay State" and once against the South in "A Rallying-Cry," he early recognized the futility of war and the truth that "Force never yet gained one true victory." His satiric poem "An Extract," written in 1848 at the close of the Mexican War, challenges all thoughtful men. What has been gained? Death and destruction, sorrow and weeping—those are the harvest of "men turned murderers." And for the country, what has been won? Lowell answers, only "A kindred people's everlasting hate" and "The bloody drain of untamed provinces."*

Lowell, as has been indicated, was not content with preaching freedom for the slaves in America; he was keenly interested also in the progress of mankind toward a better life everywhere. The previously collected writings show this, of course, more clearly than the poems which appear in this volume. However, even here we find a poem addressed to the memory of the Italian patriots, showing his sympathy with their struggle against Austrian oppression. In a letter written to Loring, August 30, 1837, the summer before his senior year at Harvard, he described a letter from his sister, who was with his parents in Ireland. The travelers had been exploring an Irish lake, and the boatman "smashed a bottle of Mountain Dew . . . on a little island and named it after her as an American lady. . . . Such is this degraded and oppressed

_____
* Cf. *Biglow Papers.* "God'll send the bill to you."

people's love for the land of so called freedom! My sister very sensibly remarks that the philanthropists of England, instead of meddling with the slavery of this country . . . would be much more profitably employed in endeavoring to ameliorate the condition of poor, starving Ireland, where the Bakers' carts are driving . . . under the protection of strong guard to keep them being robbed in ye streets."* A year later to the same friend Lowell wrote of the Manchester riots: "It almost brings tears to my eyes when I think of this vast multitude starved, trampled upon, meeting to petition the government which oppressed them, and which they supported by taxes wrung out of the very children's life blood." The bitterly satiric poem in this volume, "Merry England," published in 1841, shows the poet's specific knowledge of the evils countenanced by England. (See Notes p. 250.) Again in the rejected half of "A Chippewa Legend," Lowell warns England to rescue her starving multitudes:

> Hear it, O England! thou who liest asleep
> On a volcano, from whose pent-up wrath,
> Already some red flashes, bursting up,
> Glare bloodily on coronet and crown
> And gray cathedral looming huge aloof,
> With dreadful portent of o'erhanging doom!
> Thou Dives among nations! from whose board,
> After the dogs are fed, poor Lazarus,
> Crooked and worn with toil, and hollow-eyed,
> Begs a few crumbs in vain!†

In addition to many references to much-needed reform abroad as well as in America, Lowell makes frequent comments on current events of a non-political nature, on progress in mechanical invention, and on such things as the fads which Americans seem so much to enjoy. In the college verses there are allusions to football, to the joys of tobacco (this Lowell writes of through all his life), to the delights of fried oysters and rosy wine, to the newly built railroad, and to the monument on Bunker Hill, half finished for lack of funds. The long poem "Our Own" contains many such amusing allusions, a few whimsical lines on the current wave of enthusiasm for everything from the Near East, some pungent comments on the Fourierites and Brook Farm (see Notes p. 259), a rollicking description of the tortures suffered by passengers in a railway coach, a number of lines of cogent satire on "humbug" of various kinds, particularly the interest in spirits, mediums, table-tipping, and the like, a very amusing passage on the Yankee's proclivity for earning money in an amazing number of ways, and many other similar references to life

* Harvard library. See also the *Class Poem* and "Epigram on J. M." in this volume.

† *Poems* (1844), p. 223.

in America. Lowell's entertaining rhymed lecture *The Power of Sound* also contains contemporary references—for example, the death of the French poet Béranger—and comments on the songs Americans were singing. One final example can be given in the poem "The Trustee's Lament," which is a half-amused account of the controversy over the Albany Observatory (see Notes p. 265). This observatory, built by popular subscription, was controlled by a council who wished to devote it solely to scientific purposes; but the general public, who had endowed it, wished to employ it for the popular amusement of star-gazing.

Critics of Lowell have frequently remarked that his innate power as a poet of nature was in conflict with his overwhelming humanitarian concern for the correction of abuses in democratic society, which expressed itself through the medium of his great satiric power. Whoever regards the nature poet as the nobler phenomenon, as Norman Foerster did,[*] will deplore Lowell's thralldom to "the paralyzing effect of the spirit of the times. He suffered a confusion of mind and heart from which he never extricated himself; although he changed, he failed to reach at any period of his life self-mastery, that concentration of his powers that alone could lend impact to his fine qualities." To the present writer it is enough that Lowell achieved poetic self-mastery as a critic of society. Nevertheless, a perusal of this volume quite as clearly as the *Collected Edition* shows the effects of this conflict in Lowell's youth and the emerging supremacy of the satirist over the lyrist of nature. Yet in his earlier as in his later work, his all-pervading sense of the beauty and authority of nature is not confined to individual poems, but acts as a leavening influence throughout the whole of his work, breaking out sporadically in the least expected places, as in the early satire, "Ye Yankees of the Bay State."

Individual poems wholly or chiefly inspired by nature occur, particularly in the earlier period, among the poems in this volume. They show how greatly he was influenced by Burns, by Wordsworth, by Keats, and, in the very beginning, by Emerson. One of the best of these nature poems is "Out of Doors," which, as Killis Campbell remarks,[†] is clearly Emersonian. Another early nature poem, "When in a book I find," contrasts the intuitional discovery of nature and life with that derived from books—an idea which came possibly from Emerson, and certainly from the transcendentalists—and the poem was published, appropriately enough, in the *Dial* in 1842.

Lowell's delight in the grandeur of American landscape furnished a field for his use of nature as a theme in many of these poems, and the beauty of the American scene is a background even for his satiric poems.

[*] *Nature in American Literature* (New York, 1923), pp. 157-58.
[†] *PMLA*, XXXVIII, no. 4 (December, 1923), p. 935.

Closely allied with this impulse in his youth was his awareness of the American Indian and his legends. One of the college poems in this collection, "To Mount Washington," is not truly a nature poem, since the landscape is used in connection with burlesque elements, but the characterization of the mountain as a bald-headed old Indian has its point. More serious use of Indian materials and references are frequently to be found, especially in "Saratoga Lake," the *Class Poem*, and "A Chippewa Legend."

Interesting information concerning a number of Lowell's friendships can be gleaned from poems in this volume and their annotations. One is the "Song" ("A pair of black eyes") which was written first in a letter to Loring and then, because Lowell liked it so much, was used as a contribution to *Harvardiana*. It was when Lowell was rusticating at Concord, during the spring and summer months of his senior year, that he met Caroline Brooks, then engaged to be married to Ebenezer R. Hoar, Lowell's friend. Lowell himself had fallen in love the summer before with Hannah Jackson. This unhappy affair affected deeply his emotional life until after he had met and learned to love Maria White. Perhaps Lowell's youthful enthusiasm in the letter to Loring enclosing his "Song" (August 9, 1838) can be understood partly as compensation for the feeling for Hannah Jackson which was still very real to him. At any rate he wrote the poem and commented to Loring: "Hoar is a pretty good sort of a fellow. He is engaged to the only girl I like in the whole place Miss Caroline Brooks. I think I could fall in love with her. . . . Hoar is a lucky man and Miss B. is the sweetest girl! She has very remarkable black eyes."

George Bailey Loring and Lowell were friends from childhood, an hereditary friendship, since Loring was the son of a clergyman at Andover who was an intimate friend of Dr. Lowell. The friendship ripened at Harvard. The correspondence between the two during vacations and subsequently, while Lowell was studying law and Loring studying medicine, sheds important light on the formative years of the young poet. Since both young men were keenly interested in literature, Lowell sent much of his early verse to Loring for criticism. Loring himself occasionally tried his hand at a poem, and one of Lowell's letters welcomes him in verse to "Muses land."

Another college friend to whom Lowell sent some of his poems was Charles Woodman Scates, one of the editors of *Harvardiana*. After graduation from Harvard, Scates went to South Carolina to study law. Unfortunately most of Lowell's letters to Scates were burned, although not until after Charles Eliot Norton had used numerous excerpts from them in the *Letters*.

Another early friendship of the young Lowell and his wife, Maria

White, strengthened the poet's humanitarian impulses and is reflected in this volume. It was that with Edward M. Davis and his family of Philadelphia. (See Notes p. 254.) Maria White was physically unable to stand the bitter New England winters, and before her marriage she had spent the winter with her mother in Philadelphia in the home of the Parkers, a family of Quakers. After their marriage on December 26, 1844, Lowell and Maria White journeyed to Philadelphia. They arrived on the first day of the new year. The Parkers and the Davises, influential members of the Society of Friends, introduced the Lowells to others who were working for the common cause of anti-slavery and reform.

Of the four children born to Maria and James Russell Lowell, Mabel, the second, was the only one to live past childhood. It was for this child, who was not yet two years old, that Lowell composed the amusing lines of "Lady Bird." During Mabel's babyhood Lowell generally called her by the nickname "Mab." In writing the poem Lowell may also have had another child in mind. The Briggs family and the Lowell family were close friends, visiting one another as often as possible, and there was a small daughter in the Briggs household who would surely have enjoyed the verses. "Hob Gobbling's Song," another child's verse in this collection, was written, as Lowell asserted, for his four nephews.

In the long poem "Our Own" Lowell makes humorous reference to "Harry Franco," the pen name used by Charles F. Briggs. Briggs's first novel, which was partly autobiographical, bore the title *The Adventures of Harry Franco* (1839). A later work, *The Trippings of Tom Pepper* (2 vols., 1847-50) has the sub-title "The Results of Romancing. An Autobiography by Harry Franco." The other editor of *Putnam's* when that magazine published "Our Own" was George William Curtis, whose nickname, "Howadji," which Lowell also employed in his poem, had been assumed as a pseudonym for the amusing impressions of his travels in the Near East as correspondent for the New York *Tribune*. (See Notes p. 259.)

As early as 1843, in his short-lived magazine *The Pioneer*, Lowell recorded his opinion of William Lloyd Garrison, "the half-inspired Luther of this reform, a man too remarkable to be appreciated in his generation, but whom the future will recognize as a great and wonderful spirit."* Five years later an article by Harrison G. Otis, attacking Garrison (see Notes p. 255), inspired two fine poems by Lowell. One, "To W. L. Garrison," in the *Collected Edition*, is a lofty acknowledgment of Garrison's magnificent leadership against the forces of slavery. The other, "The Ex-Mayor's Crumbs of Consolation," is a keen satiric attack on Otis, containing lines which show Lowell's appreciation of what had been accom-

* *Pioneer*, I, no. 2 (February, 1843), p. 92.

plished by "one man and a boy in a garret," as Otis disparagingly recalled Garrison's origins as a pamphleteer in the cause of reform.

The biographers have made a point of Lowell's wide reading of the literature of the past, beginning perhaps with Spenser's *Faerie Queene*, which was frequently read to him as a child. The poems in this collection are remarkable for the richness of their allusion to English and continental literature and to the classics. It is of course natural to find Lowell's college reading primarily among the great English writers. Shakespeare, Milton, Sheridan, Wordsworth, Keats, Coleridge, Shelley, Byron, Dickens, Carlyle, and many others are mentioned in Lowell's early letters and poems, particularly the *Class Poem*. Lowell's knowledge of *Sartor Resartus* is clear in the first of the college verses, a burlesque account of a "new poem of Homer" supposedly discovered by the great Teufelsdröckh. From the evidence in this volume, however, it can be seen that contemporary American figures were also read by Harvard students, although necessarily on their own initiative. The reference to N. P. Willis in "Saratoga Lake" is particularly interesting. In the ten years from Lowell's graduation to the publication of *A Fable for Critics* it is obvious that he read with sure understanding contemporary American writers.

The evidence of this volume shows how thoroughly Lowell read and admired Burns. An amusing invitation to W. H. Shackford, soliciting his subscription to *Harvardiana* and beginning "Dear Shack, a circular I send ye" (see Notes p. 278), is in imitation of the style of Burns; and the next month, September 1837, Lowell published in the college magazine "In Imitation of Burns," a poem written in the stanza of "To a Mouse." The introductory quotation to "Song" ("A pair of black eyes") is from Burns, and again there is the strong influence of the Scottish poet in the stanzas. One recalls, of course, the evidence of Burns's influence in a number of the poems in the *Collected Edition*, such as "An Incident in a Railroad Car" and "At the Burns Centennial." There are lines describing and commenting on Burns in the *Class Poem* and *The Power of Sound*. A random jotting in one of Lowell's notebooks (Harvard library) reads: "Burns scooped up the stream life in his bare hands where it gushed from the rock fresh and foamy."

Lowell's early love for Tennyson is shown in the copies he made for himself and for his sister of Tennyson's 1833 volume. In a letter to Evert A. Duyckinck, December 5, 1841,* Lowell begs him not to reprint Tennyson because the English poet is about to publish a new and correct edition of his poems, and an earlier American edition would deprive Tennyson of any profit in this country. In the same letter Lowell wrote: "Your notice of Keats . . . a poet whom I especially love and whom I consider to be one of the true old Titan brood—made me wish to see

* New York Public Library, Duyckinck Collection.

two of my own sonnets enshrined in the same volume." The sonnets were "Sunset and Moonshine" (in this edition) and "To the Spirit of Keats," which the poet preserved in his *Collected Edition*. Less than a month later, Lowell's "Sonnet—To Keats," which is in this text, appeared in the *Boston Miscellany of Literature*.

In "Extracts from a 'Hasty Pudding Poem'" the line, "Light Somnus greets one with Pickwickian smile," suggests that Lowell, while in college, was reading *Pickwick Papers* as it appeared in monthly installments. His continued admiration for Dickens led him years afterward to write the sonnet "Charles Dickens" in defense of the English novelist just after his death, when his reputation was being subjected to savage attack on personal as well as critical grounds.

The reader will also find in this volume two sonnets addressed to Wordsworth. Just as his sonnets to Keats show fine critical understanding of the poet, so in writing of Wordsworth, Lowell was able to catch the essence of the "Poet of the lofty brow! far-sighted seer!" Significantly it was the combination of nature with reflectiveness in Wordsworth that Lowell praised. A comparison of these sonnets with those to Wordsworth in Lowell's *Collected Edition* affords an interesting example of his critical discrimination and fair-mindedness. The six sonnets "On Reading Wordsworth's Sonnets in Defense of Capital Punishment" were printed in May 1842. Lowell, who disapproved of capital punishment, did not hesitate to show his dismay at the stand Wordsworth took. The young poet wrote: "And always 'tis the saddest sight to see/ An old man faithless in Humanity." Yet the following March appeared the two sonnets in this text defending and praising the English poet. Obviously Lowell was able to disagree on one issue but retain his admiration for the man as a whole.

Also in this volume will be found a sensitive tribute in verse to Shakespeare, and a fine eight-line poem, "Inscription for a Memorial Bust of Fielding," which magnificently sums up the novelist: "Who loves a Man may see his image here." The sonnet "In a Volume of Sir Thomas Browne" is good literary criticism also, showing appreciation for the epithetic sensitiveness and beautiful cadence of Browne's prose.

Lowell's constant references to subjects of classical mythology and his use of Latin and Greek quotations and phrases are illustrated in this volume, as would be expected. His knowledge of classical authors is not merely superficial. "He knows Vergil and Homer best of all, but Horace, Juvenal, Martial, Cicero are evidently old friends. . . . To be as clever at the expense of the classics as Lowell was requires a thorough classical training."* In this text the poem "Orpheus" is a retelling of the classical

* Edmund G. Berry, "Lowell and the Classics," *Classical Weekly*, XXXVIII, no. 2 (October 9, 1944), pp. 11-12.

story, just as are "Prometheus" and "The Shepherd of King Admetus" in the *Collected Edition*. In his use of the classics, as in his reference to later literature, Lowell was seldom the mere imitator, if we except his juvenilia. He had a way of absorbing what he read and transmuting it to his own tongue, and his critical acumen frequently transformed his use of literary allusion into a new act of creation. As early as 1842 he wrote, in a sonnet in this volume,

> If some small savor creep into my rhyme
> Of the old poets . . .
> It is not pride, God knows, but reverence.

An effort has been made to confine this introduction to comments on the poems in this text. It has been seen that they bear relationships to many aspects of Lowell's life and career and to the poems which he gathered together in the *Collected Edition*. It is perhaps fitting to conclude with an epitaph which Lowell wrote in 1845:

> Here lies that part of J. R. L.
> Which hampered him from doing well;
> Here lies that film of muddy clay
> Which kept the sight of Heaven away:
> If now his faults thou canst not brook,
> Into his heart a moment look;
> If still to judge him thou incline,
> O, Unforgiving, look in thine!

Note on the Text

This volume contains two kinds of notation. The footnotes at the bottom of the text page show Lowell's occasional notes and all variant readings, including those found in manuscripts, with the exception of unimportant variations in punctuation and spelling. The notes at the end of the volume give the location of manuscript sources, where available, together with the place and date of publication for each poem, and other relevant data. The poems, except the juvenilia placed at the end of the volume, are arranged chronologically by date of composition, when known, otherwise by date of printing.

TEXT OF THE POEMS

"These verses once seemed lava hot,
Or molten gold or God knows what;
Now, stiffened in the mould of print,
If fire there be, 'tis that of flint;
Therefore, good reader, steel thy brain;
To strike with lead were all in vain."

Lowell MS.

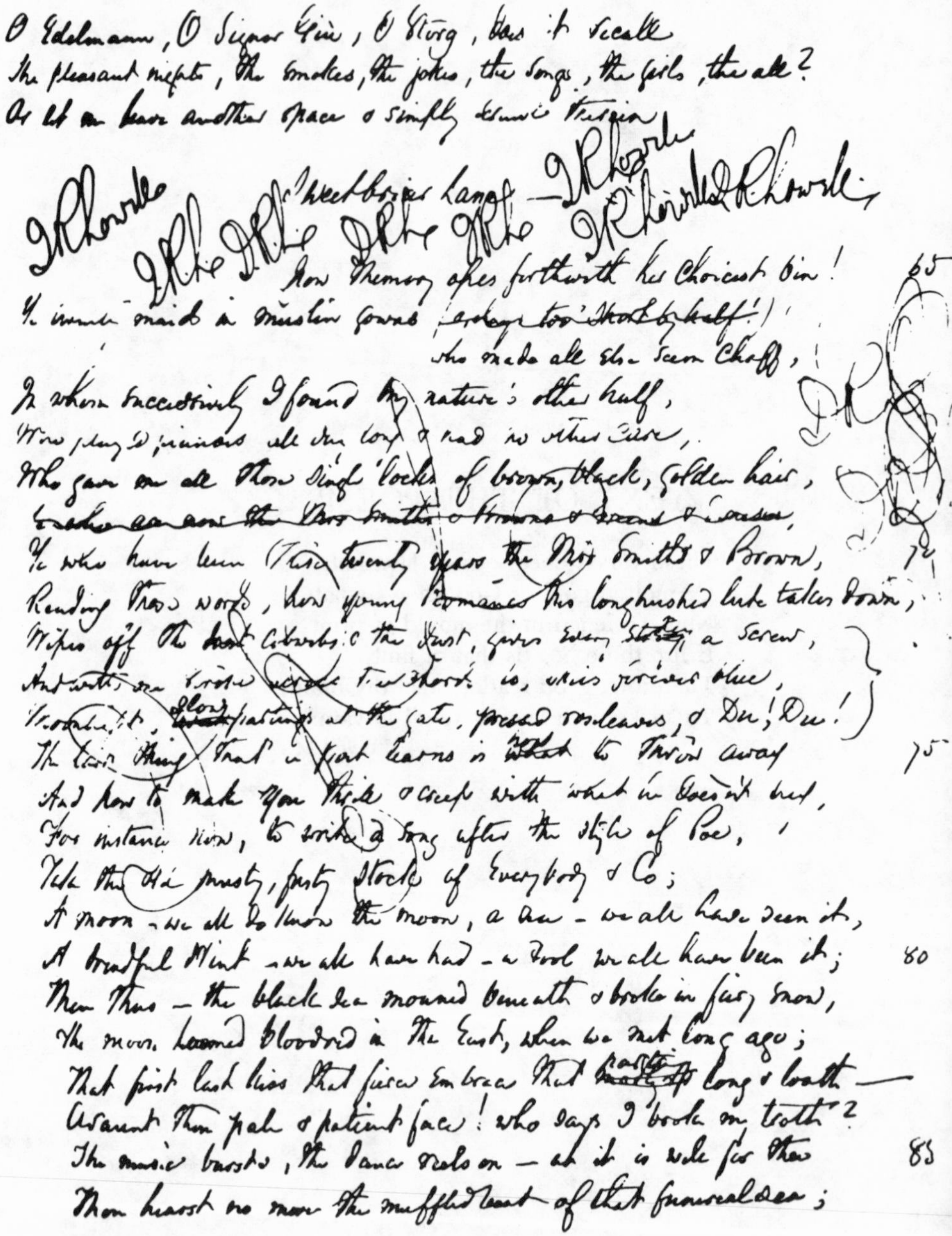

O Edelmann, O Signor Giu, O Storg, hast it recall
The pleasant nights, the smokes, the jokes, the songs, the girls, the ale?
Or let me leave another space & simply dismiss them——

[illegible scrawled word repeated several times] Sweetbrier Lane *[illegible scrawls]*

Now Memory opes forthwith her choicest bin!   65
Ye innate maids in muslin gowns (perhaps too short by half!)
                    who made all else seem chaff,
Ye whom unceasingly I found my nature's other half,
Now playd guineas all day long & had no other care,
Who gave me all those dingy locks of brown, black, golden hair,
~~and are now the Miss Smiths & Browns & ~~
Ye who have been (this twenty years) the Miss Smiths & Browns,   70
Reading these words, how young Romance this longhushed lute takes down;
Wipes off the ~~dust~~ cobwebs & the dust, gives every string a screw,
And with one stroke ~~sets~~ the book is, which revives thee,
~~Nodding it? contemplating~~ at the gate, pressed rose-leaves, O Die! Die!)
The last thing that a poet learns is what to throw away   75
And how to make you think & creep with what he doesn't best,
For instance now, to write a song after the style of Poe,
Take the Ha' musty, fusty stock of Everybody & Co;
A moon — we all do know the moon, a sea — we all have seen it,
A dreadful Wind — we all have had — a fool we all have been it;   80
Then thus — the black sea moaned beneath & broke in fiery snow,
The moon loomed bloodred in the East, when we met long ago;
That first last kiss that fierce Embrace that ~~lasted~~ long & loath ——
Avaunt! then pale & patient face! who says I brook no truth?
The music bursts, the Dance reels on — ah it is well for thee   85
Thou hearst no more the muffled beat of that funereal sea;

From "Our Own," p. 102.

"YE YANKEES OF THE BAY STATE"

1

Ye Yankees of the Bay state,
  With whom no dastards mix!
Shall Everett dare to stifle
  The fire of seventy-six?
Up with the tough old pine-tree*
  As it proudly waved of yore,
Though its gnarled roots be watered
  With the dearest of our gore!
Then up with the pine tree,
  The tall New England pine!
We'll fight beneath its shadow,
  As it waves above the line!

2

Where Warren fell for freedom,
  His spirit lingers still,
And freemens' hearts beat proudly
  Round glorious Bunker Hill.
The hireling foe would gladly
  That death stained hill forget—
Their red coats shall be redder
  Ere many suns have set.
The pine-tree! the pine-tree!
  The tall New England pine!
We'll shrink but from dishonor
  As it waves above the line!

3

The spirit of the pilgrims
  Still liveth in their sons,
And it shall live forever—
  Stern granite hearted ones!
Our motherland is rocky,
  But we love her rugged face;
Like her she rears her children
  A free and toughknit race.
Hurrah for the pine-tree!
  The tall New England pine!
It tells us of the Pilgrims
  As it waves above the line!

* The pine was on the flags at Bunker Hill. [Lowell's note.]

4

By every hill and valley
  Where Pilgrim blood hath flowed,
And where their martyr spirit
  Hath still its old abode—
We will not let the red coats
  Set foot within our soil!
We'll teach them that we Yankees
  Can FIGHT as well as toil!
Kneel, kneel round the pine-tree!
  The tall New England pine!
Its strong trunk points to Heaven
  As it waves above the line!

5

Then up with the pine-tree!
  Its boughs shall wave again,
And quiver with the shoutings
  Of lion-hearted men!
For while our fathers' hearts blood
  Yet calleth us aloud,
Before the storm of battle
  Its crest shall ne'er be bowed!
Shout, shout for the pine-tree!
  It waveth o'er us now—
In the dreadful storm of battle
  Its head shall never bow!

THE LOVER'S DRINK-SONG

"Drink to me only with thine eyes."

Pour me a cup of sunniest hue,
Of woman's love, oh, let it be!
    The ecstasies
    Of thy great eyes,
Thine eyes divine of peaceful blue,
Pour out, that I may drink to thee!

And with those smiles the beaker wreathe
That grow within thine eyes for me;
    Oh! scatter showers
    Of those bright[1] flowers,

[1] MS: "dear."

Which in Love's sunshine[2] live and breathe,
That I may fitly drink to thee!

And let eye-spoken thoughts be there,
That not in words may languaged be;
    Rain, rain them down,[3]
    The cup to crown,
Of thy soul's valley lilies fair,
That I may fitly drink to thee!

Sing now of dear[4] rememberings,
For love is born of harmony;
    Sing with thine eyes
    That I may rise
To thy soul's height on music's wings,
And be lift up beholding thee!

AGATHA

'Neath her long lashes veiled, her gentle eyes,
In deep and earnest thought, are downward bent,
Filled with her soul's own light, as the moonrise
Fills with pale gleams the ample firmament.
Mildness and meekness make their dwelling there,
And gentle feelings without variance;
While human firmness hath a generous share,
Which lifts the spirit out of change and chance.
Not from her weakness hath her mildness grown,
But from a deep, unsounded strength of will,
And a strange earnestness her soul doth fill,
Bearing the virtues of the bezoar stone,
To sin's foul poison antidote and test;
An inward instinct, lurking in her breast,
Deeper than all her judgments, doth she own,
Which, touching the marked form of specious good,
Detects it, as the fallen Satan stood
Before Ithuriel's heavenly spear confess'd.

[2] MS read "That in Love's sunlight"; then substituted "Which" for "That."
[3] MS: "Oh rain them down."
[4] MS: "sweet."

Few rules hath she, for she believes, in sooth,
That our best safeguard is unconsciousness;—
That innocence hath a perpetual youth,
Which weareth not away 'neath Time's rough stress;
That all temptations which around us press,
Shine dazzled from the glorious shield of Truth.
Thus unsuspicious onward doth she move,
Without the dimmest shadow of a fear,
Through Love's serene and golden atmosphere.
A golden Hope shines ever on her path,
The clear reflection of a trustful Faith,
Which doubts not, wavers not, through joy and woe,
An inward light, which, whether tempests blow,
Or night come on, a flame forever hath.

Yet, though her spirit is so vast and full,
There is no sense of pride to mar and blot;
All souls agree that she is beautiful,
Yet she alone doth seem to know it not.
Herself she seemeth ever to forget,
And as the stars shine in the unfathom'd night,
Her virtues in an infinite Peace are set.
An understanding open, broad and bright,
Pierces through error at the instant sight,
So that her judgments never run astray,
While her mild temper, genial as the day,
Keeps the whole world in pure Elysian light.

She hath a natural sense of poetry,
Which weds her to the beautiful and true;
All noble deeds and thoughts that ever grew
Out of strong, fearless spirits, loveth she.
Nature is something other than a fact;
For love doth make from out each common thing
The fragrant blossom of a thought to spring,
Which lends a perfume to her every act.

Yet though so distant from the touch of sin,
The humblest spirit doth she not disdain,
But soothing with a tender care each pain,
The erring spirit gently doth she win
Into the path of duty back again.
Ever her best rebuke to sin is found

Within her piety,—a soul-sung psalm,
Breathed in her life, all undisturbed and calm,
That with its circle every act doth bound.
While through the saddest phase of human life,
And through the fret of every day's annoy,
The living token of her being,—Joy,—
Is borne upon the restless waves of strife,
Her anchored spirit's ever floating buoy.

Her utmost pleasure is self-sacrifice;
And though within her deep and saint-like eyes
The pensive shade of dreamy thought doth hover,
Yet it but softens, not obscures their light,
And hallows that which else had been too bright,
Like some blue haze that shrouds the landscape over.

Few be there upon earth more fair and sweet,
In whose ripe age so much of childhood lies,
So much of that strange fragrance from the skies
That circles every gentle child we greet.
For she is one the soul might rather meet
In the dim land of dreams and memories;
Like some fair picture hanging in the rare
And mournful twilight, doth her spirit seem,
When the young moon pales in the purple air,
And the heart, reaching out in many a dream,
Sees o'er the canvass many a shadowy gleam
Floating across the features strange and dim.

The steadfast path of duty doth she tread,
Strengthening her life of fact by that of thought,—
Ever the light into her spirit shed,
Into each common deed and act is wrought.
High doth her spirit fly, both strong and free,—
Clear, undismayed, whatever chances be;
No storm doth beat her down, her unquailing eye
Sees God through sorrow, smiling peacefully,
—Knows the stars shine behind the clouded sky.

But blessed is she, for she ever maketh
All virtue beautiful, all goodness fair,
And sin seems but a shadow while she speaketh,
That melts away into the thinnest air.

But dearest, happiest, in the quiet grace
She sendeth into life in every place,
Like some wild lute that lends the common breeze
Its own soul, filling it with harmonies.

THE TWO

Soon each the other knew,
But love grew up more slowly;
Firmly and fair it grew,
Watered with Heaven's dew,
That plant so pure and holy.

Thereon burst forth a flower,
To fuller beauty moulded
By sunshine, shade and shower,
In which all seeds of power
And mystery were folded.

They saw the flower rare,
And loved it for its beauty;
They watcht it with sweet care
Till, ere they were aware,
It grew to be a duty.

Then started they in fear
And gazed upon each other:
They said, "Why lose our cheer?
We only will be dear
As sister and her brother."

So dwelt they late and soon
In love's unclouded weather:
They loved the self-same tune,
And underneath the moon
'T was bliss to be together.

From all the world so wide
Each soul the other singled;
Something within did guide
Their life-streams side by side
Until at length they mingled.

And now they cannot part,
But must flow on forever,—
Two streams that rose apart,
Joined in the mighty heart
Of one calm-flowing river.

CALLIRHÖE

Whence art thou bright Callirhöe,
Calm, Heré-eyed Callirhöe?
Art thou a daughter of this earth,
That, like myself, had life and birth,
And who will die like me?
Methinks a soul so pure and clear
Must breathe another atmosphere,
Of thought more heavenly and high,
More full of deep serenity,
Than circles round this world of ours;
I dare not think that thou shouldst die,
Unto my soul, like summer showers
To thirsty leaves thou art,—like May
To the slow-budding woodbine bowers.
Oh no! thou canst [not] pass away.
No hand shall strew thy bier with flowers!
Those eyes, as fair as Eve's, when they,
Untearful yet, were raised to pray,
Fronting the mellow sunset glow
Of summer eve in Paradise,
Those bright founts whence forever flow
Nepenthe-streams of ecstacies.
It cannot be that Death
Shall chill them with his winter breath,—
What hath Death to do with thee,
My seraph-winged Callirhöe?

Whence art thou? From some other sphere,
On which, throughout the moonless night,
Gazing, we dream of beings bright,
Such as we long for here,—
Or art thou but a joy Elysian,
Of my own inward sight,

A glorious and fleeting vision,
Habited in robes of light,
The image of a blessed thing,
Whom I might love with wondering,
Yet feeling not a shade of doubt,
And who would give her love to me,
To twine my inmost soul about?
No, no, these would not be like thee,
Bright one, with auburn hair disparted
On thy meek forehead maidenly,
No, not like thee, my woman-hearted,
My warm, my true Callirhöe!

How may I tell the sunniness
Of thy thought-beaming smile?
Or how the soothing spell express,
That bindeth me the while,
Forth from thine eyes and features bright,
Gusheth that flood of golden light?
Like a sun-beam to my soul,
Comes that trusting smile of thine,
Lighting up the clouds of doubt,
Till they shape themselves, and roll
Like a glory all about
The messenger divine.—
For divine that needs must be
That bringeth messages from thee.
Madonna, gleams of smiles like this,
Like a stream of music fell,
In the silence of the night,
On the soul of Raphael.
Musing with a still delight,
How meekly thou did'st bend and kiss
The baby on thy knee,
Who sported with the golden hair
That fell in showers o'er him there,
Looking up contentedly.
Only the greatest souls can speak
As much by smiling as by tears.
Thine strengthens me when I am weak,
And gladdens into hopes my fears.
The path of life seems plain and sure,
Thy purity doth make me pure

And holy, when thou let'st arise
That mystery divine,
That silent music in thine eyes.
Seldom tear visits cheek of thine,
Seldom a tear escapes from thee,
My Hebé, my Callirhöe!

Sometimes in waking dreams divine,
Wandering, my spirit meets with thine,
And while, made dumb with ecstacy,
I pause in a delighted trance,
Thine, like a squirrel caught at play,
Just gives one startled look askance,
And darteth suddenly away,
Swifter than a phosphor glance
At night upon the lonely sea,
Wayward-souled Callirhöe.
Sometimes, in mockery of care,
Thy playful thought will never rest,
Darting about, now here, now there,
Like sun-beams on a river's breast,
Shifting with each breath of air,
By its very unrest fair.
As a bright and summer stream,
Seen in childhood's happy dream,
Singing nightly, singing daily,
Trifling with each blade of grass
That breaks his riples as they pass,
And going on its errand gaily,
Singing with the self-same leap
Wherewith it merges in the deep.
So shall thy spirit glide along,
Breaking, when troubled, into song,
And leave an echo floating by
When thou art gone forth utterly.
Seeming-cheerful souls there be,
That flutter with a living sound
As dry leaves rustle on the ground;
But they are sorrowful to me,
Because they make me think of thee,
My bird-like, wild Callirhöe!

Thy mirth is like the flickering ray
Forthshooting from the steadfast light

Of a star, which through the night
Moves glorious on its way,
With a sense of moveless might.
Thine inner soul flows calm forever;
Dark and calm without a sound,
Like that strange and trackless river
That rolls its waters underground.
Early and late at thy soul's gate
Sits Chastity in maiden wise,
No thought unchallenged, small or great,
Goes thence into thine eyes;
Nought evil can that warder win,
To pass without or enter in.
Before thy pure eyes guilt doth shrink,
Meanness doth blush and hide its head,
Down through the soul their light will sink,
And cannot be extinguished.
Far up on poiséd wing
Thou floatest, far from all debate,
Thine inspirations are too great
To tarry questioning;
No murmurs of our earthly air,
God's voice alone can reach thee there;
Downlooking on the stream of Fate,
So high thou sweepest in thy flight,
Thou knowest not of pride or hate,
But gazing from thy lark-like height,
Forth o'er the waters of To Be,
The first gleam of Truth's morning light
Round thy broad forehead floweth bright,
My Pallas-like Callirhöe.

Thy mouth is Wisdom's gate, wherefrom,
As from the Delphic cave,
Great sayings constantly do come,
Wave melting into wave;
Rich as the shower of Danäe,
Rains down thy golden speech;
My soul sits waiting silently,
When eye or tongue sends thoughts to me,
To comfort or to teach.

Calm is thy being as a lake
Nestled within a quiet hill,

When clouds are not, and winds are still,
So peaceful calm, that it doth take
All images upon its breast,
Yet change not in its queenly rest,
Reflecting back the bended skies
Till you half doubt where Heaven lies.
Deep thy nature is, and still,
How dark and deep! and yet so clear
Its inmost depths seem near;
Not moulding all things to its will,
Moulding its will to all,
Ruling them with unfelt thrall.
So gently flows thy life along
It makes e'en discord musical,
So that nought can pass thee by
But turns to wond'rous melody,
Like a full, clear, ringing song.
Sweet the music of its flow,
As of a river in a dream,
A river in a sunny land,
A deep and solemn stream
Moving over silver sand,
Majestical and slow.

I sometimes think that thou wert given
To be a bright interpreter
Of the pure mysteries of Heaven,
And cannot bear
To think Death's icy hand should stir
One ringlet of thy hair;
But thou must die like us,—
Yet not like us,—for can it be
That one so bright and glorious
Should sink into the dust as we,
Who could but wonder at thy purity?
Not oft I dwell in thoughts of thine,
My earnest-souled Callirhöe;
And yet thy life is part of mine.
What should I love in place of thee?
Sweet is thy voice, as that of streams
To me, or as a living sound
To one who starts from fev'rous sleep,
Scared by the shapes of ghastly dreams,

And on the darkness stareth round,
Fancying dim terrors in the gloomy deep.
Then if it must be so,
That thou from us shalt go,
Linger yet a little while;
Oh! let me once more feel thy grace,
Oh! let me once more drink thy smile!
I am as nothing if thy face
Is turned from me!
But if it needs must be,
That I must part from thee,
That the silver cord be riven
That holds thee down from Heaven,
Not yet, not yet, Callirhöe,
Unfold thine angel wings to flee,
Oh! no, not yet, Callirhöe!

SONNET—TO KEATS

Thine eyes, I know, with earnestness were fraught,
Thy brow a pale and musing hue had ta'en,
And a mild frown, from watching not in vain
The patient dawn and sunrise of great thought;
Thy soul seemed listening still as if it caught,
Through castle hall, or arches dim and long,
The mail-clad tramp of old heroic song,
Or heard, through groves of moss-grown oak trees brought,
Mysterious tones from the lone pipe of Pan;
While thy dark eyes glowed mellowly to see
Coy nymphs, as down thick-leavèd dells they ran,
And backward glanced with[1] longing eyes at thee,
Whose gracious heart, in its most Grecian mood,
Ran red and warm with right good English blood.

MERRY ENGLAND

Hurrah for merry England,
Queen of the land and sea,
The champion of truth and right,
The bulwark of the free!

[1] MS: "from."

Hurrah for merry England!
  Upon thy seagirt isle
Thou sittest, clothed in righteousness,
  Secure of Heaven's smile!

When ruled the fairhaired Saxon,
  Yes, thou wert merry then;
And, as they girt their bucklers on,
  Thy meanest serfs were men;
And merry was the castle-hall
  With jest and song and tale,
When bearded lips with mead were white
  And rang the loud Washael!

And, when grim Denmark's black-browed prows
  Tore through thine Emerald sea,
And many a wild blue eye was turned
  In savage lust on thee,—
When, in the greenest of thy vales,
  The gusts of summer air
Blew out in long and shaggy locks
  The sea-king's yellow hair,—

Yet Alfred was in England,
  And merry yet again
Thy white-armed Saxon maidens were
  When, on the drunken Dane,
The sudden thunders of thy war
  With arrowy hail did pour,
And grim jaws dropt that quivered yet
  With savage hymns to Thor.

Thy merry brow was fair and free,
  Thine eye gleamed like a lance,
When thy good ash and yew did crush
  The gilded knights of France;
When Paris shook within her walls
  And trembled as she saw
Her snow-white lilies trampled down
  Beneath thy lion's paw.

Queen Bess's days were merry days,
  Renowned in song and tale,

Stout days that saw the last brown bead
  Of many a tun of ale;
Queen Bess's days were golden days
  And thou full proudly then
Did'st suckle at thy healthy breasts
  The best of Englishmen.

Thou hast been merry, England,
  But art thou merry now,
With sweat of agonizing years
  Upon thy harlot brow,
Grimed with the smoke of furnaces
  That forge with damned art
The bars of darkness that shut in
  The poor man's starving heart?

Oh free and Christian England!
  The Hindu wife no more
Shall burn herself in that broad realm
  Saint George's cross waves o'er;
Thou art the champion of the right,
  The friend of the opprest,
And none but freemen now shall tread[1]
  Thine Indies of the West.

But thou canst ship thy poison,
  Wrung from lean Hindu slaves,
To fill all China with dead souls
  That rot in living graves;
And, that thy faith may not be seen
  Barren of goodly works,
At Saint Jean D'Acre thou sent'st up
  To Heaven three thousand Turks.

Fling high your greasy caps in air,
  Slaves of the forge and loom,
If on the soil ye're pent and starved
  Yet underneath there's room;
Fling high your caps, for, God be praised,
  Your epitaph shall be,
"Who sets his foot on English soil
  Thenceforward he is free!"

[1] MS: "And no black slave shall longer tread."

Shout too for merry England
  Ye factory-children thin,
Upon whose little hearts the sun
  Hath never once looked in;
For, when your hollow eyes shall close
  The poor-house hell to balk,
(Thank God for liberty of speech)
  The parliament will talk.

Thank God, lean sons of Erin,
  Who reverence the Pope,
In England consciences are free
  And ye are free—to hope;
And if the Church of England priest
  Distrain—why, what of that?
Their consciences are freer still
  Who wear the shovel-hat.[2]

The poet loves the silent past,
  And, in his fruitful rhyme,
He sets the fairest flowers o'er
  The grave of buried time;
But, from the graves of thy dark years,
  The night-shade's ugly blue
And spotted henbane shall grow up
  To poison Heaven's dew.

[2] MS interpolates following two stanzas:
> Ye are not wholly friendless,
>   For, o'er your life-deep cares,
> Sleek men will murmur gently
>   In after-dinner chairs,
> And, from their cornlaw gains, will give
>   Some shilling, at the least,
> To have Christ's blessed gospel preached
>   In the benighted East;
>
> And, though both cold and hunger are
>   The obstinatest facts,
> Good men will never let you starve
>   For want of wholesome tracts;
> Besides, they are so eloquent
>   In speech or wise review,
> Methinks 'twere very bliss to live
>   Upon a roasted shoe.

[In this interpolation Lowell rejected "To" as the first word in line 8 and "godly" as the fourth word in line 12.]

Woe to thee, fallen England,
  Who hast betrayed the word,
And knelt before a Church when thou
  Shouldst kneel before the Lord!
And, for that scarlet woman
  Who sits in places high,
There cometh vengeance swift to quench
  The lewdness in her eye.

Woe to thee, fallen England,
  Who, in thy night-mare sleep,
O'er a volcano's heart dost toss
  Whence sudden wrath shall leap
Of that forgotten Titan
  Who now is trodden down
That one weak Guelphic girl may wear
  Her[3] plaything of a crown!

That Titan's heart is heaving now,
  And, with its huge uprise,
On their sand basements lean[4] and crack
  The old moss-covered lies;
For freedom through long centuries
  Lives in eternal youth,
And nothing can forever part
  The human soul and truth.

"I LOVE THOSE POETS, OF WHATEVER CREED"

I love those poets, of whatever creed,
  Who bring such holy tears into mine eyes
As are the pledge of sweetest charities,
  And of a love wherein lies wrapt ripe seed
Of the white flow'r of high unconscious deed;
  Who make me to hold up a manly head
And put a firmer muscle in my tread,
  Even by one little word that fits my need:
And I must love such deep and solemn lines,
  As give me that strong tenderness of heart

[3] MS rejects "The."
[4] MS rejects "heave."

I feel within a wood of ancient pines,
For then I know that Nature did her part
Towards the filling of that harmony,
Which finds so true an answering chord in me.

SONNET

"To die is gain."

Where are the terrors that escort King Death,
That hurl pale Reason from her trembling throne?
Why should man shudder to give up his breath?
Why fear the path, though naked and alone,
That *must* lead up to scenes more clear and bright,
Than bloom amid this world's dim clouded night?
Is not his God beside, around, above,
Shall he not trust in His unbounded love?
Oh, yes! Let others dread thee if they will,
I'll welcome thee, O death, and call thee friend,
Come to release me from these loads of ill,
These lengthened penances I here fulfil,
To give me wings, wherewith I may ascend,
And with the soul of God my soul may blend!

SONNET

Whene'er I read in mournful history
How all things crumble at the touch of time,
And even great deeds renowned in mighty rhyme
Show but as cities buried 'neath the sea
Which in calm days men gaze on awfully,
My heart grows heavy; but one thought sublime
Rises, and therewith the uplifting chime
Of morning stars comes back rememberingly;
Woman, thou art that thought, in whom I know
That I alone gave Time his tyrant might,
Drooping my foolish lids of clay too low,
For, looking up, I see great Love, far, far,
Above all changes, like a steadfast star
Behind the pulsings of the northern light.

SONNET

Like some black mountain glooming huge aloof,
Grassed with tall pines, friend of the thoughtful crowd
Of stars, yet thereof seeming nothing proud,
Calm granite pillar of God's own home-roof,
Thrilling me through with infinite reproof,
Yet so wrapt round with twilight's awful shroud
That I may wellnigh deem it but a cloud
Or even some strand of fantasy's vast woof
Wrought by the lurid moonrise,—even so
Stands the great asking for some afterwork,
Which Earth and Custom vainly strive to shirk,
Making all other toils seem mean and low,
And sweetest rhymes of what I am or was,
A cricket's chirp among the easeful grass.

THE LESSON—TO IRENE

I

Thou openest wide thy heart,
    All-hopeful flower,
Thou dost not give a part
Nor askest aught for dower;
    In sun or shower,
    Like a true soul,
    Thou giv'st the whole,
Not waiting for a better hour;
    With thee I feel my earth
    That it is full and fair,
And often muse upon my place of birth
    Because my home's not there:
Thou sayest—'The stars are far above me,
    Are greater much than I,
    Yet, if thou wilt not love me
    As I love, I must die
    And give my God the lie!'

II

Thou lookest with calm eyes,
  Unwaning star,
On thee my spirit cries
For hopes that greatest are,
  With thee it doth arise
  And shine afar,
Knowing that wherewith its hope
At the strongest could not cope;
Thou sayest—'Give me reverence
  Or I must fade;
  I was not made
To glimmer on a gross and bodily sense!'

III

The great soul pines alone;
  How lonely only they,
True brother-souls, have known
But never yet could say,
Lone as a corpse on its death night,
When it first begins to have
Some fore-feeling of the grave,—
Lone as the first world, I wis,
That groped the yet unsunned abyss
Ere Love had smiled and it was light;
But when, in its fulfilling hour,—
Like the thought of some great poem,
When the bard, in calm of power,
Folds the vast heart of All unto him,—
  Comes forth its spirit bride,
With a perfectness of dower
  As the blue heaven wide,
Dear God, could it forget
The lessons thou had'st set
In thy star and flower?

BALLAD

Gloomily the river floweth,
  Close by her bower door,
And drearily the nightwind bloweth
  Across the barren moor.

It rustles through the withered leaves
Upon the poplars tall,
And mutters wildly 'neath the eaves
Of the unlighted hall.

The waning moon above the hill
Is rising strange and red,
And fills her soul, against her will,
With fancies lone and dread.

The stream all night will flow as drearful,
The wind will shriek forlorn,
She fears—she knows that something fearful
Is coming ere the morn.

The curtains in that lonely place
Wave like a heavy pall,
And her dead mother's pale, pale face
Doth flicker on the wall.

And all the rising moon about
Her fear did shape the clouds,
And saw dead faces staring out
From coffins and from shrouds.

A screech-owl now, for three nights past,
Housed in some hollow tree,
Sends struggling up against the blast
His long shriek fearfully.

Strange shadows waver to and fro,
In the uncertain light,
And the scared dog hath howled below
All through the weary night.

She only feels that she is weak
And fears some ill unknown,
She longs, and yet she dreads to shriek
It is so very lone.

Her eyeballs in their sockets strain,
Till the nerves seem to snap,
When blasts against the window-pane
Like lean, dead fingers tap.

And still the river floweth by
   With the same lonely sound,
And the gusts seem to sob and sigh,
   And wring their hands around.

Is that a footstep on the stair,
   And on the entry-floor?
What sound is that, like breathing, there?
   There, close beside the door!

Hush! hark! that was a dreadful sigh!
   So full of woe, so near!
It were an easier thing to die
   Than feel this deadly fear.

One of her ancestors she knew
   A bloody man had been,
They found him here, stabb'd through and through,
   Murdered in all his sin.

The nurse had often silenced her,
   With fearful tales of him—
God shield her! did not something stir
   Within that corner dim?

A gleam across the chamber floor—
   A white thing in the river—
One long, shrill, shivering scream, no more,
   And all is still forever!

"MY FATHER, SINCE I LOVE, THY PRESENCE CRIES"

My Father, since I love, thy presence cries
To me from every smallest thing I see;
There is no flower but hath its pray'r to thee,
No river but upon whose full heart lies
The skiey shadow of thy mysteries;
No leaf that fluttereth on any tree,
But thou thereon hast written wondrously
Thy gospels evident to loving eyes:

Thy truth I will not call thy testament,
For I most truly know that thou dost live;
Thy life is mine, for I on thee have leant,
And down Time's current all things fugitive
Have drifted from me, leaving me alone
(So best companioned) with the ETERNAL ONE.

SONNET—SUNSET AND MOONSHINE

The sunset hath a glory for the soul,
Uplifting it from all earth's things apart
And building it a palace of pure[1] Art
Where it doth sit alone in crown'd control
And o'er all space its eyes unsealed[2] roll;
But the dear moonshine looks in on the heart,
Giving each kindly blood-drop warmer start,
And knits me with humanity's great whole;
It doth not bear me, as the sunset doth,
Forth of the city, but, on dull brick walls,
Silverly smileth, as 'twere nothing loath
To sanctify all that whereon it falls,
And with it my full heart goes[3] forth and broods
In love o'er all life's sleeping multitudes.

THE LOVED ONE

The loved one, the loved one!
    Unseen but never far—
All souls must have a loved one,
    Though haply but a star.

And thou, most blessed woman,
    When first I looked on thee,
Wert in thy heavenly lustre
    Only a star to me.

[1] MS rejects "all."
[2] MS: "unscaled."
[3] MS: "grows."

I gazed on thee so distant,
  And with such truth did long,
That, in my earnest loving,
  My soul grew high and strong.

And in its deep abysses
  Thy shade slept silverly;
Seen only in calm weather,
  As stars are in the sea.

So kept I ever quiet,
  That it might rest therein;
For thine unconscious shadow
  Was utmost bliss to win.

I know not how it happened—
  For we can never know
The channel whereby Heaven
  Into the soul doth flow;

But, while I yet was gazing,
  I was methought lift up!
My soul was filled with splendor,
  Like an o'er brimming cup;

And ere I ceased from wonder,
  Next to this burning heart
I prest thee, truest woman,
  All glorious as thou art;

And, now thou art my loved one,
  Thou art my star no less;
For Heaven and Earth are married
  In thy full loveliness.

THE BALLAD OF THE STRANGER

The wind is moaning sadly among the pine trees high,—
But that was not it, surely, so like a human sigh.

Her list'ning face she lifted, put back her scattered hair,
And, in the growing twilight, she saw her loved one there.

"Why cam'st thou not more early? Where tarried'st thou so long?
I have waited thee from sunset till dusky even-song;

"The stars came out so slowly! It was a weary time;
I almost thought I *never* should hear the vesper chime.

"And I have had strange fancies, dim thoughts that seemed like fears,
Not sad,—yet, when they left me, mine eyes were salt with tears;

"I thought of my dead mother, her pale face I could see
Between me and the starlight, as if she waited me;—

" 'Now, wherefore, blessed mother, say wherefore art thou here?
Most sure, if I had sinned, my heart would chill with fear.'

"Her lips moved not to answer, but glimmered with a smile,
That seemed to say, 'my daughter, wait yet a little while.'

"With that no more I saw her; the Pleiades alone
I saw, all dim and misty, as through my tears they shone.

"And now, when thou art with me, when I should be most glad,
I yet do feel a something that makes me well nigh sad.

"Why lookest thou so mournful? Such face to thee is new;
And why dost thou not kiss me, as thou art used to do?"

Long time his lips seemed moving, as if unwont to speak,
And, when at length he answered, his voice was dim and weak.

"Now, dearest, if thou'lt listen, I will make plain the truth;
As I to thee did hasten, I met a stranger youth;

"He seemed of other country, and he was pale and fair;
His eyes were very mournful, yet kind as thine eyes are;

"He sang to me full sweetly the songs of his own clime,
And, all along, the music interpreted the rhyme;

"They were of unknown language, yet ever, more and more,
They grew to sound like something that I had heard before;

"His face did shine so brightly, he sang so silverly,
I knew he was an angel come down for love of me,—

"A mild and gentle spirit, and in his earnest eyes
I read the seeming riddle of all life's mysteries.

"His voice went through and through me, it was so soft and low,
And it was very mournful, but not as if with woe;

"The voices of the lost ones, of those who've gone before,
Seemed woven with it strangely to charm me more and more.

"With his mild eyes he drew me, he took me by the hand,
I could not choose but follow into his pleasant land;

"And so with him I journeyed, in that fair clime to dwell,
But of its wondrous beauty only that youth can tell;

"The gate whereby we entered, it is both green and low,
And up beyond the church door 'tis scarcely a stone's throw.

"I shall be with thee often, but never as before,
For I wear not the vestments of clay which I once wore;

"We will not break our troth plight, though time can never bring
The day when I may claim thee, to wed thee with a ring;

"For that kind youth hath promised that, on a certain day,
He will go forth and bring thee to dwell with me alway."

His words to silence faded, when he so far had said,
And mingled with the murmur of the pine trees overhead.

She did not sink with sorrow, nor weep when he was gone,
But patiently she waited until five moons had shone.

She kept her ever ready to greet the stranger youth,
Drest in her wedding garment of purity and truth.

And, when those days were numbered, the stranger came once more,
With gentlest look, to lead her in at the low, green door;

With joy she gave him welcome, all robed in snowy white,
Her heart had told her surely that he would come that night;

A bridal wreath of amaranth he twined about her head,
And then the fair betrothed all silently forth led.

She followed him right gladly, it was not far to go
To meet and dwell forever with him who loved her so.

With many tears they prayed her to stay, but all in vain;
Long waited they her coming, but she never came again.

SONNET

Only as[1] thou herein canst not see me,
Only as thou the same low voice canst hear
Which is the morning-song of every sphere
And which thou erewhile heardst beside the sea
Or in the still night flowing solemnly,
Only so love this rhyme and so revere;
All else cast from thee, haply with a tear
For one who, rightly taught, yet would not be
A voice obedient; some things I have seen
With a clear eye, and otherwhile[2] the earth
With a most sad eclipse hath come between
That sunlight which is mine by right of birth
And what I know[3] with grief I ought to have been,—
Yet is short-coming even something worth.

SONNET

When in a book I find a pleasant thought
Which some small flower in the woods to me
Had told, as if in straitest secrecy,
That I might speak it in sweet verses wrought,
With what best feelings is such meeting fraught!
It shows how nature's life will never be
Shut up from speaking out full clear and free
Her wonders to the soul that will be taught.
And what though I have but this single chance
Of saying that which every gentle soul

1 MS rejects "Only herein."
2 MS: "otherwhiles."
3 MS rejects "I to know."

Shall answer with a glad, uplifting glance?
Nature is frank to him whose spirit whole
Doth love Truth more than praise, and in good time,
My flower will tell me sweeter things to rhyme.

TO AN ÆOLIAN HARP AT NIGHT

There is a spirit in thee,
A spirit wild and lone,
As of a fallen star;
And when the night-winds win thee
To muse of thy lost throne,
Thy voice is sunken far
In the night's vast hollow
So deep and low,
That the soul dare not follow
Its wandering woe:
Thine anguish sharp
Doth wring the harp
Where bitter fate hath bound thee,
And countless wings
Of dreamy things
Rustle the dark around thee,
Bending to hear
The music clear
Thy hopeless woe hath found thee.

Up from the wondrous past
When thou an angel wast,
Shapes of dim hugeness rise
Through the darkness yonder;
And the old mysteries
With awfully calm eyes
All about thee wander:
Faces of dumb distress
Without a hope of balm;
Of fiery gentleness
In agony kept calm;
Of wisdom deep as death,
Older than oldest star,
O'er which a pale gleam wandereth

From suns long set afar;
Creatures of love and awe,
Dark with the aged woe
Of Godhead long brought low,
Such as the young earth saw
In temples long ago,
When beauty gave unbroken law
And great thoughts into Gods did grow.

In thy heart's abysses
Darkness dwells forever:
Memory of old blisses
Parteth from thee never:
Thinking of thy former light
Deepeneth thy deepest night,
And puts a sadness in thy wail
So utterly forsaken,
That my hope turns deathly pale,
Doubtful of her skyey mail,
When thy moans awaken.

There is a night in thy dark heart
Which longeth for no morrow,
A glorious and awful sorrow
Wherewith thou would'st not part
Though thou could'st so regain
The ancient fulness of thy reign;
Thou hast learned in thine unnumbered years
Of loneliness and woe
That the soil must be wet with many tears
Where the soul's best flowers grow.

There are unworded pains
Whereby the spirit gains
Home in the deepest deep;
Our sorrow and annoy
High as the angel's joy
On wings of patience sweep;
In joy our bodies shine,
Grief makes our souls divine,
Clay washeth from us with each tear we weep.

Woe is more glorious
Than deepest gladness,

Great thoughts look on us
With eyes of sadness;
The mournfullest melodies
Still are the mildest,
Filling the soul with ease
When it is wildest;
There is a joyous gain
In our tears' fiery rain,
And well we can languish
In sorrow and anguish
While the soul maketh music and song of its pain.

SONNET

If some small savor creep into my rhyme
Of the old poets, if some words I use,
Neglected long, which have the lusty thews
Of that gold-haired and earnest hearted time,
Whose loving joy and sorrow all sublime
Have given our tongue its starry eminence,—
It is not pride, God knows, but reverence
Which hath grown in me since my childhood's prime;
Wherein I feel that my poor lyre is strung
With soul-strings like to theirs, and that I have
No right to muse their holy graves among,
If I can be a custom-fettered slave,
And, in mine own true spirit, am not brave
To speak what rusheth upward to my tongue.

SONNET

Thou art a woman, and therein thou art
Fit theme for poet's songful reverence;
Thou art the clear and living evidence
That God will never leave the human heart;
And, being so, should'st thou not do thy part,
For Him and for his blessed cause of Truth?
I fear not that thy crystal dew of ruth
Will be dried from thee in the dusty mart,

Or that thou wilt outwear thy womanhood;
No; where the jar of tongues swells angrily,
Thy gentleness shall clip thee with a ring
Of guardian light,—be the more calm, and good,
And clearlier, like a white angel sing,
Knowing that all shall one day angels be.

FANCIES ABOUT A ROSEBUD,

Pressed in an Old Copy of Spenser

Who prest you here? The Past can tell,
    When summer skies were bright above,
And some full heart did leap and swell
    Beneath the white new moon of love.

Some Poet, haply, when the world
    Showed like a calm sea, grand and blue,
Ere its cold, inky waves had curled
    O'er the numb heart once warm and true;

When, with his soul brimful of morn,
    He looked beyond the vale of Time,
Nor saw therein the dullard scorn
    That made his heavenliness a crime;

When, musing o'er the Poets olden,
    His soul did like a sun upstart
To shoot its arrows, clear and golden,
    Through slavery's cold and darksome heart.

Alas! too soon the veil is lifted
    That hangs between the soul and pain,
Too soon the morning-red hath drifted
    Into dull cloud, or fallen in rain!

Or were you prest by one who nurst
    Bleak memories of love gone by,
Whose heart, like a star fallen, burst
    In dark and erring vacancy?

To him you still were fresh and green
　As when you grew upon the stalk,
And many a breezy summer scene
　Came back—and many a moonlit walk;

And there would be a hum of bees,
　A smell of childhood in the air,
And old, fresh feelings cooled the breeze
　That, like loved fingers, stirred his hair!

Then would you suddenly be blasted
　By the keen wind of one dark thought,
One nameless woe, that had outlasted
　The sudden blow whereby 'twas brought.

Or were you pressed here by two lovers
　Who seemed to read these verses rare,
But found between the antique covers
　What Spenser could not prison there:

Songs which his glorious soul had heard,
　But his dull pen could never write,
Which flew, like some gold-winged bird,
　Through the blue heaven out of sight?

My heart is with them as they sit,
　I see the rose-bud in her breast,
I see her small hand taking it
　From out its odorous, snowy nest;

I hear him swear that he will keep it,
　In memory of that blessed day,
To smile on it or over-weep it
　When she and spring are far away.

Ah me! I needs must droop my head,
　And brush away a happy tear,
For they are gone, and, dry and dead,
　The rose-bud lies before me here.

Yet is it in no stranger's hand,
　For I will guard it tenderly,
And it shall be a magic wand
　To bring mine own true love to me.

My heart runs o'er with sweet surmises,
　The while my fancy weaves her rhyme,
Kind hopes and musical surprises
　Throng round me from the olden time.

I do not care to know who prest you:
　Enough for me to feel and know
That some heart's love and longing blest you,
　Knitting to-day with long-ago.

FAREWELL

Farewell! as the bee round the blossom
Doth murmur drowsily,
So murmureth round my bosom
The memory of thee;
Lingering, it seems to go,
When the wind more full doth flow,
Waving the flower to and fro,
But still returneth, Marian!
My hope no longer burneth,
Which did so fiercely burn,
My joy to sorrow turneth,
Although loath, loath to turn,—
I would forget—
And yet—and yet
My heart to thee still yearneth, Marian!

Fair as a single star thou shinest,
And white as lilies are
The slender hands wherewith thou twinest
Thy heavy auburn hair;
Thou art to me
A memory
Of all that is divinest:
Thou art so fair and tall,
Thy looks so queenly are,
Thy very shadow on the wall,
Thy step upon the stair,
The thought that thou art nigh,
The chance look of thine eye

Are more to me than all, Marian,
And will be till I die!

As the last quiver of a bell
Doth fade into the air,
With a subsiding swell
That dies we know not where,
So my hope melted and was gone:
I raised mine eyes to bless the star
That shared its light with me so far
Below its silver throne,
And gloom and chilling vacancy
Were all was left to me,
In the dark, bleak night I was alone!
Alone in the blessed Earth, Marian,
For what were all to me—
Its love, and light, and mirth, Marian,
If I were not with thee?

My heart will not forget thee
More than the moaning brine
Forgets the moon when she is set;
The gush when first I met thee
That thrilled my brain like wine,
Doth thrill as madly yet;
My heart cannot forget thee,
Though it may droop and pine,
Too deeply it had set thee
In every love of mine;
No new moon ever cometh,
No flower ever bloometh,
No twilight ever gloometh
But I'm more only thine.
Oh look not on me, Marian,
Thine eyes are wild and deep,
And they have won me, Marian,
From peacefulness and sleep;
The sunlight doth not sun me,
The meek moonshine doth shun me,
All sweetest voices stun me,—
There is no rest
Within my breast
And I can only weep, Marian!

As a landbird far at sea
Doth wander through the sleet
And drooping downward wearily
Finds no rest for her feet,
So wandereth my memory
O'er the years when we did meet:
I used to say that everything
Partook a share of thee,
That not a little bird could sing,
Or green leaf flutter on a tree,
That nothing could be beautiful
Save part of thee were there,
That from thy soul so clear and full
All bright and blessed things did cull
The charm to make them fair;
And now I know
That it was so,
Thy spirit through the earth doth flow
And face me whereso'er I go,—
What right hath perfectness to give
Such weary weight of wo
Unto the soul which cannot live
On anything more low?
Oh leave me, leave me, Marian,
There's no fair thing I see
But doth deceive me, Marian,
Into sad dreams of thee!

A cold snake gnaws my heart
And crushes round my brain,
And I should glory but to part
So bitterly again,
Feeling the slow tears start
And fall in fiery rain:
There's a wide ring round the moon,
The ghost-like clouds glide by,
And I hear the sad winds croon
A dirge to the lowering sky;
There's nothing soft or mild
In the pale moon's sickly light,
But all looks strange and wild
Through the dim, foreboding night:
I think thou must be dead

In some dark and lonely place,
With candles at thy head,
And a pall above thee spread
To hide thy dead, cold face;
But I can see thee underneath
So pale, and still, and fair,
Thine eyes closed smoothly and a wreath
Of flowers in thy hair;
I never saw thy face so clear
When thou wast with the living,
As now beneath the pall, so drear,
And stiff, and unforgiving;
I cannot flee thee, Marian,
I cannot turn away,
Mine eyes must see thee, Marian,
Through salt tears night and day.

THE TRUE RADICAL

Some men would prune off the limbs of the plant whose summit is dying;—
Water thou well its roots, that new leaves and blossoms may grow:
Often new life may lie waiting, hidden and dead 'neath the surface,
So shall thy name be blest of thousands that rest in its shade.

HYMN

One house, our God, we give to thee:
One day in seven, Eternity
Floods all our souls, and in our eyes
Some thanks for thy great goodness rise.

Let us not think thy presence falls
Only within these narrow walls,
Nor that this handiwork of clods
Can prison up the God of gods.

Let us not think that only here
Thy being to our own is near;
But let us find thee every day
Forth in the fields, or by the way.

The world too many homes doth own,
Shall God the Father have but one?
Shall we his loving presence seek,
But one poor day of all the week?

O, let us feel thee every where
As common as the blessed air,
Among our neighbors and our friends,
The shaper of our rough hewn ends.

Here let us only need to meet,
Because our service is more sweet
When many hearts as one adore,
And feel thee through each other more.

Thy presence here we then shall seek,
As but an emblem of the week;
Secure that thou wilt bless us when
We strive to bless our fellow men.

Then shall this house indeed be thine,
A visible and outward sign
Of that unseen, encircling love,
Which doth in all our spirits move.

SONNET

Poet, if men from wisdom turn away,
And are so wiled with idle gauds of Time,
They will not list the everlasting chime
Of beautiful things, that let in God's clear day,
Through every inlet to this hut of clay,
Think not Truth's sun can ever reach his west;
Nor let one holy longing in thy breast
Fade with long watching dawn's slow-whitening gray:
No! late and early, let thy soul sing clear,
Gushing with prophesy of growing light;
Sing to the hearing of the Eternal ear,
Keep day at noon *within*, though murkest night
Wrap all *without;* for, ere 'tis long, our sphere
Shall hymn once more amid his brethren bright!

VOLTAIRE

Heaven shield me from ambition such as his—
To weigh a pun against Eternal bliss
And scoff at God for an antithesis.

THE FOLLOWER

To one who drifteth with opinion's tide
Things on the firm shore seem to shift and glide,
While he, his fantasy's unwitting thrall,
Seems the sole thing that moveth not at all.

THE POET AND APOLLO

"O, master of the golden lyre,
    Dread twanger of the golden bow,
I call upon thee, mighty sire,
    Old, outcast, blind, and full of woe.

"I have poured out my soul like rain
    Upon the dry and withered earth;
And what has been my luckless gain?
    A wrinkled heart and honor's dearth.

"All earthly things have I explored,
    Sounded the deeps of love and hate,
And often hath my spirit soared
    High o'er the dark abyss of fate.

"Now therefore grant me what I seek,
    Some gift that none with me may share,
A larger vision than these weak
    Unaided eyes could ever dare."

So prayed a poet once of old,
    A poet wise, without a peer,
By long-pent agony made bold
    To seek his father's pitying ear.

Apollo heard, and sadly smiled,
   Then, murmuring scarce above his breath,
"Bear thou," he sighed, "unto my child
   My last and greatest gift, oh Death."

A LOVE THOUGHT

In my walks the thought of thee
Like sweet music comes to me;
Music sweet I knew not whence,
Ravishing my soul and sense,—
As if some angel with droopt eyes
Sat at the gate of Paradise,
And let his hand forgetfully
One after one his harpstrings try.

WORDSWORTH

Poet of the lofty brow! far-sighted seer!
Whose gifted eye on mountain peak and plain,
The eternal heavens and never-sleeping main,
Mysterious writings saw and read with fear!
In the deep silence of the night thine ear
Heard from the earth a "still, sad music" rise,
Nor less the anthem caught that midnight skies
Pour through the soul from each rejoicing sphere;
But most thou lov'st, with solemn steps, to take
Down through the awful chambers of the soul
Thy dreadful way, and hear the billows roll
Of that deep ocean whose far thunders break
Upon the everlasting shores, and wake
Echos that wiser make whom they control.

Thy song sublime, the tinkling charm disdains,
And painted trappings of the gaudy muse,
And in such dress as Truth and Nature use
Majestic mounts in high Miltonic strains,
And pours its strength along the ethereal plains,
Solemn and grand as when the hills reply

To the full chorus of a stormy sky,
Or ocean round his rock-bound shores complains;
Yet not the highest heaven amid the "quire
Of shouting angels and the empyreal thrones,"
Nor lowest Erebus, nor Chaos old,
Thy chiefest haunt: but, with sublimer tones,
Through the dark caverns of the mind are rolled
The mighty thunders of thy master lyre.

WINTER

The bird sings not in winter-time,
  Nor doth the happy murmur of the bees,
Swarm round us from the chill, unleav'd lime,
And shall ye hear the poet o'sunny rhyme,
  Mid souls more bleak and bare than winter trees?

As a lone singing bird that far away,
  Hath follow'd north the fickle smiles of spring,
Is ambush'd by a sudden bitter day,
And sits forlorn upon a leafless spray,
  Hiding his head beneath his numbed wing.

So is the poet, if he chance to fall
  'Mong hearts by whom he is not understood,
Dull hearts, whose throbbing grows not musical,
Although their strings are blown upon by all
  The sweetest breezes of the true and good.

His spirit pineth orphan'd of that home
  Wherein was nursed its wondrous infancy,
And whence sometimes 'neath night's all quiet dome,
Swiftly a winged memory will come,
  And prophesy of glory yet to be.

Then knows he that he hath not been exiled
  From those wide halls his own by right of birth;
But hath been sent, a well-beloved child,
A chosen one on whom his father smiled,
  And blest, to be his messenger on Earth.

Then doth his brow with its right glory shine,
  And stretching forth his strong, undaunted wings,
He soareth to an atmosphere divine,
Whence he can see afar that clime benign,
  His father land, whose mystic song he sings.

So in his eyes there doth such blessings grow,
  That all those faces erst so hard and dull,
With a sweet warmth of brotherhood do glow,
As he had seen them glisten long ago,
  In that old home so free and beautiful.

A RALLYING-CRY FOR NEW-ENGLAND, AGAINST THE ANNEXATION OF TEXAS

[By a Yankee]

Rouse up, New-England! Buckle on your mail of proof sublime,
Your stern old hate of tyranny, your deep contempt of crime;
A traitor plot is hatching now, more full of woe and shame,
Than ever from the iron heart of bloodiest despot came!

Six slave States added at a breath! One flourish of a pen,
And fetters shall be rivetted on millions more of men!
One drop of ink to sign a name, and slavery shall find
For all her surplus flesh and blood a market to her mind!

A market where good Democrats their fellow-men may sell!
O, what a grin of fiendish glee runs round and round through hell!
How all the damned leap up for joy and half forget their fire,
To think men take such pains to claim the notice of God's ire!

Is't not enough that we have borne the sneer of all the world,
And bent to those whose haughty lips in scorn of us are curled?
Is't not enough that we must hunt their living chattels back,
And cheer the hungry bloodhounds on that howl upon their track?

Is't not enough that we must bow to all that they decree,—
These cotton and tobacco lords, these pimps of slavery?
That we must yield our conscience up to glut Oppression's maw,
And break our faith with God to keep the letter of Man's law?

But must we sit in silence by, and see the chain and whip
Made firmer for all time to come in Slavery's bloody grip?
Must we not only half the guilt and all the shame endure,
But help to make our tyrant's throne of flesh and blood secure?

If hand and foot we *must* be bound by deeds our fathers signed,
And *must* be cheated, gull'd and scorn'd, because they too were blind,
Why, let them have their pound of flesh—for that is in the bond—
But woe to them if they but take a half hair's-breadth beyond!

Is water running in our veins? Do we remember still
Old Plymouth rock, and Lexington, and glorious Bunker Hill?
The debt we owe our fathers' graves? and to the yet unborn,
Whose heritage ourselves must make a thing of pride or scorn?

Gray Plymouth rock hath yet a tongue, and Concord is not dumb,
And voices from our fathers' graves, and from the future come;
They call on us to stand our ground, they charge us still to be
Not only free from chains ourselves, but foremost to make free!

The homespun mail by mothers wove, that erst so freely met
The British steel, clothes hearts as warm with Pilgrim virtues yet,
Come, Brethren, up! Come, Mothers, cheer your sons once more to go
Forth to a nobler battlefield than with our olden foe!

Come, grasp your ancient buckler, gird on your ancient sword,
Let freedom be your bastion, your armory God's word,
Shout "God for our New-England!" and smite them hip and thigh,
The cursed race of Amalek, whose armor is a lie!

They fight against the law of God, the sacred human heart,
One charge from Massachusetts, and their counsels fall apart!
Rock the old Cradle yet once more! let Faneuil Hall send forth
The anger of true-hearted men, the lightning of the North!

Awake, New-England! While you sleep the foes advance their lines,
Already on your stronghold's wall their bloody banner shines,
Awake! and hurl them back again in terror and despair,
The time has come for earnest deeds, we've not a man to spare!

ANTI-TEXAS

Written on Occasion of the Convention
in Faneuil Hall, January 29, 1845

O spirit of the noble Past, when the old Bay State was free,
When her soil was uncontaminate from Berkshire to the sea,
When her sons beneath a foreign sky could answer bold and loud
Of the land that held their fathers' bones within her bosom proud,—

O, for a moment, wake again! rise from thy ancient deep,
Where, in their waving sea-weed shrouds, are swung to dreamless sleep
Her tawny-visaged mariners, within whatever nook
Old Ocean with his moaning surge in farthest seas hath shook!

Awake! arise! O, come again, called up from every sod
Where the moss-gray headstones cluster round the humble house of God,
Where rest the stern old Pilgrims, each little hamlet's pride,
Now, for the first time, sleeping with no weapon by their side!

O, come from where the same good blood, sworn foe to slavery still,
Came oozing through the homespun frock on that world-famous Hill,
And choked his voice whose last faint prayer was for his country's health,—
From being slave or making slave God save the Commonwealth!

O, come from every battle-field, from every famous scene,
Where any blood for Freedom shed hath made the grass more green,
Where, if there be one darker spot and greener than the rest,
It marks where Pilgrim blood hath flowed from a Massachusetts breast!

Rouse! for the Massachusetts men are crowding, one and all,
To look at the corpse of Freedom, where she lies in Faneuil Hall,
Where she lies in her cradle stark and stiff, with death-damp on her brow,
Though cravens would have us think her heart beat never so strong as
    now!

From clanging forge, from humming mill, from work-shop and from loom,
From ploughing land and ploughing sea, from student's lonely room,
They're coming with the will in their eyes, the Puritan-hearted men,—
At sound of their footsteps, the blood shall rush to Freedom's cheek again!

Not now, as in the olden time, with braced-up hearts they come,
While King Street echoes jarringly the roll of British drum;

Not now prepared to grasp the sword, and snatch the firelock down
From where it had hung since the old French war, with dust and cobwebs
    brown;—

They're coming but to speak one word, they're coming but to say,—
"Poor minions of the tyrant's cause, your grovelling hearts obey!
But, hear it, North, and hear it, South, and hear it, East and West,
We will not help you bind your slaves! In God's name, we protest!"

And, though all other deeds of thine, dear Father-land, should be
Washed out, like writing upon sand, by Time's encroaching sea,
That single word shall stand sublime, nor perish with the rest,—
"Though the whole world sanction slavery, in God's name, we protest!"

If hand and foot we must be bound by deeds our fathers signed,
And must be cheated, gulled, and scorned because they too were blind,
Why, let them have their pound of flesh,—for that is in the bond,
But woe to them, if they but take a half-hair's breadth beyond!

Is water running in our veins? Do we remember still
Old Plymouth rock, and Lexington, and glorious Bunker Hill?
The debt we owe our fathers' graves, and to the yet unborn,
Whose heritage ourselves must make a thing of pride or scorn?

Gray Plymouth rock hath yet a tongue, and Concord is not dumb,
And voices from our fathers' graves and from the future come;
They call on us to stand our ground, they charge us still to be
Not only free from chains ourselves, but foremost to make free!

If we[1] must stand alone, what then? the honor shall be more;—
But we can[2] never stand alone, while heaven still arches o'er,
While there's a God to worship, a devil to be denied:
The good and true of every age stand with us[3] side by side!

Or,[4] if it must be, stand alone! and stronger we shall[5] grow
With every coward that deserts to join the tyrant foe;
Let wealth and trade and empire go for what the dross is worth,
One man that stands for right outweighs the guilt of all the earth.

[1] Newspaper text: "thou."
[2] Newspaper text: "thou can'st."
[3] Newspaper text: "us."
[4] Newspaper text: "Well."
[5] Newspaper text: "thou wilt."

No, if the old Bay State were sunk, and, as in days of yore,
One single ship within her sides the hope of Freedom bore,
Run up again the pine-tree flag, and on the chainless sea
That flag should mark, where'er it waved, an[6] island of the free!

A MYSTICAL BALLAD

I

The sunset scarce had dimmed away
Into the twilight's doubtful gray;
One long cloud o'er the horizon lay,
'Neath which, a streak of bluish white
Wavered between the day and night;
Over the pine-trees on the hill
The trembly evening star did thrill,
And the new moon, with slender rim,
Through the elm arches gleaming dim,
Filled memory's chalice to the brim.

II

On such an eve the heart doth grow
Full of surmise, and scarce can know
If it be now or long ago,
Or if indeed it doth exist;—
A wonderful, enchanted mist
From the new moon doth wander out,
Wrapping all things in mystic doubt,
So that this world doth seem untrue,
And all our fancies to take hue
From some life ages since gone through.

III

The maiden sat and heard the flow
Of the west wind, so soft and low
The leaves scarce quivered to and fro;
Unbound, her heavy golden hair
Rippled across her bosom bare,
Which gleamed with thrilling snowy white
Far through the magical moonlight:
The breeze rose with a rustling swell,

6 Newspaper text: "the."

And from afar there came the smell
Of a long-forgotten lily-bell.

IV

The dim moon rested on the hill,
But silent, without thought or will,
Where sat the dreamy maiden still;
And now the moon's tip, like a star,
Drew down below the horizon's bar;
To her black noon the night hath grown,
Yet still the maiden sits alone,
Pale as a corpse beneath a stream,
And her white bosom still doth gleam
Through the deep midnight like a dream.

V

Cloudless the morning came and fair,
And lavishly the sun doth share
His gold among her golden hair,
Kindling it all, till slowly so
A glory round her head doth glow;
A withered flower is in her hand,
That grew in some far distant land,
And, silently transfiguréd,
With wide, calm eyes, and undrooped head,
They found the stranger-maiden dead.

VI

A youth, that morn, 'neath other skies,
Felt sudden tears burn in his eyes,
And his heart throng with memories;
All things without him seemed to win
Strange brotherhood with things within,
And he forever felt that he
Walked in the midst of mystery,
And thenceforth, why, he could not tell,
His heart would curdle at the smell
Of his once cherished lily-bell.

VII

Something from him had passed away;
Some shifting trembles of clear day,
Through starry crannies in his clay,

Grew bright and steadfast, more and more,
Where all had been dull earth before;
And, through these chinks, like him of old,
His spirit converse high did hold
With clearer loves and wider powers,
That brought him dewy fruits and flowers
From far Elysian groves and bowers.

VIII

Just on the farthest bound of sense,
Unproved by outward evidence,
But known by a deep influence
Which through our grosser clay doth shine
With light unwaning and divine,
Beyond where highest thought can fly
Stretcheth the world of Mystery,—
And they not greatly overween
Who deem that nothing true hath been
Save the unspeakable Unseen.

IX

One step beyond life's work-day things,
One more beat of the soul's broad wings,
One deeper sorrow, sometimes brings
The spirit into that great Vast
Where neither future is nor past;
None knoweth how he entered there,
But, waking, finds his spirit where
He thought an angel could not soar,
And, what he called false dreams before,
The very air about his door.

X

These outward seemings are but shows
Whereby the body sees and knows;
Far down beneath, forever flows
A stream of subtlest sympathies
That make our spirits strangely wise
In awe, and fearful bodings dim
Which, from the sense's outer rim,
Stretch forth beyond our thought and sight,
Fine arteries of circling light,
Pulsed outward from the Infinite.

NEW YEAR'S EVE, 1844

A Fragment

The night is calm and beautiful; the snow
Sparkles beneath the clear and frosty moon
And the cold stars, as if it took delight
In its own silent whiteness; the hushed earth
Sleeps in the soft arms of the embracing blue,
Secure as if angelic squadrons yet
Encamped about her, and each watching star
Gained double brightness from the flashing arms
Of winged and unsleeping sentinels.
Upward the calm of infinite silence deepens,
The sea that flows between high heaven and earth,
Musing by whose smooth brink we sometimes find
A stray leaf floated from those happier shores,
And hope, perchance not vainly, that some flower,
Which we had watered with our holiest tears,
Pale blooms, and yet our scanty garden's best,
O'er the same ocean piloted by love,
May find a haven at the feet of God,
And be not wholly worthless in his sight.

O, high dependence on a higher Power,
Sole stay for all these restless faculties
That wander, Ishmael-like, the desert bare
Wherein our human knowledge hath its home,
Shifting their light-framed tents from day to day,
With each new-found oasis, wearied soon,
And only certain of uncertainty!
O, mighty humbleness that feels with awe,
Yet with a vast exulting feels, no less,
That this huge Minster of the Universe,
Whose smallest oratries are glorious worlds,
With painted oriels of dawn and sunset;
Whose carved ornaments are systems grand,
Orion kneeling in his starry niche,
The Lyre whose strings give music audible
To holy ears, and countless splendors more,
Crowned by the blazing Cross high-hung o'er all;
Whose organ music is the solemn stops
Of endless Change breathed through by endless Good;

Whose choristers are all the morning stars;
Whose altar is the sacred human heart
Whereon Love's candles burn unquenchably,
Trimmed day and night by gentle-handed Peace;
With all its arches and its pinnacles
That stretch forever and forever up,
Is founded on the silent heart of God,
Silent, yet pulsing forth exhaustless life
Through the least veins of all created things.

Fit musings these for the departing year;
And God be thanked for such a crystal night
As fills the spirit with good store of thoughts,
That, like a cheering fire of walnut, crackle
Upon the hearth-stone of the heart, and cast
A mild home-glow o'er all Humanity!
Yes, though the poisoned shafts of evil doubts
Assail the skyey panoply of Faith,
Though the great hopes which we have had for man,
Foes in disguise, because they based belief
On man's endeavor, not on God's decree,—
Though these proud-visaged hopes, once turned to fly,
Hurl backward many a deadly Parthian dart
That rankles in the soul and makes it sick
With vain regret, nigh verging on despair,—
Yet, in such calm and earnest hours as this,
We well can feel how every living heart
That sleeps to-night in palace or in cot,
Or unroofed hovel, or which need hath known
Of other homestead than the arching sky,
Is circled watchfully with seraph fires;
How our own erring will it is that hangs
The flaming sword o'er Eden's unclosed gate,
Which gives free entrance to the pure in heart,
And with its guarding walls doth fence the meek.

Sleep then, O Earth, in thy blue-vaulted cradle,
Bent over always by thy mother Heaven!
We all are tall enough to reach God's hand,
And angels are no taller: looking back
Upon the smooth wake of a year o'erpast,
We see the black clouds furling, one by one,
From the advancing majesty of Truth,

And something won for Freedom, whose least gain
Is as a firm and rock-built citadel
Wherefrom to launch fresh battle on her foes;
Or, leaning from the time's extremest prow,
If we gaze forward through the blinding spray,
And dimly see how much of ill remains,
How many fetters to be sawn asunder
By the slow toil of individual zeal,
Or haply rusted by salt tears in twain,
We feel, with something of a sadder heart,
Yet bracing up our bruised mail the while,
And fronting the old foe with fresher spirit,
How great it is to breathe with human breath,
To be but poor foot-soldiers in the ranks
Of our old exiled king, Humanity;
Encamping after every hard-won field
Nearer and nearer Heaven's happy plains.

. . . . . .

Many great souls have gone to rest, and sleep
Under this armor, free and full of peace:
If these have left the earth, yet Truth remains,
Endurance, too, the crowning faculty
Of noble minds, and Love, invincible
By any weapons; and these hem us round
With silence such that all the groaning clank
Of this mad engine men have made of earth
Dulls not some ears for catching purer tones,
That wander from the dim surrounding vast,
Or far more clear melodious prophecies,
The natural music of the heart of man,
Which by kind Sorrow's ministry hath learned
That the true sceptre of all power is love
And humbleness the palace-gate of truth.
What man with soul so blind as sees not here
The first faint tremble of Hope's morning-star,
Foretelling how the God-forged shafts of dawn,
Fitted already on their golden string,
Shall soon leap earthward with exulting flight
To thrid the dark heart of that evil faith
Whose trust is in the clumsy arms of Force,
The ozier hauberk of a ruder age?
Freedom! thou other name for happy Truth,

Thou warrior-maid, whose steel-clad feet were never
Out of the stirrup, nor thy lance uncouched,
Nor thy fierce eye enticed from its watch,
Thou hast learned now, by hero-blood in vain
Poured to enrich the soil which tyrants reap;
By wasted lives of prophets, and of those
Who, by the promise in their souls upheld,
Into the red arms of a fiery death
Went blithely as the golden-girdled bee
Sinks in the sleepy poppy's cup of flame;
By the long woes of nations set at war,
That so the swollen torrent of their wrath
May find a vent, else sweeping off like straws
The thousand cobweb threads, grown cable-huge
By time's long-gathered dust, but cobwebs still,
Which bind the Many that the Few may gain
Leisure to wither by the drought of ease
What heavenly germs in their own souls were sown;—
By all these searching lessons thou hast learned
To throw aside thy blood-stained helm and spear
And with thy bare brow daunt the enemy's front,
Knowing that God will make the lily stalk,
In the soft grasp of naked Gentleness,
Stronger than iron spear to shatter through
The sevenfold toughness of Wrong's idle shield.

THE HAPPY MARTYRDOM

It is not that the wicked hate,
And that the foolish ones deride,
It is not that so long we wait
To see our Master glorified;—
Let hatred, scorn, and sorrow come,
These do not make our martyrdom.

Father! we know our cause is Thine;
Though every earthly hope departs,
We ask of Thee no clearer sign
Than the sweet promise in our hearts:
Error may win the world's applause,—
Peace watches with the righteous cause.

And, if this blessing Thou hast given,
Why should we heed the bigot's scorn?
He cannot bar the gates of Heaven,
Nor bribe the sunset or the morn
Their consolation to deny,
Because his soul is niggardly.

Love, Faith, and Peace, Thy lilies three,
Bloom on a single heart's frail stem
That dares Truth's unpaid bondman be;—
Father! what lack we, having them?
Though unbelief's bleak winter freeze,
Thy quiet sunshine fences these.

Then, Lord, what martyrdom have we,
Whose pride of self grows less and less,
Who, from a vain world's din, can flee
Into thy guarded silentness,
Content, if we, from year to year,
May save mankind a single tear?

And yet what pang so sharp as this,—
To see our brother sit in night,
Shut out and exiled from the bliss
Of giving all to serve the Right?
To see the seed thy hand hath sown
With the World's darnels overgrown?

To see the Church hold up Thy Book
To keep thy light from bursting in?
To see Thy priests with patience brook,
For the rich sinner's sake, the sin?
To see the red-eyed vengeance creep
Upon our nation in its sleep?

O, let these make our faith more strong,
And make our hope more sure and high;
Except our brother do us wrong,
How could'st Thou teach us charity?
Except we feel our utter weakness,
How could'st Thou strengthen us with meekness?

Still give us trials such as these,
That we may learn to lean on Thee;
Still humble us, till, by degrees,

LEARNING RESOURCES CENTER
NAZARETH COLLEGE

Proof against self our mail may be;
So shall peace, hope, and patience come
Seven-fold from this our martyrdom.

AN EPIGRAM,

On Certain Conservatives

In olden days men's ears were docked
For thinking, and for other crimes;
And now, some worthies overstocked
With these commodities are shocked
At the false mercy of the times,
Which spoils their chance of being shortened
In their own feature most important.

NOW IS ALWAYS BEST

Dreamy river of the Past,
Flowing into darkness slowly,
Many a blossom I have cast
On thy waters, now made holy
By an idle melancholy;
Give me but a leaflet back,
Though quite wilted, ere thy track
Shall be lost in midnight wholly!
Give me one, I ask no more,
Though it be but from the store
Of some childish, by-gone folly!

Ah me! in a heavy mood,
Such as I to-night am bearing,
Any thing that's past is good;
All the present is but caring,
All the future more despairing,
And the past is sweet alone,
Where, although the sun be gone,
Half the sky is warm with wearing
His last kiss, and in the East
A faint glow, of lights the least,
Tells that moon-rise is preparing.

When was ever joy like thine,
Whose memory, even, is juvenescent?
Then my blood was more than wine,
Then I slumbered like a peasant,
Then my hope was like a crescent
That could never come to full,
Then, if ever, life looked dull,
Dulness must for once be pleasant,
Then my heart so lightly beat
That the sunshine seemed more sweet
Even for being evanescent.

Idle fancies! would I change
The hard present, with its swinking,
With its hopes of broader range,
Past and Future strangely linking
By their privilege of thinking,—
Would I change it for their Old,
Which, for all its cups of gold,
Gives us but poor dregs for drinking?
Would I change it for the past?
Make ease first, and labor last?
Out on such unmanly shrinking!

Mine the Present! That is best,
Let what will have gone before it;
Here my heart shall build her nest,
With green leaves to rustle o'er it;
When there's sunshine, she shall store it
As the moss does, 'gainst the hour
When the clouds come'into power,
And from her own garners pour it
All around, until the sun
Come again, ere half's outrun,
And with tenfold grace restore it.

After both are over and gone,
What care I for sun or shower?
While there's earth to stand upon,
Spite of both the heart can flower;
In herself is all her power;
Fancy, too, can build a home
Higher than where change can come,

And the soul hath still her dower
Of high faith and purpose vast,
Where, though earth in night be cast,
She waits firm as in a tower.

ORPHEUS

I

Earth, I have seen thy face,
And looked upon it so,
That what before was barren of all grace,
Did with delight o'erflow.

II

So generous was my glance,
So kingly and so free,
O, mother Earth, thy wo-worn countenance
Lit up for love of me.

III

I looked as doth the sun
Who leaps up, and, behold,
The dark and shaggy hill-tops, one by one,
Beneath his gaze turn gold.

IV

The largess of mine eye
On humblest things I poured,
And still, the more I scattered lavishly,
The fuller grew my hoard.

V

O, Heaven's o'erfolding blue!
I had not loved thee long
Ere royal shapes of gods did glimmer through
And deepen all my song.

VI

Thence leaned the golden-haired
Apollo and the rest,

The forms of power and grace that long had shared
The worship of my breast.

VII

They seemed but dim at first
Till, by my love made wise,
I saw them in all higher moods, and durst
Face their strength-giving eyes.

VIII

From me my brethren learned
To name them, and to praise
One sunlike god, that in calm centre burned,
And shot forth many rays.

IX

Thy love, Eurydice,
To me was shield and helm,
And, when thou wentest forth, it was the key
That oped the spirit-realm.

X

Then did I know at last
What I had dreamed before,
What the tried heart would patiently forecast—
New life when this is o'er.

XI

What hope had argued long
Thereof brought sorrow proof,
And heights of calm that erst hemmed in my song
No longer loomed aloof.

XII

O, Earth, I roam again
Thy hills and woods and glades;
Thy oceans heave, thy forests wave in vain;
Thou art the land of shades!

XIII

Where my beloved is,
And whither now I go,
There only is the solid form of bliss
Whose shadow here is wo.

XIV

Earth, thou hast lent me much
Yet thine is all the debt—
For, where my heedless feet have chanced to touch,
The spot is holy yet.

AN EXTRACT

Force never yet gained one true victory:[1]
The outward man, by pike and ball o'er-argued,[2]
Bends low his politic will; but still, within,
The absolute Man, on whom the basis rest,[3]
Deep under-ground, of the infrangible State,[4]
Stands up defiant, plotting loyalty
To[5] one poor banished, homeless, hunted thought,
The dethroned image of a native land.

Never was city-wall so strong as Peace;
This, founded sure[6] on the soul's primitive rock,
Smiles back upon the baffled engineer;
The mine at its foundations tugs in vain;[7]
An olive-wreath, stretched harmlessly across
Its open gates, enchants all[8] enemies,
So that the trumpet baulks the knitted lips
That would have jarred it with the trampling charge,
And, hushing back its hoarse and quarrelsome voice,
Like a disbanded soldier when he sees
The nestled hamlet of his unstained youth,
With its slim steeple quivering in the sun,[9]
Pipes with repentant note the gay recall.[10]

[1] MS rejects "Force never yet hath conquered any man."
[2] MS rejects "out argued."
[3] MS rejects "on whom convictions rest."
[4] MS rejects "The unseen basis of a true State's weal."
[5] MS: "For."
[6] MS rejects "deep."
[7] MS rejects "The mine its sure foundations lifts in vain."
[8] MS rejects "lets in no."
[9] MS rejects "in the sun quivering."
[10] MS read "Pipes with a softened tone the glad recall"; then substituted "Pipes with repentant tone the glad recall."

What hath the conqueror for all his toil?
So many men from men turned murderers;
So many spoiled[11] in the fierce[12] apprenticeship;
So many sacred images of God,
Sons, fathers, brothers, husbands, trampled down
Into the red mud of the plashy field;
So many vultures gorged with human flesh;
So many widows made, so many orphans;
So many cinders for so many homes;
So many caps flung up as there are fools;[13]
And, when his shattering and ungoverned course
Is run at length, he drops, a mass inert,
Like[14] a spent cannon-ball which the child's foot
Spurns at in play,—what further need of him?
Peace will not brook to have her snowy leaves
Turned rudely[15] by those crimson-smutching[16] thumbs;
The smooth civilian elbows him aside;[17]
Like an old armor he is hung in the hall,
For idle men to count the dints upon,
A buttress for the siper's [*sic*][18] hanging-bridge.

And for his country what hath this man conquered?[19]
A kindred people's everlasting hate,
The bloody drain of untamed[20] provinces;
Those are ill crops whose sickle is the sword.[21]
And for himself? I never heard that any
Dared knock at Heaven's gate with his reeking sword,
Or lift the next life's latch with bloody hands.[22]

11 MS: "slain."
12 MS rejects "red."
13 MS rejects "So many empty show as there are fools."
14 MS omits "Like."
15 MS: "roughly."
16 MS rejects "dropping."
17 This line in MS appeared 3 lines earlier (after "need of him?"); and was transposed in MS draft.
18 MS: "spider's."
19 MS: "gained."
20 MS: "conquered."
21 MS: "An endless condemnation to yᵉ sword."
22 MS interpolates the following lines:
    The soft palmed tradesman coming home at eve
    Gathers his wondring (wide-eyed) children round the hearth,
    Reads o'er the lists of wounded and of killed
    To tell (And tells) them this is glory, says with (modest) pride
    "I knew Jones well—the man who lost his leg,"
    And, fired with honest rivalry, bestrides

The merry plough-boy whistling to his team,
The noisy mason and the carpenter
Efface the ruinous letters wherewith he
Essayed to carve an everlasting name.
The tyrannous lion preys upon the lamb;
Men fear him and install him king of beasts,
Yet prize the wool above the ravening claws.

THE EX-MAYOR'S CRUMBS OF CONSOLATION:
A PATHETIC BALLAD

Two Governors once a letter writ
    To the Mayor of a distant city,
And told him a paper was published in it,
That was telling the truth, and 'twas therefore fit
That the same should be crushed as dead as a nit
    By an Aldermanic Committee;
        "Don't say so?" says Otis,
        I'll inquire if so 'tis;
Dreadful! telling the truth? what a pity!

"It can't be the Atlas, that's perfectly clear,
    And of course it isn't the Advertiser,
'Tis out of the Transcript's appropriate sphere,
The Post is above suspicion; oh dear,
To think of such accidents happening here!
    I hoped that our people were wiser:
        While we're going," says Otis,
        "*Faustissimis votis,*
How very annoying such flies are!"

The ungoverned hackney on the musterfield
With hands that long yet dread to clutch the mane.

He hath his fame tis true; and parodied
In many a dim and fly blown lithograph
His features struggle through the barroom's smoke,
Trimmed round the edges with some topers score,

Was on the jury that could not agree
When he was tried for petty larceny
A hero now—what constable would dare
To clasp a fetter round that wooden leg?

So, without more ado, he inquired all round
  Among people of wealth and standing;
But wealth looked scornful and standing frowned,
At last in a garret with smoke imbrowned,
The conspirators all together he found,—
  One man with a coloured boy banding;
    " 'Pon my word," says Otis,
    "Decidedly low 'tis,"
As he groped for the stairs on the landing.

So he wrote to the Governors back agen,
  And told them 'twas something unworthy of mention,
That 'twas only a single man with a pen,
And a font of types in a sort of a den,
A person unknown to Aldermen,
  And, of course, beneath attention;
    "And therefore," wrote Otis
    Annuentibus totis,
"There's no reason for apprehension."—

But one man with a pen is a terrible thing,
  With a head and heart behind it,
And this one man's words had an ominous ring,
That somehow in peoples' ears would cling;—
"But the mob's uncorrupted; they've eggs to fling;
  So 'tis hardly worth while to mind it;
    As for Freedom," says Otis,
    "I've given her notice
To leave town, in writing, and underlined it."

But the one man's helper grew into a sect,
  That laughed at all efforts to choke or scare it,
Old parties before it were scattered and wrecked
And respectable folks knew not what to expect;—
" 'Tis some consolation, at least to reflect,
  And will help us I think to bear it,
    That all this," says Otis,
    Though by no means *in votis,*
"Began with one man and a boy in a garret."

THE BURIAL OF THEOBALD

They heard it in[1] the lulls of the blast,[2]
  In the pauses[3] strange and dreary
That come[4] when a wave of the storm has past,
Through the hollow midnight void and vast,
  They heard the plaint[5] of the *Miserere*.

Up the mountain-side came a sound of wail[6]
  Wavering and struggling against the gale
Gathering[7] to a choral swell,
  Blown by the tyrannous gust away,[8]
Dropped full-toned in the sheltered dell,
  Over the sharp cliff whirled in spray;[9]
One shepherd to another called,
  " 'Tis the burial-chant of Theobald,"
Then listened to catch the faint reply,
  "May he plead for our souls with the saints on high!"[10]

In the Abbey Church the body lay,
  And[11] the monks kept watch in turn
That holy candles in due array[12]
  At head and feet should burn.

"Hush! heard you naught?" whispered brother Paul,
  And fearfully glanced behind
Tow'rd the darkness that seemed to thicken and fall[13]
  Nearer and nearer, and shift and crawl[14]
With weird shapes and faces,—" 'Tis only the wind,"[15]

1 MS rejects "between."
2 In the MS this is line 5. The first 4 lines are those of stanza 3 in the present text
with the variants as indicated.
3 MS: "silence."
4 MS: "Comes."
5 MS rejects "wail."
6 MS gives alternate reading "a deep toned wail."
7 MS rejects "Now loudering."
8 MS: "Then blown by the tyrannous wind away."
9 MS read "Or against the steep cliff whirled in spray"; then substituted "Or
over . . ."
10 MS omits this line and the preceding.
11 MS omits "And."
12 MS rejects "That at head and feet in due array."
13 MS: "crawl."
14 MS: "Nearer and nearer; 'Tis only the wind."
15 MS omits this line.

Muttered brother Giles, his awe[16] dissembling,
But the shake of his beads betrayed his trembling.

As the lumberers' log-fire melts the snow
  And slowly bares its circle of ground,[17]
So the flame[18] of the candles seemed melting slow
  Through the chancel's deep-drifted gloom profound,
And figures of saints peered stony and grim
  Round the shivering[19] halo's outer rim,
Now hid in their niches, now starting out,
As the wind tossed the island of light about.

"There! there!" gasped Paul, "it sounded again,[20]
  Something between a groan and a sigh!"
They listened, but[21] only heard the rain
Dashed spattering against the oriel-pane
  By a flap of the storm's wing[22] rushing by.[23]

There are two to knoll the bell have gone,
For the sacristan dared not go alone,
  And in many a winter evening cold,
In after years they have both of them told
  How behind them, over the floor,
They heard the patting of clammy feet
And the trail, as it were of a winding-sheet
  As far as the outer door.

The censers sweet meanwhile were swung
  And the dirge for the holy dead was sung;
"God rest his soul!" said the Abbot then;
  Much monkish blood was running chill,
As the roof gave back the words agen,
  And all once more was still.

16 MS: "fear."
17 MS read "And bares its arch of ground"; then interpolated "slowly" as in present reading.
18 MS read "In the light"; then substituted "In the flame."
19 MS rejects "wavering."
20 MS rejects "I heard it again."
21 MS: "and."
22 MS rejects present reading and substitutes "As the storm flapped its broad wing."
23 MS ends here.

"Amen!" and the lank corpse sate upright
  Upon the bier, the cerements white
Fell backward as it raised
  Its shrunk arm in the ghastly light
And on the Abbot gazed;
  Ice crept round the roots of the Abbot's hair,
As he met the dead man's frozen stare.

The blue lips stir not, but the words
  Upon the darkness fall,
As flit the shapes of twilight birds
  From some long-ruined hall.

"*Justo judicio*," thus groaned he,
  "*Dei damnatus sum,*"
And then sank backward silently,
  To be forever dumb.

He lived a lone and prayerful life,
  Penance was his and gnawing fast,
Much wrestling with an inward strife
  To win the crown at last;
Full oft his rebel flesh had known
  Sharp scourge-sores festering to the bone.

No sound of earth could pierce his cell,
  He sought not fame nor pelf,
Below he saw the fires of hell,
  And prayed and scourged and fasted well
  Therefrom to save himself;
His heart he starved and mortified;
  Love knocked and turned away denied.

Such graces rare, and such an end
  God grant us all our lives to mend!
Was not a monk among the whole
  Could read this riddle for his soul;
Some hinted at a secret crime,
  A vow unpaid, a penance broke,
But clearer views and more sublime
Prevailed, and all agreed in time,
  'Twas Satan, not their saint, that spoke.

KING RETRO

I

There lived once, and perhaps lives still,
   A monarch brave and mighty,
A prince of energy and will
   Compact as *lignum vitæ*,
Who, among other treasures great,
   Whereof he had profusion,
(As well beseemed his birth and state),
   Possessed an Institution.

II

A King's whole outfit was, years back,
   A people and a saddle;
Enough if he could spur and whack,
   Although his brains were addle;
But now these good old times are gone,
   And kings, grown wisely heedful,
Find that, to keep their saddles on,
   A bridle too is needful.

III

Just now 'tis kingcraft's highest art
   Itself to bit and bridle,
Yet kings will sometimes set their heart
   Upon a whimsy idle;
One for a brimstone match stakes all,
   For a frail woman's kiss one,
One won't let last year's dead leaves fall,
   And so it was with this one.

IV

Although his hobby asked no good
   To give it expedition,
But bare him straight along the road
   To double-distilled perdition,
Although his revenues incurred
   An hourly diminution,
His Trojan horse he whipped and spurred,
   And blessed his institution.

V

Riches have been but flighty things,
  From our day up to Adam,
But, if a treasure e'er had wings,
  This institution had 'em;
Or rather, what was just as good
  As wings, however supple,
It had ('tis true by holy rood!)
  Of legs three million couple.

VI

Whereof each being stout and tough
  As those of Bishop Burnet,
Its share of body would take off
  Forgetting to return it,
And, what was worse, both clothes and shoes
  Went off with every biped,
For whose evasive, larcenous use,
  The monarch (with a sigh) paid.

VII

Our king, but that his eyes were dim,
  Had thought it quite a blessing
To see his ruin leaving him
  And cheap reform progressing,
To lose this rust which nothing did
  But eat into his riches,
And of this hobby-horse get rid
  Which wore out all his breeches.

VIII

But some his title to the thing
  Denied, or picked a hole in it,
Nay, even hinted that the king
  His grandfather had stolen it,
And when the wandering pieces got
  Beyond his kingdom's borders,
The neighbor Powers said, *"Go to pot!"*
  To all his threats and orders.

IX

This made his kingship very wroth,
  He growled like baited Bruin,

Swearing a great and solemn oath
That he would have his Ruin;
And, when his Council next time sate,
His fist he struck the board on
And bade them to prepare him straight
A sanitary *cordon.*

X

"Liege friends," (they all hummed *vivat rex!*)
"I wish your calm solution
Of what disease infects the legs
Of this my institution;
It must and shall be put to rout,
And all of you I'll gibbet if—
That is—I'll thank you to make out
Some penal law prohibitive.

XI

"Although my honoured sire and those
Who lived and reigned before him,
Have been a tariff's deadly foes,
Both fixed and *ad valorem,*
Yet, rather than these insults bear,
I will impose a tariff,
Which whoso breaks shall straightway wear
A neckcloth *à la sheriff!*"

XII

Then rose the Minister of Law
And begged he might disclose his—
"Well," growled the king, "why hem and haw?
Let's have your *diagnosis!*"
"This epidemic so malign,
I think, if I might venture I
Should say bore every mark and sign
Of chronic Nineteenth Century."

XIII

"That's the disease beyond a doubt,"
Broke in the king, "that's firstly,
But secondly's *how keep it out?*
And that does pose me curstly;"

It bursts in like another flood
And drowns all earth in troubles,
Thrones that since Noah's time have stood
It trifles with like bubbles;

XIV

"Nay, that huge image of men's fears,
That spiritual domination
Clamped down with sixteen hundred years
Of iron association,
It has torn up (unless, indeed,
There's taken place of late a
Recoil) and tossed it like a weed
To crumble at Gaëta."

XV

"First," said the minister, "we ought
To fix our scale of duties;
Old forms, while Speech is free and Thought,
Are not worth my cast shoe-ties;"—
"Well, tax 'em, then," the king replied,
"If taxing will prevent 'em;
Say, *ad valorem* (you decide)
Fifty or so *per centum.*"

XVI

"May't please you, as those articles
Are quoted now, a higher
Rate will be needed, for all else
Is squirting on hell-fire;
For now-a-days they're both so poor,
So in the making blundered,
That our *percent* to make all sure,
Must be some fifty hundred.

XVII

"Then there's a book which now-a-days
Is turned into a libel,"—
"Its name? Who wrote it?" "Please your grace,
I mean—a—a—the Bible."
"The what? O, atheistic wound!
O, stab in part most vital!
Why, on that Book, you know, we found
Our Institution's title."

XVIII

"Yes, but 'tis made a nuisance now
   By Fourierites and fanatics,
Creatures who live, one knows not how,
   On bran bread up in attics."
"Well, then, if fiends in human shape
   Their vile eyes have intruded
Upon the text, there's no escape,
   The Book must be excluded!

XIX

"And yet it harrows my soul's core
   To lose this Widow Cruise's
Pitcher, this never-emptied store
   Of precedent for abuses;
Used prudently, it does no harm,
   And, given in cautious doses,
It is a safe and sovereign charm
   To lead men by their noses."

XX

"There's yet one more new-fangled thing
   That's always mischief hatching,
And, what is worse (God save the King!)
   'Tis desperately catching;
They call it Light,"—"By all that's good,
   Keep *that* out, Mister Minister,
Of all the new-loosed Satan's brood
   Not one is half so sinister."

XXI

Here rose an ancient Counsellor
   With all men's reverence valanced,
A soul 'twixt After and Before,
   In perfect quiet balanced;
When Memory, over ninety years
   Can make her retrogressions,
Experience, manifold appears
   But backward-looking Prescience.

XXII

He, rising, stood there, hoar and blind,
   'Mid much applausive murmur,

Seeking some staff wherewith his mind
  Might safelier tread and firmer,
Then straightening, seemed to lay one hand
  Upon the Future's shoulder,
One on the Past's, and so to stand
  Majestically bolder.

XXIII

"What must that be, O King, think yet,
  Which thou are thus protecting,
With every fence around it set
  Its weakness more detecting?
All good things strike firm roots below,
  The whirlwind with them wages
A fruitless war, and can but blow
  Their seeds along the Ages.

XXIV

"What shall thy safeguard be against
  Those forces ever living
Whose ordered march thou marr'st and pain'st
  Thus vainly with them striving?
Can'st thou shut Love out? Can'st thou bar
  Those endless aspirations
Which, upward from the things that are
  Lead poets first, then nations?

XXV

"Thou may'st exclude the written Word
  And muzzle dead Apostles,
But can'st thou gag the mocking bird,
  The robins and the throstles?
These by the lonely rice swamp sing
  Or 'mid the bursting cotton,
And tidings of the Father bring
  To those by Man forgotten.

XXVI

"The Letter's narrow grave no more
  Confines the heart of Jesus;
From whip-scarred flesh the soul can soar
  To him who made and sees us;

The air we breathe takes Freedom's part,
  Prompts wanderings and departures,
Filled with the spirit and the heart
  Of prophets, saints and martyrs.

XXVII

"Your tariff may be strong and tight,
  But, if you keep out Heaven, you
Must have men swifter than the light
  For officers of revenue;
It floods, it bursts, and eddies in,
  Or, on the wings of silence,
Floats down o'er walls of want and sin,
  In spite of watchful violence.

XXVIII

"Call back, thou may'st, the martyr age,
  Heap faggots for the firing,
Yet think against your futile rage
  What traitors are conspiring;
Still shines the sun, still roves the wind,
  And, since the earth had motion,
The stars to human hearts have shined
  Hope, courage, and devotion.

XXIX

"Against the bestial and the false,
  The Kingdom of Unreason,
All Nature gathers force and falls
  At once to plotting treason;
Hush every voice you start at now,
  Bring Slavery to perfection,
And every leaf upon the bough
  Would whisper insurrection.

XXX

"Put trust, my Liege, while yet you can,
  In the soul's inborn beauties;
Write first your debt to brother-man,
  Upon your scale of duties,
Or keep all dark and close, to work
  Brewing explosive vapour,
And woe betide, who in that murk
  First lights Hope's farthing taper!"

XXXI

He ceased, and straight the King broke out,
Amid much tongue-confusion,
"What! one of us with sneer and doubt
Blaspheme my Institution!
Thou crazy Fawkes, I'll find out soon
A bedlam to clap you in;
Things must be sadly out of tune
If I can't have my Ruin!"

"LADY BIRD, LADY BIRD, FLY AWAY HOME"

Lady Bird, lady bird, fly away home!
Your house is on fire, your children will burn!
Send for the engines, and send for the men,
Perhaps we can put it out agen;
Send for the ladders, and send for the hose,
Perhaps we can put it out, nobody knows;
Sure, nobody's case was ever sadder,
To the nursery-window clap the ladder,
If they are there, and not done brown,
They'll open the window and hopple down!

Splish, splash! fizz and squirt!
All my 'things' ruined with water and dirt,
All my new carpets torn to flinders,
Trodden in with mud and cinders!
My mirrors smashed, my bedsteads racked,
My company tea-set chipped and cracked!
Save my child—my carpets and chairs,
And I'll give you leave to burn my heirs,
They are little six-legged, spotted things,
If they have any sense, they'll use their wings;
If they have any sense, they'll use their legs,
Or, at worst, it is easy to lay more eggs.

OUT OF DOORS

'Tis good to be abroad in the sun,
His gifts abide when day is done;

Each thing in nature from his cup
Gathers a several virtue up;
The grace within its being's reach
Becomes the nutriment of each,
And the same life imbibed by all
Makes each most individual:
Here the twig-bending peaches seek
The glow that mantles in their cheek—
Hence comes the Indian-summer bloom
That hazes round the basking plum,
And, from the same impartial light,
The grass sucks green, the lily white.

Like these the soul, for sunshine made,
Grows wan and gracile in the shade,
Her faculties, which God decreed
Various as Summer's dædal breed,
With one sad color are imbued,
Shut from the sun that tints their blood;
The shadow of the poet's roof
Deadens the dyes of warp and woof;
Whate'er of ancient song remains
Has fresh air flowing in its veins,
For Greece and eldest Ind knew well
That out of doors, with world-wide swell
Arches the student's lawful cell.

Away, unfruitful lore of books,
For whose vain idiom we reject
The spirit's mother-dialect,
Aliens among the birds and brooks,
Dull to interpret or believe
What gospels lost the woods retrieve,
Or what the eaves-dropping violet
Reports from God, who walketh yet
His garden in the hush of eve!
Away, ye pedants city-bred,
Unwise of heart, too wise of head,
Who handcuff Art with *thus and so,*
And in each other's foot-prints tread,
Like those who walk through drifted snow;
Who, from deep study of brick walls
Conjecture of the water-falls,

By six feet square of smoke-stained sky
Compute those deeps that overlie
The still tarn's heaven-anointed eye,
And, in your earthen crucible,
With chemic tests essay to spell
How nature works in field and dell!
Seek we where Shakspeare buried gold?
Such hands no charmed witch-hazel hold;
To beach and rock repeats the sea
The mystic *Open Sesame;*
Old Greylock's voices not in vain
Comment on Milton's mountain strain,
And cunningly the various wind
Spenser's locked music can unbind.

THE NORTHERN SANCHO PANZA AND HIS VICARIOUS CORK TREE

If any age or any zone
Hath zeal for Christian doctrines shown,
Zeal proved by deeds, not word of mouth,
Sure the North shows it toward the South;
Ere from one cheek the smart hath burned,
The other to the palm is turned;
Soon as the coat is asked for, lo!
The cloak must from our shoulders go;
And now they bid us, for our sins,
To Compromise—what's left? our skins.
Our cheeks, *our* cloaks, *our* skins, suppose
They should be some one's else, who knows?
Well, well, we're not our brother's keeper,
And *such* self-sacrifice is cheaper.

"Brethren," says Sancho, meekly, "this is
The price we pay for prejudices;
Some views prevailed in Pagan times
Which our more light convert to crimes;
The stranger found the ancient roof
'Gainst every harm a shield of proof,
And even a foe, become a guest,
Was sure of shelter, food and rest;

But, my good friends, this heathen virtue
In its pure form would surely hurt you,
Though, watered well with compromise,
The stomach finds it very nice;
Christ came, as Paul's Epistles state,[1]
The Ethnic law to abrogate,
Which means—that is—in short, the fact is
Virtue is good in all but practice,[2]
And we have all of us gone wrong,
I almost blush to say how long.
We must obey God's laws, no doubt,
As fast as we can find them out,
That truth is marked by every steeple—
But if we are God's chosen people?
If Cuffee here is just the ram
Jehovah sent to Abraham
In Isaac's stead, by whom is meant
Our party and our ten per cent?[3]

"When the wise men of Gotham found
Their townhouse leaked, they looked around
Some lasting remedy to find
Such as would suit the Gotham mind;
After ten years of speeches, lectures,[4]
Specifications, doubts, conjectures,
And quarrelings among electors,
A very wise and reverend man
Proposed, as all agreed, *the* plan—
A roof that[5] won't keep out the weather
Had best[6] be torn down altogether;
When we've no roof, 'tis very plain
There'll be no leak to let in rain.[7]

"So we have tried our small concessions,
And given the lie to our professions,
Yet, spite of all our strength and skill,[8]

[1] MS begins here.
[2] MS omits this line and the preceding.
[3] MS omits the above 8 lines.
[4] MS: "plans and lectures."
[5] MS: "Since the roof."
[6] MS: "Let it."
[7] MS omits this line and the preceding.
[8] MS rejects "Yet, spite of all that we could do."

The South is discontented still;
Now let us no more play the dunce,[9]
But fairly give up all at once,
And fitting[10] penance do, what's more,
For not inventing it[11] before;
My private feelings I surrender,
Although my flesh, like yours, is tender;
Let all the people, far and near,
The thong[12] across my shoulders hear!"

O, generous Sancho, cut and thrash![13]
The cork-tree will[14] not hurt the lash;
Lay on and spare not, soundly thwack![15]
Remember that the bark is black;[16]
Keep up the sacrifice, 'tis brave,
When no one feels it but the slave;
Till dooms-day give up all to others,
When all you give up is—your brother's.

A DREAM I HAD

I read one fine evening how Socrates,
Making ready for old Davy's locker at ease,
So grandly contrived a reply to
The reasons and temptings of Crito,
Who urged 't would be acting imbecilely
If, before came from Delos the vessel, he
Did not quickly slip off to Thessaly,
And wait till the fickle Athenians
Had time to get wiser opinions,
Instead of remaining a fixture
Just to drink up the City's vile mixture,
And the, *sans* his fleshly surtout (Oh
Dreadful!), sneak shivering to Pluto,
Kicked, as 't were, by the general shoe-toe.

[9] MS rejects "Now let us give up all at o . . ."
[10] MS rejects "And let us."
[11] MS: "this."
[12] MS read "whacks"; then substituted "lash."
[13] MS: "thrash and thrash.
[14] MS rejects "does."
[15] MS rejects "Lay all your feelings, do not falter."
[16] MS rejects "Thus nobly on the public altar."

Love of life—what a cowardly mocker it is!
But it wasted its breath upon Socrates;
Though he saw Death just lifting the knocker at his
Door, with a stern *I must lead ye hence,*
Yet he argued so well for obedience
To the law, and showed how on principle
Men must gulp, and not even wince, a pill
Prepared by the rightful authorities,
No matter how dreadful a bore it is,
And how for himself it was proper
(If some friend would lend him a copper
To defray the expenses of Charon,
An abuse he should waive comment there on,
Since he soon should have time, if he wanted it,
To row up the people who granted it),
It was proper—if he but obeyed his
Conscience—to go down to Hades
(Hope, doubtless, threw in some suggestions
How he'd bother the ghosts with his questions),
And fulfil there his proper vocation
As a live note of interrogation;
He, I say, argued all this so strongly
That his friends were convinced they'd done wrongly,
The more since no jailor could them lock
In at night, nor were they to drink hemlock.

Methought 't was a grand thing in Socrates
Thus to sanctify law in Democraties,
And I mused, with my feet on the fender's
Bright rim, about other surrenders
Of self to the infinite Splendors,
And of some to the Darknesses also,
Wondering how people could fall so
As to change a true soul for a sham one,
And become the poor Levites of Gammon,
Making one shame a mere cotyledon
For the seed of another to feed on,
Or rather, like that little dumb bug,
Lifelong rolling pellets of humbug;
And it struck me—would men but consider
Which truly goes highest as bidder
For their services here, God or Satan—
But they will not; our Age is the great one

Of quick returns and small prophets
With no faith in Heavens or Tophets.

Then I thought of those countless epistles,
Flying thick as balloon-seeds from thistles,
Those pleas of the Great Defender's
Where (as boys play at kittledybenders)
One is forced to skim quick o'er the frail ice
Of logic as brittle as Paley's,
Because, if one stop for a moment
To put in a doubt or a comment,
He goes slap through to get a blind seasoning
In the thick mud beneath the thin reasoning.
Well, I bravely went o'er the whole batch (or all
Up to date), and then, as was natural,
Fell asleep, and my brain took to breeding
A dream out of what I'd been reading.

I thought that the sun had just risen
When, I, Crito, went to the prison
To visit (so dreams often whisk us)
The condemned son of old Sophroniscus,
Who somehow was Webster—drest oddly
In a queer want of costume ungodly,
Such as never is seen but on statues
(An invention of sculptors for that use),
No coat, breeches, waistcoat, shirt, hat, shoes,
Just a kind of a sheet flung about him;
Such a garb as was ne'er worn by sane gents,
Save in stone, whether modern or ancients.

Well, Daniel played Socrates nicely,
Talking cheerfully, bravely and wisely,
And spoke of the hemlock precisely
As if any true man would think it
A privilege only to drink it,
And would just as soon wish to say Ah no
To a *fiasco* of Montepulciano.

The calm sage grew no whit the paler,
When the door creaked and in walked the jailer
With a glass of vile stuff on a waiter;
Unmoved as a Jupiter Stator,

He said, "I regard it as all some
Delicious conservative balsam,
Which to swallow (by proxy) is wholesome—
For the patriot true and self-scorner"—
Just then came a moan from the corner,
. And I looked and saw Ellen Craft kneeling,
With a face full of hopeless appealing,
And found that (dreams mix things so drolly)
Daniel did not play Socrates solely;
The talking part—*that* was his wholly,
And performed with no womanly shrinking;
But as soon as it came to the drinking,
Why, the hemlock was handed to Ellen—
And the roof of my dream-building fell in.

ON RECEIVING A PIECE OF FLAX-COTTON

While we, with human rage and heat,
Would make the world forego its ill,
Behold with what unnoticed feet
God's passionless reformers still
Come unaware and have their will.

Tough roots hath profitable wrong
That blunt too long the leveller's axe;
God touches them with naught more strong
Nor sharper than a stem of flax,—
The iron fibres melt as wax.

Thou soft and silken Garrison!
Light as thou liest in my hand,
By thee great marvels shall be done,
For thou shalt snap the Circe-wand
And disenchant the grovelling land.

By many a rushing waterfall
I hear the spindles buzz aloud,
Twining the cords that bind us all;
I see our dear New England bowed
To weave the web of Freedom's shroud.

How quietly upon her side
Doth Fate the hostile force enlist!
Perchance, ere long, with us allied,
Those wheels with every thread they twist
Shall make an Abolitionist.

I hear our pines, with horrent thrill,
Sigh dreading that their doom may be
From 'neath the shade of Bunker Hill,
To bear across the spurning sea
The human flesh-tax of the free.

Come swiftly happy change and bless
Our longing sight before we die;
Set free our pulpit and our press,
Relume the ancient fires that die,
In fallen New England's downcast eye!

Or come in God's own season; swift
In sickly ripeness, stung by wasps;
The hand of God from each good gift
One finger at a time unclasps,
And shuts from him who rashly grasps.

Then let our banyan empire shoot
Such knitted stems as earth ne'er saw,
O'er half a world; and let its root
From Shakspeare's tongue and Alfred's law
The everliving forces draw!

OUR OWN,

His Wanderings and Personal Adventures

Πολλῶν δ'ανθρώπων ἴδην ἀστεα, καὶ νοον ἔγνω.
Quae regio in terris NOSTRI non plena laboris?

Full many cities he hath seen and many great men known;
What place on earth but testifies the labors of OUR OWN?

DIGRESSION A
Our Own in mounting Pegasus,
Takes such impetuous stride

That, with a downcome ominous,
He falls o' the other side.

Sirs, Editors of Putnam's (if it's right to use the plural),
I wish to recommend myself to—*tooral, looral, looral!*
This strikes you as an oddish way of winding up a distich?
As something rather wild, incomprehensible, and mystic?
Well, to confess the truth at once, I'm something new at verses,
No fairy gave me rhymes at birth in Fortunatus-purses;
Rhymes, I opine, like Plato's souls, are born in incompleteness,
Pining, mere bachelors, till they meet their destined linkéd sweetness;
And some men, never finding halves *sans* those they should be pinned to,
Scrawl rhyme as easily as Jack Frost scrawls rime upon a window:
That's not my luck;—the prior verse, before I've time to think, 's at hand,
While that which ought to marry it plays spinster in my inkstand,
Immovable as the proverb's horse that can both nod and wink stand;
So, having written my first line, and ended it with *plural,*
I could not light on any mate but *Ural, mural, crural,*
All very crooked sticks (just try yourselves, good Messieurs Editors,—
When you have turned it twenty ways, you'll own I might have said it
     worse);
So baffled like poor Nap. the Third, for fear of worse miscarriage,
I sought some friendly assonance, a morganatic marriage;
Failing in that, with Butler's rule I can my weakness bolster,
And 'gainst a lock-less pistol match the flask in t'other holster,
Or, better yet, with Tennyson's authority can cure all,—
If *he* says *tirra-lirra,* why mayn't *I* say *tooral-looral?*

DIGRESSION B
With foot in stirrup, hand on mane,
     Our Own makes prudent pause,
Swings o'er the careful leg again,
     And tight the curb-rein draws.

There's naught so hard, Lord Byron says, as getting under way;[1]
The wilted sails droop from the yard, oil-smooth the windless bay,
The tide slips wimpling by, the same that weeks ago, perhaps,
Round coral-reefs in Indian seas, shimmered with whispering lapse;
The same that, sweeping northward still, to Arctic snows may bear
Great leaves, scarce disenchanted yet of drowsy tropic air,
Such as may vex stout Franklin's dreams, where unrelenting lines
Of icepeaks whitening endlessly o'ertop his useless[2] pines;—

[1] MS I entitled "Setting Sail."
[2] MS I: "helpless."

The tide slips by and there you lie, the anchor at the peak,
The captain swearing inwardly, the mate with quid in cheek;
There's not a hope of any breeze before, beside, behind,
And, though with ingots laden deep, you cannot[3] raise the wind;
Fair cousins, kissed and bid good-bye, gaze awkward from the pier,
Sorry they wiped their eyes so soon, because their second tear
Declines to fill the other's place; the cambric from the bags
Is taken once again and waved; the slow time drags and dra-a-ags;
He (whom in childhood's guileless prime, you used to lick),[4] your
    brother,
Spells this exhausted leg, or that, with the exhausted other;
The children go too near the edge, and fuss, and screw, and wriggle;
Tommy's best cap falls overboard and no one dares to giggle;
You strive to make the feeling stay that misted both your eyes,
But thoughts of luggage intervene, and the tired feeling dies;
The farewell, mixed of smiles and tears, so painful-sweet before,
Drawn out into an hour, becomes impertinence and bore,
As if too literal Jove should grant the lovers' prayed-for bliss,
And glue them Siamesely tight in one eternal kiss;[5]
In such case what do captains, even of clippers swift as arrows?
They take a prosy steam-tug till they get beyond the Narrows;
That's what I've done, and, being now safe in the open main,
Set stu'nsails (that is, mend my pen), and take my start again.

PROGRESSION A—THE INVOCATION
He now, with wise spurs so inclined
    That each the flank evades,
Nor gives a mettle undesigned,
    Invokes two mighty blades.

Sirs, Editors of Putnam's, then, if you indeed be plural,
Or if you the Howadji be, who, sitting crucicrural
(A habit learned in Egypt), through the anaconda coils,
Of his *effendi* sucks the rare *ulemah's* fragrant spoils,
And on the best papyrus with a split reed splutters down
An article on Banking that will startle half the town,
(Proving our system all is due to some old Coptic file
Because before that Ramsay reigned, who helped at Babel's pile,
Deposits constantly were made on both banks of the Nile);
Then claps hands languidly (hands lotus-soft) to bring A lad in,
Allah ed deen he calls him—'tis a dyed Milesian clad in

[3] MS I: "could not."
[4] MS I: "thrash."
[5] In MS I Digression B ends here.

A bloomer bought in Chatham-street and a bandanna turban,
Pure Saracenic in his style like certain cots suburban:—
Or if you Harry Franco be, who, though he e'er so far goes,
Remembers in his secret heart the dear, flat, dull sea's Argos,
And, as a mild suggestion of the customs of Nantucket,
To any kind of elbow-chair prefers an o'erturned bucket;
Who (as the Persian Envoy to old Louis the Magnificent
A turf brought with him piously, that he might always sniff a scent
Of the *natale solum*) keeps an oilcask in the closet,
(One that has made a v'y'ge, too), lays a harpoon across it,
And with strange rites, left wisely to the fancy of my Reader,
Consults the bunghole's Delphic deeps before he writes a leader;—
Or if you be that gentle youth, so tall and slim and pale,
Who fitted to his Pegasus a Scandinavian Tale,
Who the Pathfinder's leaders made, yet could not find the way
With next-day-after-never to displace our poor to-day,
And nothing met but humbergs, where Charles Fourier (on his slate)
Had cleared the Northwest Passage to a better Social State;—
Or if you be that Moses who, from Modern Egypt's wrecks adust,
Unto their Canaan of Brook Farm the New Lights safely Exodused;
Where life's clean page was never more to be defaced with fresh spots,
As soon as Theory could be made as fattening as the flesh-pots;
Where the new manner, dropt from heaven, should so nerve hand and
    brain,
That he who nothing did before, should do't as well again;
Where with fresh water from the spring they warmed their stoic lunch,
Biding the time when Fourier said the sea would be milk-punch,
When gold into the public chest like water was to run
For phalansterian beets (that cost two shillings every one),
And Time should wander Ripleying along o'er golden sand,
When forty heads could dig as well as one experienced hand;—
If you are one or all, or if you're ne'er a one of those,
Hear, by what title suits you best, the plan I now propose!

PROGRESSION B LEADING TO DIGRESSION C
Our Own then states his business,
Sets forth the why and how,
Begins in safety to progress
But brings up in a slough.

I am a man of forty, sirs, a native of East Haddam,
And have some reason to surmise that I descend from Adam;
But what's my pedigree to you? That I will soon unravel;
I've sucked my Haddam-Eden dry, therefore desire to travel,

And, as a natural consequence, presume I needn't say,
I wish to write some letters home and have those letters ° ° °
[I spare the word suggestive of those grim Next thorns[6] that mount,
Clump, clump, the stairways of the brain with—sir, *my small account,*
That,[7] after every good we gain—Love, Fame, Wealth, Wisdom—still,
As punctual as a cuckoo clock, hold up their little bill,
The *garçons* in our Café of Life, by dreaming us forgot—
Sitting, like Homer's heroes, full and musing God knows what,—
Till they say, bowing, *s'il vous plait, voilà, Messieurs, la note!*]
I should[8] not hint at this so soon, but in our callous day,
The tollman Debt, who drops the[9] bar across the world's highway,
Great Cæsar in mid-march would stop if Cæsar could not pay;
Pilgriming 's dearer than it was: men cannot travel now
Scot-free from Dan to Beersheba upon a simple vow;
Nay, as long back as Bess's time, when Walsingham went over
Ambassador to Cousin France, at Canterbury and Dover
He was so fleeced by innkeepers that, ere he quitted land,
He wrote to the Prime Minister to take the knaves in hand: °
If I with staff and scallop-shell should try my way to win,
Would Bonifaces quarrel as to who should take me in?
Or would my pilgrim's progress end where Bunyan started his on,
And my grand tour be round and round the backyard of a prison?
I give you here a saying deep and therefore, haply true;
'Tis out of Merlin's prophecies, but quite as good as new:
𝕿𝖍𝖊 𝖖𝖚𝖊𝖘𝖙𝖎𝖔𝖓 𝖇𝖔𝖆𝖙𝖍 𝖋𝖔𝖗 𝖒𝖊𝖓 𝖆𝖓𝖉 𝖒𝖊𝖆𝖙𝖊𝖘 𝖑𝖔𝖓𝖌𝖊 𝖇𝖔𝖞𝖆𝖌𝖊𝖘 𝖞𝖙 𝖇𝖊𝖌𝖎𝖓𝖓𝖊
𝕷𝖞𝖊𝖘 𝖎𝖓 𝖆 𝖓𝖔𝖙𝖘𝖍𝖊𝖑𝖑, 𝖗𝖆𝖙𝖍𝖊𝖗 𝖘𝖆𝖞𝖊 𝖑𝖞𝖊𝖘 𝖎𝖓 𝖆 𝖈𝖆𝖘𝖊 𝖔𝖋 𝖙𝖎𝖓𝖓𝖊.
But, though men may not travel now, as in the middle ages,
With self-sustaining retinues of little gilt-edged pages,
Yet one may manage pleasantly, where'er he likes to roam,
By sending his small pages (at so much per small page) home;
And if a staff and scallop-shell won't serve so well as then,
Our outlay is about as small—just paper, ink, and pen.
Be thankful! Humbugs never die, more than the wandering Jew;
Bankrupt, they publish their own deaths, slink for a while from view,
Then take an *alias,* change the sign, and the old trade renew;
Indeed, 'tis wondrous how each Age, though laughing at the Past,
Insists on having its tight shoe made on the same old last;
How it is sure its system would break up at once without

6 MS I: "Morns."
7 MS I: "And."
8 MS I: "would."
9 MS I: "his."

* See the COMPLEAT AMBASSADOR, 1655, p. 21. [Lowell's note. MS I omits.]

The bunnian[10] which it *will* believe hereditary gout;
How it takes all its swans for geese, nay, stranger yet and sadder,
Sees in its treadmill's fruitless jog a heavenward Jacob's-ladder,
Shouts—*Lo, the Shining Heights are reached! one moment more aspire!*
Trots into cramps its poor, dear legs, gets never an inch the higher,
And, like the others, ends with pipe and mug beside the fire.
There, 'tween each doze, it whiffs and sips and watches with a sneer
The green recruits that trudge and sweat where it had swinked whilere,
And sighs to think this soon spent zeal should be in simple truth
The only interval between old Fogyhood and Youth:
"Well," thus it muses, "well, what odds? 'Tis not for us to warn;
" 'Twill be the same when we are dead, and was ere we were born;
"Without the Treadmill, too, how grind our store of winter's corn?
"Had we no stock, nor twelve *per cent.* received from Treadmill shares,
"We might . . . . but these poor devils at last will get our easy-chairs;
"High aims and hopes have great rewards, they, too, serene and snug,
"Shall one day have their—soothing pipe and their enlivening mug;
"From Adam, empty-handed Youth hath always heard the hum
"Of Good Times Coming, and will hear until the last day come;
"Young ears hear forward, old ones back, and, while the earth rolls on,
"Full-handed Eld shall hear recede the steps of Good Times Gone;
"Ah what a cackle we set up whene'er an egg was laid!
"*Cack-cack-cack-cackle!* rang around, the scratch for worms was stayed,
"*Cut-cut-ca-dah-cut!* from *this* egg the coming cock shall stalk!
"The great New Era dawns, the age of Deeds and not of Talk!
"And every stupid hen of us hugged close his egg of chalk,
"Thought,—sure, I feel life stir within, each day with greater strength,
"I have not sat these years in vain, the world is saved at length;—
"When lo, the chick! from former chicks he differed not a jot,
"But grew and crew and scratched and went, like those before, to pot!"
So muse the dim *Emeriti*, and, mournful though it be,
I must confess a kindred thought hath sometimes come to me,
Who, though but just of forty turned, have heard the rumorous fame
Of nine and ninety Coming Men, all—coming till they came.
Pure Mephistophiles all this? the vulgar nature jeers;
Good friend, while I was writing it, my eyes were dim with tears;
Thrice happy he who cannot see, or who his eyes can shut,
Life's deepest sorrow is contained in that small word there—But!

DIGRESSION D
Caught in the mire, he argufies,
Shows how 'twas done by rules,

10 MS I: "bunnion."

And proves outright that nonsense lies
Beyond the reach of fools.

That's pure digression, then, you think? Now, just to prove 'tis *not*,[11]
I shall begin a bigger one upon this very spot:
At any rate, 'tis naught, you say; precisely, I admit it,
For, in convicting it of that, you virtually acquit it;
You have conjectured, I suppose,—(come, never look despondent!)
That I intend to offer as an OUR OWN CORRESPONDENT,
And by what method more direct could I avouch my fitness
Than by exhibiting such art as the above may witness?
I had one Nothing; and, by dint of turning and displaying it,
I've occupied the time thus far in seeming to be saying it,
And have it, good as new, till comes the moment for conveying it.
Each creature must get forward in his own peculiar sort;
The crab slants sideway to his end, and finds the way as short,
You'd make him go forth rightly, eh? pray try your hand, Sir dab,[12]—
Well, you have bettered Providence, but Nature wants her crab;
Sir, in that awful Congress there, where sit th' assembled Fates,
Of which the unconscious newspapers report the slow debates,
Thank God, you can't be lobbying, log-rolling, and all that;—
A world that suited you, O Smith, might be a trifle flat.
Fate, Idiosyncrasy, or what is just the same thing, custom,
Leads every mortal by the ear, though he be strong as Rustem,
Makes him do quite impossible things,—then, with a spear of grass
Marks the thin line none else can see, but which he cannot pass;
That son of yours, so pale and slim, with whom the master fails,
What claps him in the fo'c'stle rude, and sends him after whales?
And Samson, there, your burly boy, what takes him by the nape
And sets him at the counter's back to measure thread and tape?
The servant-man you hired last year, who, for a paltry fee
Surrendered all his nature up, and would if he'd had three,
To suit your whimsies, and who seemed to find all drudgery sweet,
Left you in tears,—he could not take *that* bundle through the street;
Centripetal, centrifugal, these the conditions two,
Some cling like moss, and other some fling off, their whole lives through;
My style's centrifugal; mark plain the settled boundary-line,
And, till it gets on t'other side, 'twill fret and fume and pine:
Or call 't the polypean style; each verse contains, at any rate,
A polypus that in its turn new polypi can generate,

[11] MS I entitled "On Digression and (Good) Humor."
[12] MS I: "Dab."

And if I the temptation strong that lurks in any verse shun,
'Tis certain that the next will breed new centres of dispersion;
A brief attempt would shortly prove that I should be much worse if
I tried to curb my natural bent of being too discursive,
But I forbear, I spare you this *experimentum crucis,*
And shall, instead, proceed to show that Nonsense hath its uses;
I mean good nonsense, there are men enough who have a leaning to
Write nonsense in great solemn tomes, nor have the wit of meaning to—
Tomes, the hop-pillows of the mind, that vanquish readers stout,
And which no gentleman's library can be complete without,
Pernoctent nobis, bedward turned, take one and feel no doubt;
What a profound narcotic spell your fading senses greets,
'Tis just like getting into bed to look between their sheets;
[I mean to make a list of them, some rainy day, to be a
Fasciculus first to my complete[13] *librorum Pharmacopœia.*]
And now, because so hard of faith, this omnibus and gas age,
From an old author I translate the following deep passage;
(See preface to the *Moriæ Encomium* of Erasmus,
Recensuit et præfationem addidit Gelasmus:
  'Tis the easiest matter, in one sense,*
  To write very passable nonsense;
  There are those who do naught but create your
  Poor stuff from mere thinness of nature;
  But to do it with art and intention,
  To never let fancy or pen shun
  Any kind of odd lurches, twists, waggeries,
  Absurdities, quibbles, and vagaries;
  To roll your Diogenes-puncheon
  The vext reader's toes with a crunch on,
  Making one quip the mere[14] cotyledon
  For the seed of another to feed on,
  Is a matter—why, just reckon how many
  Have fared well enough with Melpomene,
  And how very few have come by a
  Mere prosperous look[15] from Thalia;
  Who since has contrived to hit off an ease

[13] MS I omits "complete."
[14] MS I: "more."
[15] MS I: "glance."

* "Nullitates scribere tam facile est quam bibere; sed scribere intelligenter quod sit inintelligibile; insanire perfrequenter, motu proprio, libenter; vertere in risibile quod plane impossible, sic ut titillat imum pectus,—hoc est summum intellectus," *et cætera.* Praefatio Gelasmi pp. XCIX. *et seqq.* [Lowell's note. MS I reads "inintelligible" and "titillet" in the two relevant words above.]

That in hard work will match A——s?†
Hath even great Swift[16] in his shabby lays
Come near the hop-skip prose of R——s?
The deep-quibbling, sage-clown of S——e,
From among all the wits can you rake his peer?
Are they not, my dear sir, *rari nantes*
Who can jingle the bells with C——s?
How many great clerks in one turn could
Be both zany and wise man as S——e could?
And who could with such a wise knack array
Great Jeames's phonetics as T——y?
Your head is too small if it happen
That you can't keep the noble fool's-cap on.
So he goes maundering on and on, he's almost worse than I am,
And every line he writes begets as many sons as Priam;
All this, good Messieurs Editors, is simply introduction
To show how nothing could be said in endless reproduction;
I also wished to smooth the way for scribbling off some jolly
Good, topsy-turvy, head-o'er-heels, unmeaning, wholesome folly;
We're pretty nearly crazy here with change and go-ahead,
With flinging our caught bird away for two ne'er caught[17] instead,
With butting 'gainst the wall which we declare shall[18] be a portal,
And questioning Deeps that never yet have said a word to mortal;
We're growing pale and hollow-eyed, and out of all condition,
With *mediums* and prophetic chairs, and crickets with a mission,
(The most astounding oracles since Balaam's donkey spoke,
'T would seem our furniture was all of Dodonean oak).
Make but the public laugh, be sure, 'twill take you to be somebody;
'Twill wrench its button from your clutch, my densely-earnest, glum
        body;
'Tis good, this noble earnestness, good in its place, but why
Make great Achilles' shield the pan to bake a penny pie?
Why, when we have a kitchen-range, insist that we shall stop,
And bore clear down to central fires to broil our daily chop?
Excalibur and Durandart are swords of price, but then
Why draw them sternly when you wish to cut[19] your nails or pen?

16 MS I: "S——."
17 MS I: "for two i' th' bush."
18 MS I: "*shall.*"
19 MS I: "trim."

† To avoid all suspicion of personality, I have omitted the names here. Though dead for centuries, an enraged satirist might revenge himself on me, nowadays, through the columns of the *Spiritual Telegraph*, or the legs of some dithyrambic centre-table. [Lowell's note.]

Small gulf between the ape and man; you bridge it with your staff;
But it will be impassable until the ape can laugh;—
No, no, be common now and then, be sensible, be funny,
And, as Siberians bait their traps for bears with pots of honey,
From which ere they'll withdraw their snouts, they'll suffer many a
    club-lick,
So bait your moral figure-of-fours to catch the Orson public.
Look how the dead leaves melt their way down through deep-drifted
    snow;
They take the sun-warmth down with them—pearls could not conquer so;
There *is* a moral here, you see; if you would preach, you must
Steep all your truths in sun that they may melt down through the crust;[20]
Brave Jeremiah, you are grand and terrible, a sign
And wonder, but were never quite a popular divine;
Fancy the figure you would cut among the nuts and wine!
I, on occasion, too, could preach, but hold it wiser far
To give the public sermons it will take with its cigar,
And morals fugitive, and vague as are these smoke-wreaths light
In which. . . . I trace . . . a . . . . let me see—bless me! 'tis out of sight.
When I my commentators have (who serve dead authors brave
As Turks do bodies that are sworn to stir within the grave,—
Unbury, make minced-meat of them, and bury them again),
They'll find deep meanings underneath each sputter of my pen,
Which I, a blissful shade (perhaps in teapoy pent, by process
Of these new moves in furniture, this wooden metempsychosis),
Accept for mine, unquestioning, as prudent Göthe choused
The critics out of all the thoughts they found for him in Faust.

PROGRESSION C

Our Own displays him just the man
    To do the thing proposed,
Though what that thing is, nor his plan,
    He hath not yet disclosed.

Travel (my theory is) suits least the race called Anglo-Saxon,
They come back loaded from each land they set their fullish[21] tracks on
With every folly they can pile their mental and bodily backs on;
So at the outset let me state I do not mean to budge
And see the persons, places, things, I shall describe and judge,
Because when men have cheated you, or when they've tea'd and fed you,
    'tis
The hardest thing to feel unbribed and clear the mind of prejudice;

---

[20] MS I: "in sunshine would you have them pierce the crust."
[21] MS I: "foolish."

Therefore, 'tis wasting honest time, this squandering round the earth,
And I, who once sold wooden clocks, should know what time is worth.
Next as to how I'm qualified,—but let us first agree
What things deserve a wise man's eyes and ears across the sea;
PERSONS: I'm forty, and have led, as you will see ere long,
A multifarious Yankee life, so there I'm rather strong;
I've tended bar, worked farms to halves, been twice to the South seas,
Sold clocks (I mentioned that before), done something in herb teas,
Hawked books, kept district school (and thus, inspired with thirst for
    knowledge,
Pegged shoes till I have saved enough to put me through Yale College),
Invented a cheap stove (the famed *Antidotum Gehennæ*,
So fuel-saving that no skill could coax it to burn any—
If you have lectured in small towns, you've probably seen many),
Driven stage, sold patent strops, by dint of interest at the White House,
Got nominated keeper of the Finback Island Light-house,
Where, just before a Northeast blow, the clockwork got ungeared,
And I revolved the light myself nine nights until it cleared;
(I took it as a quiet place to invent perpetual motion,—
This large dose of the real thing quite cured me of the notion;
It was, perhaps, the bitterest drop e'er mingled in my cup,
I rowed ashore so thoroughly sick, I threw the light-house up;)
Then I went through the Bankrupt Act, merely from general caution—
For, if you're prudent, you'll take heed, and every chance's claws shun,
Nor leave old blankets lying about for adverse fates to toss ye on;
Then I stood round a spell, and then bought out an Indian Doctor,
Then—but I have a faint surmise your credence may be shocked, or
I might go on, but I have said enough, no doubt, to show
That, to judge characters and men, I need not wait to grow;—
PERSONS thus well provided for, the next thing is the strictures
On works of Art in general; and first, we'll take the PICTURES.
Even here you cannot turn my flank,—I began life a painter,
Worked 'prentice first, then journeyman, with Major-General Taintor,
And did, myself, the sausages and the great round of beef
On the new market-house's sign, still prized for bold relief;—
SCULPTURE: I think that more than half the Sculptors that have risen
Should hammer stone to some good end, sent all to Sing Sing prison;
I'm sick of endless copyings of what were always bores,
Their dreary women on one toe, their Venuses by scores;
(That's in the ignorant, slashing style,—if you prefer a judge
Mildly appreciative, deep,—just give my tap a nudge,
'Twill run æsthetic folderol, and best high-German fudge;)—
MUSIC: when cousin Arad Cox at muster hurt his hand,

I played the bass-drum twice or more in the East Haddam band;—
BUILDINGS: I saved them till the last, for there I feel at home—
Perhaps you never heard about the city of New Rome?
'Twould not disgrace you deeply if you hadn't, for, you see,
It stayed in the potential mood, and was but going to be;
We merely staked a pasture out, christened the poor thing Forum,
And chose two natural architects—OUR OWN was *unus horum;*
'Twas he who planned the Meeting-house, a structure pure and winning,
With specimens of every style 'twixt vane and underpinning;
Unhappily it ne'er was built; New Rome, with nine good hills,
Remains unsettled to this day,—so do, alas! its bills,—
But the experience thus obtained entitles me to hope
My architectural criticism will be allowed full scope.

PROGRESSION D
Our Own, his various qualities
And aptitudes defined,
Descends, and makes more close replies
To the inquiring mind.[22]

But what, in these your voyagings, do you propose to do?
I might retort, O, highborn Smythe, with—what is that to you?
These twenty times I've bit my nails, and my left ear-tip scratched,
Wondering why *you* should wish to count *my* chickens ere they're
hatched;
But, if you further will insist, I'll answer (if I can);
My plan is—let me see—my plan is just to have no plan;
In laying out a pleasure-ground (the rule is not in Price),
Be tipsy when you mark the paths, or you'll be too precise;
And do it upon Burgundy, 'twill give a curvi-line
More sure of gentlemanly grace than any thinner wine;
Precision is a right good thing, like olives, in its place,
But (still like olives) it comes in a long way after Grace.
Suppose I told you that I meant (as vines do, when they climb)
To wander where my clasp was wooed by any jutting rhyme?
Or said that, like a river deep, lost first in bogs and sedges,
I soon should march to meet the sea with cities on my edges?
(This seemingly mixed simile, at which the Highborn frowns,
Refers to sketches I shall give of European towns;)
However, you shall have a peep; come, children, form a ring,

[22] MS II: "Childe Outis now, his qualities
And aptitudes defined
Meets other queries that may rise
To the inquiring mind."   [MS II rejects in first line (1) "Having
his various qualities" and (2) "He, having now, his qualities."]

I'll lift the crust, and let you see the birds are there to sing;
Now then—I shall appear to go from capital to capital,
Pick up what's worth the picking up, and in my letters clap it all;
When aught of interest shall occur, as certain as a star,
I, in our happy western phrase, shall be precisely *thar;*
If Paris, for example, which is very likely, chooses
To have the periodic fit she's subject to—the Blouses,
And there should be a general row, I, from the very thick of it,
Shall send home thrilling narratives till you are fairly sick of it;
I shall have interviews with kings and men of lower stations,
(Authors—of course,) and send reports of all the conversations;
Shall visit the cathedrals, and, for fear of any blunder,
Call each the finest in the world, a mountain of carved wonder;
Of every building, thing, and scene, that comes within my view,
I shall say something different, something so simply new,
The very Is upon my page shall with surprise grow round,—
And, by the way, lest any one should base enough be found
To steal the phrases got by me at cost of thought profuse,
I here put in a *caveat,* for some I mean to use,—

As—*Architecture's music cooled to zero point of Reaumur;*

A *statue is a song in stone (the chisel was its Homer);*

St. *Peter's has an epic dome, beneath whose deeps profound
The papal choir, on Easter eve, build up a dome of sound;*

Art *is the soul's horizon broad, and, as we onward go,
It moves with us and still recedes, until life's sun is low;*

You call those rather goodish thoughts? I have them by the score,
Ne'er yet by mortal man or maid put into words before;
Life's sun I feel quite sure is new; I got it by hard thinking
Only last night at half-past five, just as the sun was sinking;
With these and other ornaments I shall enrich my text,
When, far across the Atlantic wave, I have to write my next.

PROGRESSION E[23]
Our own unfolds another coil
Of his portentous tale,
And shows the torture and the toil
Of riding on a rail.

I left East Haddam by the train—a mode of torture worse
Than any Dante conjured up[24]—the case I will rehearse:

23 MS II entitles this section "Progression D" and omits the opening quatrain.
24 MS II: "dreamed about."

I found the car, then, occupied (I got in rather late,
And 'twas hermetically closed[25]) by victims fifty-eight,
Each one of whom[26] looked headachy and parboiledy and pale,
Having less air a-piece, perhaps, than Jonah in his whale;[27]
They[28] seemed a troop of convict souls let out in search of bail[29]
And, lest they might[30] a mouthful get of unbedevilled[31] air,
A Stygian sheriff's officer went with them every where,
Whose duty[32] was[33] to see that they no atmosphere should know
Cooler than that which Minos' tail had doomed[34] them to below:
In shape he seemed a kind of stove, but by degrees my head
Was squeezed into an iron cap and screwed till I was dead
(Or thought I was), and then there came strange lights into my brain,[35]
And 'neath his[36] thin sheet-iron mask the tipstaff imp was plain.
At intervals another fiend—by mortals Brakeman hight—
Would rouse his fellow[37]-torturer into a fierce delight,
Punching[38] his ribs, and feeding him with lumps of anthracite;
The demon's single eye grew red, and with unholy glee
Exulted as it shrivelled up[39] the very soul in me.[40]
I would have shrieked a maniac shriek, but that I did not dare;
I thought of turning madly round, and seizing by the hair
A soul unblest that sat by me, only[41] somehow I got
A notion that his treacherous scalp[42] would prove to be red-hot.
I sprang to raise the window, but a female spirit of ill

[25] MS II: "sealed."
[26] MS II rejects "them."
[27] MS II omits this line.
[28] MS II: "It."
[29] MS II rejects ". . . a penal colony of convict souls in hell."
[30] MS II: "should."
[31] MS II gives first reading "the pure"; then gives alternate reading "unbedevilled."
[32] MS II rejects "office."
[33] MS II: "'twas."
[34] MS II rejects "sent."
[35] MS II rejects "eyes."
[36] MS II rejects "the."
[37] MS II rejects "brother."
[38] MS II rejects false start "By."
[39] MS II: "Seemed by its glare to shrivel up."
[40] MS II interpolates on the margin at this point the following lines:
"The effect was made quite perfect by three subalterns whose use
Was on the iron hot, in turn, to squirt a yellow juice."
[In this interpolation Lowell rejected "three marksmen known and true/ Who deluged the hot iron with a yellow juice by turns."]
[41] MS II rejects "but that."
[42] MS II: "spectral wig."

Who all the space around her soured, sharp-nosed, close-lipped, and
    still,[43]
(A vinegar-cruet incarnate) said, "No *gentleman* would place
A lady in a thorough-draught that had a swollen face!"
If you have ever chanced to bite a nice unripe persimmon,
You'll have some notion of her tone, but still a faint and dim one
No patent stove can radiate a chill more like the pole
Than[44] such a lady, whose each act true views of grace control,
In doubt about her bonnet-box, secure about her soul.[45]
Thenceforward all is phantasm dire; I dimly recollect
A something 'twixt[46] a nose and voice that said " 'most there, I 'xpect,"—
Heavens![47] almost WHERE? a pang, a flash of fire[48] through either eye
    shoots,
And I looked[49] momently to see the last scene of Der Frieschutz;[50]
The bland conductor will become[51] that flame-clad individual
Who stamping, Earth will gape,[52] and "Gentlemen, I bid you all,"
He'll shriek, "to lava tea at six," then crashing[53] through the floor
With a strong smell of brimstone,—but[54] all swam, I saw no more,
Only I vaguely seem to have seen the attendant fiend excite
His principal with further pokes and lumps of anthracite,
While faces featureless as dough, looked on serene and placid,
And nine and fifty pairs[55] of lungs evolved carbonic acid.
There was a scream, but whether 'twas the engine, or the last
Wild prayer for mercy of those eight and fifty as they passed
Down to their several torturings in deepest Malebolge,
As I myself am[56] still in doubt, can't certainly be told ye;
I only know they vanished all, the silent ghastly crew,
But whither, how, why, when,—these things I never fully knew;[57]

---

43 MS II read "Who on the seat behind me gloomed, severe, thin-lipped, and
still"; then substituted "Who all the space around her soured, severe, close-lipped,
and still."
44 MS I: "As."
45 MS II omits above 5 lines.
46 MS II rejects "like."
47 MS II: "We're"; then substitutes "Gods!"
48 MS II: "fear."
49 MS II rejects "expected."
50 MS I: "Der Freischutz."
    MS II: "Der Freischütz."
51 MS II rejects "shout."
52 MS II rejects false start "As when"; then read "Who stamping his feet, Earth
gapes in flames"; then substituted "Who stamping, Earth will gape in flames."
53 MS II rejects "sinking."
54 MS II: "then—but."
55 MSS I and II: "pair."
56 MS II rejects "was myself."
57 MS II: "But whither, why, how, when—these things I never wholly knew."

I stood with carpet-bag in hand, when the strange spell unbound me.
And five[58] score yelling cabmen danced their frenzied war-dance round
   me.[59]

PROGRESSION F

Our own, howe'er with Bryon's verse
   He may enchanted be,
Finds that he likes the ocean worse,
   When trying it *per se.*

When I was a beggarly boy,
   And lived in a cellar damp,
I had not a friend nor a toy,
   But I had Aladdin's lamp;
When I could not sleep for cold,
   I had fire enough in my brain,
And built, with a roof of gold,
   My beautiful castles in Spain!

Since then I have toiled day and night,
   I have money and power good store,
But I'd give all my lamps of silver bright
   For the one that is mine no more;
Take, Fortune, whatever you choose,
   You gave, and may snatch again;
I have nothing 'twould pain me to lose,
   For I own no more castles in Spain!

So mused a poet, quite as wise as either you or I,
Coughing with dust, as Crassus' coach rolled smoothly-swinging by;
And, if I understand his thought, which may be something trite,
He was (which for a poet's much) within two-thirds of right;
Fond youth, be abstinent, pull not that Hesperidean fruit,
One bite, and you repent too late, and lame your jaw to boot:
Thank God for the Unattainable, it leaves you still a boy,
The wishing for the wishing-cap is that which makes the joy;
Privation gives their charm to things, the glory and the grace,
Beckon and flee—ah, fool, that would'st their frozen zones embrace!
In winter, summer seems most fair, and what enchantment glows
In August o'er those mountain-peaks, ermined with rounding snows!
The frozen Samoiede makes his heaven a place of endless fire,

[58] MS II: "six score."
[59] MS II rejects "danced their frightful war dances fitly round me."

And, when kind fortune heaps the board, to glut the soul's desire,
Apicius Bufo starves and sighs, and wonders what it means,—
Nectar? Ambrosia?—hum, so-so, but no pig's head and greens?
And thou, oh hero, who hast climbed to scarce-dreamed fame and power,
Think'st only of a little mound which dusky yews embower,
And, sighing, musest what are all these idle sands[60] to me
Since those blue eyes are closed with dust that should be here to see?
Ah, happy eyes that shut so soon, ye only have the might
To keep undimmed the olden spell, for ever warm and bright!
Had village Alice lived, poor fool, thou would'st without remorse
Be sighing for a bride of State, and planning a divorce.

This train of thought I've fallen on, far out here on the sea,
Coiled up, half-frozen underneath the weather-bulwark's lee.
And (faith that last wave soused me through)—and writing on my knee;
The application of it is, that when you're on the land
The sea is every thing that's bright, and broad, and blue, and grand,
And that you'd change what Wordsworth calls your glorious second berth
(Now that you've tried it) for a grave, because 'twould be firm earth;
Perhaps in some October night, when the roused south o'erwhelms,
With surge on surge rolled gathering down the night, the shuddering
      elms,
You have lain fancying what wild joy there must be in the motion
Of a brave vessel plunging through the broken coils of ocean;
Your mind ran forth and back again, like a fly-watching spider,
Upon that line in Byron of the *steed that knows its rider,*
And, in your bath next morning, you splash[61] with double glee,
Humming, dear Barry Cornwall's song—*the sea! the o-pen sea!*
I wish that Barry and Byron both were only here with me!
All well enough this sentiment and stuff upon the shore,
But, when the sea is smoothest, 'tis an Erymanthian bore,
And when 'tis rough, my brace of bards, you'd neither of you sing
Of hands on manes, or blue and fresh, but quite another thing,—
Flat on your backs in jerking berths you scarce could keep your place in,
You'd moan an Amboean[62] sad—*quick, steward! quick! a basin!*
(Queen's counsel most delectable, I still seem hearing thee
Sing *Cameriere* through the rain along the Bieler sea.)

How easy 'tis to tyrannize over Taste's hapless lieges!
The poor *Achivi* still are plucked *quidquid delirant reges;*

[60] MS I: "gauds."
[61] MS I: "splash round."
[62] MS I: "Amobean."

If Hamlet says he sees a whale, Polonius must follow,
And what A swears is beautiful, all down to Z will swallow;
None dares confess he cannot see what great Flapdoddle spies,
And, like potatoes, fools are bred from one another's eyes;
Dear Nyncombe, what sharp agonies I've seen you going through with
Before a statue which your soul had naught on earth to do with,
And what could e'er be finer than your awed, assenting "Oh!"
When I suggested that deep thought in the Apollo's toe?
Don't come to Rome for nothing, man, with some likeminded crony,
Go valiantly and eat a steak down at the Gabione;
'Tis in this way that men are made to say they like the sea,
Flam says he does, and all the rest will be as good as he.
I heard a great man once declare that he had never found
A sailor, yet, who loved the fate to which his life was bound,
And when I asked our brown first-mate, a seaman good and brave,
On shore as helpless as a fish, a viking on the wave,
What life would please him most? he sighed, looked at his tattooed arm,
Studied its hieroglyphs awhile, and said—an inland farm.
And he was right; I cannot, for example, see the least
Pleasure in walking on a deck that's drunk as any beast,
A wet plank, scarcely larger than a white bear's sloppy pen,
That tips you here and slips you there, and trips you back again;
That cheats you with a moment's lull, and, when you think you feel
Quite sure of the companionway, half breaks you on the wheel,
Then slants until you need both hands to keep your hold on that,
And pins you helpless while the wind blows off your second hat.
The steed that *throws* his rider would be nearer to the fact:
To me it gives no pleasure to be swashed and washed and racked;
To have a three weeks' tipsiness on cold saltwater merely,
With legs that seem like some one's else, they bother you[63] so queerly
Taking you *here* when you mean *there*,[64]—no, no, it has no charm,
Although the loveliest cousin may be hanging on your arm.
Of course, I am not seasick, for although that epidemic
(Hic) prostrates all my friends, yet *(hic)* I only pity them *(hic)*.
Indeed, in this life's pilgrimage, I[65] found this maxim true:
There are four common weaknesses no mortal ever knew,
A headache that was caused by wine, drowsiness late at night,
Seasickness, and a corn that came from wearing boots too tight.
A seasick man I never saw; Our Own leans o'er the rail,
Muses awhile, and then comes back with features doughy pale;

[63] MS I: "one."
[64] MS I: "Taking one *here* when one means *there*."
[65] MS I: "I've."

But he had only wandered aft, a Parthian glance to take
At those strange coils of moony fire that mark the writhing wake.
With ghastly calm he takes a pipe; in minutes five (or less) hence,
He'll feel again that ecstasy produced by phosphorescence.

Conceive of an existence in which the great events
Are breakfast, luncheon, dinner, tea, in which, when Fate relents,
She sends a string of porpoises, perhaps a grampus, too,
Who blunders up beneath the stern, and gives a *poo-oo-ooh!*
While we immortal souls crowd aft and crush each other's toes
To see this stupid creature blow what he esteems a nose;
Why, I blew thrice my moral and accountable proboscis,
But found no fish so *blasé* that it ever came across his
Waterlogged brain that it was worth his while to turn and come anon,
Lest he should miss the witnessing of that sublime phenomenon;
Nor would it, though your nose were like fray John's, or even had you a
Verissimo fazzoletto of Saint Antony of Padua,
The Apostle who in Finland had a cure of souls, and sent
Conviction to his hearers that 'twas good to fry in Lent.
There are some goodish things at sea; for instance, one can feel
A grandeur in the silent man for ever at the wheel,
That bit of two-legged intellect, that particle of drill,
Who the huge floundering hulk inspires with reason, brain and will,
And makes the ship, though skies are black and headwinds whistle loud,
Obey her conscience there which feels the loadstar through the cloud;
And when by lusty western gales the full-sailed barque is hurled
Toward the great moon which, sitting[66] on the silent underworld,
Rounds luridly up to look on ours, and shoots a broadening line,
Of palpitant light from crest to crest across the ridgy brine,
Then from the bows look back and feel a thrill that never stales
In that full-bosomed, swan-white pomp of onward-yearning sails;
Ah, when dear cousin Bull laments that you can't make a poem,
Take him aboard a clipper-ship, young Jonathan, and show him
A work of art that in its grace and grandeur may compare
With any thing that any race has fashioned any where;
'Tis not a statue, grumbles John; nay, if you come to that,
We think of Hyde Park corner, and concede you beat us flat
With your equestrian statue to a Nose and a Cocked-hat;
But 'tis not a cathedral; well, e'en that we will allow,
Both statues and cathedrals are anachronistic now;
Your minsters, coz, the monuments of men who conquered you,

[66] MS I: "setting."

You'd sell a bargain, if we'd take the deans and chapters too;
No; mortal men build now-a-days, as always heretofore,
Good temples to the gods which they in very truth adore;
The shepherds of this Broker Age, with all their willing flocks,
Although they bow to stones no more, do bend the knee to stocks,
And churches can't be beautiful though crowded, floor and gallery,
If people worship preacher, and if preacher worship salary;
'Tis well to look things in the face, the god o' the modern universe,
Hermes, cares naught for halls of art and libraries of puny verse,
If they don't sell, he notes them thus upon his ledger—say, *per
Contra* to loss of so much stone, best Russia duck and paper;
And, after all, about this Art men talk a deal of fudge,
Each nation has its path marked out, from which it must not budge;
The Romans had as little art as Noah in his ark,
Yet somehow on this globe contrived to make an epic mark;
Religion, painting, sculpture, song—for these they ran up jolly ticks
With Greece and Egypt, but they were great artists in their politics,
And if we make no minsters, John, nor epics, yet the Fates
Are not entirely deaf to men who *can* build ships and states;
(I waive the literary point, contented with observing
That *I* like Hawthorne, Longfellow, Emerson, Bryant, Irving,)[67]
The arts are never pioneers, but men have strength and health
Who, called on suddenly, can improvise a commonwealth,
Nay, can more easily go on and frame them by the dozen,
Than you can make a dinner-speech, dear sympathizing cousin:
And, though our restless Jonathan have not your graver bent, sure he
Does represent this hand-to-mouth, pert, rapid, nineteenth century;
This is the Age of Scramble; men move faster than they did
When they pried up the imperial Past's deep-dusted coffin-lid,
Searching for scrolls of precedent; the wire-tamed[68] lightning now
Replaces Delphos—men don't leave the steamer for the scow;
What hero,[69] were they new to-day, would ever stop to read
The Iliad, the Shanàmeh, or the Nibelungenlied?
Their public's gone, the artist Greek, the lettered Shah, the hairy Graf—
Folio and plesiosaur sleep well; *we* weary o'er a paragraph;
The mind moves planet-like no more, it fizzes, cracks, and bustles;
From end to end with journals dry the land o'ershadowed rustles,
As with dead leaves a winter-beech, and, with their breath-roused jars
Amused, we care not if they hide the eternal skies and stars;

[67] MS I omits this and the preceding line.
[68] MS I: "wire-leashed."
[69] MS I: "public."

Down to the general level of the Board of Brokers sinking,
The Age takes in the newspapers, or, to say sooth unshrinking,
The newspapers take in the Age, and Stocks do all the thinking.

. . . . .

There's something in a clean fresh page (and I have here begun one)
That sets one thinking of the goods and ills that have been done one,
For all the good books and the bad were first but so much paper
As would have curled Belinda's lock, or lit a bedward[1] taper;
The bit of paper smooth and white is gifted with a spell[2]
Of Mahomet's carpet, and can take[3] the prisoner from his cell,
Can bear him to La Mancha's hills to dream beneath the trees,
Hearing far bells of muleteers, or fitful hum of bees;
'Tis quite a simple *recipe*—a jail, ink, paper, pen,—
Yet, mixed, they make Don Quixote,—do you think they would agen?
Go steal a trifle, Reader,[4] to put you in the
And see if you can get a lift upon the prophet's rug.
The sheet that's in your desk,[5] dear Sir, potentially contains
More wisdom than has ever yet got out of human brains,
You,[6] young Lorenzo yet may write your billy dukises sweet
On that poor Paddy's tattered shirt, that's digging in the street;
You, Doctor Dodd, may write thereon a very simple note
That singularly shall affect your Reverence's throat;
Yea, on that triangle that shows where he can't see, poor fellow
A greater Shakspeare may begin, a perfecter Othello;
There's magnetism in paper fair that rapidly draws down
The particles of thought that lie stuck fast beneath our crown;
The brain is scrawled with characters in[7] sympathetic ink,
Which with the heat show clearly forth[8] when we begin to think,—
Thoughts, fancies, feelings, memories, just now in darkness shrinking,—
For the imperative paper there compels us into thinking;
Begin; and then Necessity will, like a corkscrew stout,
From the brain's narrow gateway draw the wooden jailor out,
And all that you have bottled there, swipes be it, or Tokay,
Gulluck—gulluck comes gurgling out to wet the reader's clay;
And then, oh Reader, haste to taste; much swipes for Tokay passes
Served up upon a silver tray and poured in Tokay glasses,

1 MS rejects "farthing."
2 MS rejects "The bit of paper small and white that lies unsullied there."
3 MS rejects (1) "will take up" and (2) "to speak."
4 The remainder of this line is incomplete, having first read "to get into the" and a fragment of a word which is illegible but annotated "dictionary and poem," indicating Lowell intended to look it up.
5 MS rejects "now before me."
6 MS rejects false start "An."
7 MS rejects "written o'er and o'er with."
8 MS rejects "come clearly out."

And thou may'st drink that golden wine with palate dull and neuter
Deeming it poorish swipes because it masquerades in pewter.
Think, pen in hand, wise Göthe said, still hoarding mental pelf
And wise in the economies that save the waste of self.
The paper's virtue being proved, 'tis rather awkward hinting[9]
That all which takes its goodness out's the writing and the printing,
That, while 'tis yet unstained, it keeps its wisdom and its wit in
Until—in short that books are good as long as they're unwritten;
No doubt pure[10] mathematics lie, the undiscovered base[11]
Of all that governs, pleases, or concerns the human race;
Our grandchildren,[12] at common school, may on the blackboard see
The mystery of love resolved by simple a plus b,
And downright[13] Hamlets may produce for exercise at college
By some fourth power of minus x, which now eludes our knowledge,
Till that time comes[14] I've often thought 'twould be a pretty plan
If some not overdeep or grave, but pleasant-thoughted man
Would publish us a small white book, and leave the pages fair,[15] ⎫
[Put?][16] a suggestive index and a title here and there,   ⎬
For Thought[17] to hitch its web upon—Jove! what a book were there! ⎭
Its name should be Blank's Essays and to it we'd surrender
Our musing after dinner minds with feet upon the fender,
Meerschaum[18] in mouth, and make the smoke[19] that wavered toward the
    ceiling
Transmute itself to every shape of fancy thought and feeling.
Twould be in Tartar Doctors' style, who write the medicine's name
Make their poor patients[20] swallow it, and the effect's the same;
Faith, we will try it on the spot, it will not take a minute
I'll leave a short[21] space blank, and write

__ auf wiedersehen __
a rivederci[22]

                                               in it
Let any reader muse on that, and it will plainly show him

[9] MS rejects "it but remains a hinting."
[10] MS rejects "Now, as pure."
[11] MS rejects "the yet uncovered base."
[12] MS rejects "And haply, our greatgrandchildren."
[13] MS rejects "perfect."
[14] MS rejects "But till that time."
[15] MS rejects (1) "leaving the pages fair" and (2) "leaving the leaves all fair."
[16] MS rejects "[Scrawl?]".
[17] Rejected phrase illegible.
[18] MS rejects "With pipe."
[19] MS rejects "curled."
[20] MS rejects "And make their patients."
[21] MS rejects "few" before "short."
[22] Apparently "auf wiedersehen" and "a rivederci" were alternatives from which Lowell intended to choose upon printing the poem.

That he contains within him all he weeps o'er in a poem;
O Edelmann, O Signor Giù, O Storg, does it recall
The pleasant nights, the smokes, the jokes, the songs, the girls, the all?
Or let me leave another space and simply scrawl therein

Sweetbrier Lane   ——

Now Memory opes forthwith her choicest bin!
Ye twenty maids in muslin gowns who made all else seem chaff,[23]
In whom successively I found my nature's other half,
Who played pianos all day long and had no other care,
Who gave me all those single locks of brown, black, golden hair,
Ye who have been these twenty years the Mrs. Smith and Brown,[24]
Reading those words, how young Romance his long hushed lute takes
    down,
Wipes off the cobwebs[25] and the dust, gives every key[26] a screw,
And with one stroke across the chords lo, skies forever blue,
Moonlight, slow[27] partings at the gate, pressed roseleaves, and Du! Du!
The last thing that a poet learns is how[28] to throw away
And how to make you thrill and creep with what he doesn't say,
For instance now, to write a song after the style of Poe,
Take the old musty, fusty stock of Everybody and Co;
A moon—we all do know the moon, a sea—we all have seen it,
A dreadful Hint—we all have had—a Fool we all have been it;
Then thus—the black sea moaned beneath and broke in fairy snow,
The moon loomed bloodred in the East, when we met long ago;
That first lush kiss that fierce embrace that parting[29] long and loath—
Avaunt thou pale and patient face! who says I broke my troth?
The music bursts, the dance reels on—ah it is well for thee
Thou hearst no more the muffled beat of that funereal sea;
The dreadful Thing is at my side, its lips are on my lips,
And the sea moans on forevermore, and the frozen seaweed drips!
Tom (nearly eighteen years of age) the dark and silent Man,
Puts on as deep and wild a frown as two white eyebrows can,
Reads it to trembling Sarah Jane, and drops a hint sublime
That he, too, bears the weary weight of some unfathomed crime
And Dick and Harry, who have each an anaconda's appetite,
Feel bound to cheat it of its due and in concealment clap it tight,

[23] MS rejects "(perhaps too short by half!)".
[24] MS rejects "Ye who are now the Mrs. Smiths and Browns and Greens and Joneses."
[25] MS rejects "Wipes off the dust."
[26] MS rejects "string."
[27] MS rejects "sweet."
[28] MS rejects "what."
[29] Rejected word illegible.

Envying dark Tom's mysterious gloom (dyspepsia of both kinds)[30]
And blushing for the stomachs strong that give them healthy minds;
Ah, my Lord Byron, it would make a nice statistic question
How many follies had their rise in your diseased digestion;—
But this Digression, banyan-like, plants colonies so fast
And those again new colonies that, on my soul, at last
'Tis only[31] with nice measuring and comparing I can see
Which my discourse's offshoot is and which the mother-tree;
Let but my Muse be once caught up by something to discuss
She's like the one Old Lady that is always in the 'bus,
Who asks the seedy foreigner soon as she takes her seat
Whether they haven't got beyond the End of Something Street,
And, helpless as a bandbox lone, whence the address is torn,
Is set down[32] everywhere except at her appropriate bourne.

.   .   .   .   .

Menenius, thou who fain wouldst know how calmly men can pass
Those biting portraits of themselves, disguised as fox or ass,
Go borrow coin enough to buy a full-length psyche-glass,
Engage a rather darkish room in some well-sought position,
And let the town break out with bills, so much per head admission,
GREAT NATURAL CURIOSITY!! THE BIGGEST LIVING FOOL!!
Arrange your mirror cleverly, before it set a stool,
Admit the public one by one, place each upon the seat,
Draw up the curtain, let him look his fill, and then retreat.
Smith mounts and takes a thorough view, then comes serenely down,
Goes home and tells his wife the thing is curiously like Brown;
Brown goes and stares, and tells his wife the wonder's core and pith
Is that 'tis just the counterpart of that conceited Smith.
Life calls us all to such a show: Menenius, trust in me,
While thou to see thy neighbor smil'st, he does the same for thee.

.   .   .   .   .

Thou Satirist, who fain would'st know how calmly men can pass⎫
Those clever sketches of themselves in guise[1] of fox or ass, ⎪
Go borrow coin enough to buy a full length psyche-glass;   ⎬
Secure a rather darkish room in some well chosen position   ⎪
Let all the town break out with bills 25 cts admission;   ⎭
Just take a look yourself, my friend, and tell me if you see
Yourself or some not quite so much admired and favored he?

.   .   .   .   .

---

[30] MS rejects "(dyspepsia undefined)."
[31] MS rejects "with."
[32] MS rejects "is carried."

---

[1] MS rejects "shape."

Go buy a mirror, Satirist, secure a good position,
And advertise a raree-show, twenty-five cents admission
Great natural Curiosity!!! a real Living Fool!!!
Arrange your mirror cleverly, before it set[1] a stool,
Admit[2] the Public one by one, place each upon the seat
Draw up the curtain,[3] let him look his fill and then retreat;
Smith mounts and takes a thorough view, then comes serenely down
Goes home and tells his wife it is[4] the strangest thing in town,
"You must go take a look at it; 'tis curiously like Brown;"
Brown goes and stares and tells *his* wife the wonder's core and pith,
Is that 'tis[5] just the counterpart of that conceited Smith;
Life calls us all to such a show: Menippus, it may be
While thou to see thy neighbor smilst, he does the same for thee.

PESCHIERA

What voice did on my spirit fall,
Peschiera, when thy bridge I crost?
" 'Tis better to have fought and lost
Than never to have fought at all."

The Tricolor, a trampled rag,
Lies, dirt and dust; the lines I track,
By sentry-boxes yellow-black,
Lead up to no Italian flag.

I see the Croat soldier stand
Upon the grass of your redoubts;
The Eagle with his black wing flouts
The breadth and beauty of your land.

Yet not in vain, although in vain
O! men of Brescia, on the day
Of loss past hope, I heard you say
Your welcome to the noble pain.

1 MS rejects "place."
2 MS rejects (1) "Admit" and (2) "Let in your."
3 MS rejects false start "And", then "Before the wonder."
4 MS rejects "he's seen."
5 MS rejects "Lies in its look."

You said, "Since it is so, good-bye
Sweet life, high hope; but whatsoe'er
May be or must, no tongue shall dare
To tell, 'The Lombard feared to die.' "

You said, (there shall be answer fit,)
"And if our children must obey
They must, but thinking on this day
'Twill less debase them to submit."

You said, (O! not in vain you said,)
"Haste, brothers, haste while yet we may;
The hours ebb fast of this one day
When blood may yet be nobly shed."

Ah! not for idle hatred, not
For honor, fame, nor self-applause,
But for the glory of your cause,
You did what will not be forgot.

And though the strangers stand, 'tis true
By force and fortune's right he stands;
By fortune which is in God's hands,
And strength which yet shall spring in you.

This voice did on my spirit fall,
Peschiera, when thy bridge I crost,
" 'Tis better to have fought and lost
Than never to have fought at all."

WITHOUT AND WITHIN

No. II

The Restaurant

That seedy chap upon the grating,
    Who sniffs the odors from the kitchen,
Seems in his hungry thoughts debating
    Of all he sees what's most bewitching.

His eyes devour the window's treasure,
    The game, the cutlet, and the salmon,—

But not the flowers, which give *me* pleasure,—
    Japonicas to him are gammon.

I hope to smashing he's not given,—
    He looks so like a hungry terrier,
For, 'twixt him and his seeming heaven,
    There's but a thin and brittle barrier.

He smacks his lips—in fancy tasting,
    And has half brought his mind to nab it—
My game he thinks the cook is basting,
    While 'tis, in fact, a poor Welsh rabbit.

The longing wretch leans o'er the railing,
    And thinks—"Is't I that am a sinner?
Or is it for my father's failing
    That I must go without a dinner?"

"Look at that scamp" (he means me), "sitting
    Cramming enough to feed a dozen,
While I my useless teeth am gritting,
    And yet his wife's my second cousin.

"Now he pours down his Medoc claret,
    Now what to order next he ponders;
Prudhon is right; we ought to share it—
    The gold he so insanely squanders!"

I think.—"O! Fortune, why presentest
    To all mankind gifts so irrelevant?
My teeth demand a constant dentist,
    While *he* is ivoried like an elephant.

"Why probe us with these sharp reminders,
    Why still *in cornu habes foenum?*
Send roasts and nuts to carious grinders,
    While millstone jaws get naught between 'em?

"By all the wealth I've been the winner,
    I would without a moment's question,
Give him my Medoc and my dinner,
    To have his molars and digestion.

"He fancies me a careless feeder,
  While the Lord knows, he's not so weary;
I'm worried for tomorrow's leader.
  And dished by that last fall in Erie."

IN-DOORS AND OUT

Within the grate, fantastic forms
  Like youthful dreams, flame bright and fair,
And burning battlements are seen
  Crumbling like "castles in the air!"

Here, in the ruddy, glowing light,
  In my warm, easy-chair I sit,
Without, the blast howls fierce tonight,
  And past, pale, haggard outcasts flit.

No glimmering beacon's love-lit rays
  Will homeward guide the wand'rer's feet;
No friendly hearth-stone's genial blaze,
  The vagrant's wistful vision greet.

Homeless, and shelterless, they glide
  Like phantoms through the drifting gloom,
Sorrow and Error, side by side—
  Down to unfathomable doom!

Cold blows the wind—fast drives the sleet,
  The grey-beard Winter shrieks aloud,
And hurries on his minions fleet,
  To wrap the dead Earth in her shroud!

Poor, faded Earth—her glowing form
  But late all radiant with life—
Bares her brown bosom to the storm,
  Heeds not the wild wind's angry strife!

With feathery flake, and frosted gem,
  They fringe her winding-sheet of snow—
A glittering, ice-bound diadem
  Surmounts her wrinkled, rugged brow!

No more with summer garlands crowned,
　Lifting her regal forehead up—
She sleeps, with frozen fetters bound,
　The dreamless sleep of Lethe's cup!

Rude, rushing winds, and howling blasts
　Shall o'er her chant their dirges drear,
Till God Omniscient, rolleth back
　The resurrection of the year!

HYMN

Friends of Freedom! ye who stand
With no weapon in your hand,
Save a purpose stern and grand,
　All men to set free,
Welcome! Freedom stands in need
Of true men in thought and deed—
Men who have this only creed,
　That they will not flee!

Though we were but two or three,
Sure of triumph we should be;
We our promised land shall see,
　Though the way seem long:—
Every fearless word we speak
Makes Sin's stronghold bend and creak—
Tyranny is always weak,
　Truth is young and strong!

All the hero-spirits vast,
Who have sanctified the past,
Bearing witness to the last,
　Fight upon our part;
We can never be forlorn:
He, who, in a manger born,
Bore the Priest's and Levite's scorn,
　Gives us hope and heart.

VERSES

Copy of verses wrote by Sir Henry Knatchbull, Bart., 1760

O, share[1] these flowers! thus Delia wrote,
  And pinned upon a tree,
With her own hands, the dainty note
  Addressed to you and me.

The trees were glad that saw her pass,[2]
  The turf embalmed her trace,[3]
The brook flowed slow and smoothed a glass
  To catch her fleeting face.

Next day the letters fair were flown;
  Who stole them? Dryads, say?
By chilling Auster were they blown,
  By Zephyr lured away?

Perhaps some bird the leaf[4] conveyed
  To line her happier nest;
O lucky eggs that shall be laid
  On such a bed to rest!

Perhaps some squirrel was the thief
  To grace his hollow tree,[5]
As with inscription and relief
  Our galleries do we.[6]

But no, the truth was simply this:
  Young Strephon, wandering by,
Saw from the stem, with sudden bliss,
  Fair Delia's ensign fly.

"And oh," he cried, "be mine the page
  That Delia's hand hath prest,
Forgive, ye Gods, his harmless rage
  Whom she hath robbed of rest!

[1] MS: "spare."
[2] MS: "The flowers looked up to see her pass."
[3] MS: "And bless their silent place."
[4] MS: "script."
[5] MS: "To grace his gallery."
[6] MS: "From Greece and Rome do we."

"The slender lines her crowquill traced
 To warn rude hands away,
Shall ne'er in bleak exposure taste
 The chance of night and day;

"But with the bud she once let fall,
 The ribbon that she wore,
Shall add to Cupid's chapel wall
 One saintly relic more!"

THE POWER OF SOUND

A Rhymed Lecture

Ladies and Gentlemen! I claim tonight
With your fair leaves, to use a poet's right:
Asked for a lecture, 'twill be no high crime
If, for a change, I give you one in rhyme.
[I come no stranger, I might fairly claim[1]
In these old streets a kind of grandchild's name,
For in your graveyard, wrapt in silence deep,
Four generations of my kindred sleep,—
Happy in dying e'er our troublous time,
Made dark and full of tears by treason's crime!
Unhappy that they did not live to see
A country worthy to be great and free,
A people dauntless in the weary fight,
Whate'er its pangs, for freedom and for right!]
At no high range I try Invention's wing,
But give you just a medley of a thing,
Part serious and part comic, both in one,
Or here all sentiment and there all fun,
Rather rhymed speech than poem, framed to sound
Well in the utterance, with its couplets round,
Not too condensed, for many a verse might fall
Dead in the closet, written for the hall,
And what brought down the house to hear,—if read,
Might bring down all the critics on one's head.
The Power of Sound the subject of my song,—
Lend me your ears, nor find my own too long!

[1] These numbers refer to Charles Eliot Norton's notes to this poem and will be found on pp. 262-65.

Promise yourselves beforehand this relief,—
I may be tedious but I will be brief.

In Nature's realm what element is found
So wide in range, so deep in power as Sound,
Whether it find in earth's weird voices vent,
Or climb to Art in tongue or instrument?
What porch of sense is earlier, later, dear
Than Love's and Music's entrance-gate, the ear?
The new-born darling, sunk in slumber deep,
Hears still his mother's singing through his sleep,
Hears it and feels, though all too young to know,
That love hangs watching o'er his cradle low;
So when at last, life's ebb almost run out,
The windows darken and the dull eyes doubt,
When faces bright to all, to us grow dim,
Seen through the flush of Heaven's auroral rim,
Then thrill our ears the murmured words of prayer,
The exulting texts that wrench us from despair,
And, last of earth, like far-heard bells of home
To shipwrecked men amid the breakers' foam,
The choking tones, half blessing, half farewell,
That woman's faith and hope and heartbreak tell.

To lead the mind from things of present view,
Backward by frail association's clue,
Not e'en the Eye its magic may compare
With charms that Hearing gathers from the air:
We climb Mont Blanc and gaze with soul aglow
On God's own Gothic marble-roofed with snow,
We watch the Staubbach trailing like a mist
O'er crags by August sun to opal kissed,
We track the torrent whirling smoothly swift
Down the primeval glacier's azure rift,—
Hark! far below the mountain's beetling eaves,
A peasant girl is singing 'mid her sheaves,
A simple song, but heard long years before
From lips, that save in Heaven, will sing no more;
Hush! as she sings, the mountains fade from view,
The stream grows silent as the heaven's own blue,
Across the eyes a veil of mist is cast,
And we but see the landscape of the past.

We roam the halls where reigns the ideal race
Of Grecian gods not yet dethroned in grace,
The beauty, inaccessible and lone,
Left locked by Athens in the Parian stone;
E'en as we gaze, a voice, behind us heard,
Dissolves the spell with some sweet English word,—
The gods have vanished,—melt the walls in air,
No statue answers to our vacant stare,
Forth from the stately solitude of Rome
That chance-spoke phrase hath borne our spirits home;
We walk the village where we first drew breath,
Dear with its memories of life and death,
We see the spire whose warning shadow slow
Moves o'er its dial green of graves below,
We hear on new-fallen leaves in silent lanes
The yellowing shagbark drop its summer gains,
Or, on the ice, the ring of gliding steel,
And the long echo from the skater's heel.

But, Nymph of Sound,—what need to prove thy gift,
The Aladdin's trapdoor of the past to lift?
To spread old scenes beneath a foreign sky,
And give the enchantment of the inward eye?
Blind Milton still, though sealed in darkness long,
Could see all springtime in the sky-lark's song;
For while we hear we are not wholly blind;
'T is the best link that binds us to our kind;
To every sense God gives its several bliss,—
The words "I love you," speak alone to this.

Walk the Spring fields and say what joys of sight
So keen, so various, as the Ear's delight?
The bird whose breast shows Autumn's russet dye,
While back and wings are steeped in May's own sky,
From post to post, the rustic fence along,
Shifts the light burden of his simple song;
O'erhead the bobolink rows against the breeze,
Quivering with dithyrambic melodies,
Meanwhile the bee, with intermission sweet,
From flower to flower flits humming at our feet,
And far from elm-embosomed farm to farm
The cock's shrill triumph sends its household charm.

Where'er we turn, to him who listens right
The earth is full of music and delight,
But music formless, void of law or bound,
A vast unconquered wilderness of sound,
A chaos waiting till the master man
Should harmonize its discords into plan,
A chaos, longing with expectant heart
For the creative will and word of Art.
And what is Art? 'tis Nature reproduced
In forms ideal, from the actual loosed;—
Nature sublimed in life's more gracious hours
By high Imagination's plastic powers,
When all the senses round one passion close
As round its golden heart the unopened rose;—
'Tis Beauty, when, her Psyche-wings set free,
She spurns her chrysalis, Utility;
And, more than all, 'tis Life, creative, warm,
That wooes the blockish thought to Grecian form.

Take any sound, a step we'll say, and see
How Art can raise it to her own degree,
Free it from triteness, commonplace, and prose,
And make it herald of sublimer woes:
Steps have their various meanings,—who can hear
The long, slow, tread, deliberate and clear,
The boot that creaks and gloats on every stair
And the firm knock which says "I know you're there!"
Nor quake at portents which so oft before
Have been the heralds of the ten-inch bore?
He enters and he sits—as crowners sit,
On the dead bodies of our time and wit,
Hopes that no plan of ours he comes to balk,
And grinds the hurdy-gurdy of his talk
In steady circles meaningless and flat,
As the broad brim that rounds a Bishop's hat.
Nature, didst thou endow him with a voice,
As mothers give great drums to little boys,
To teach us sadly how much outward din
Is based on bland vacuity within?
He goes at last, and once again we wait
To hear the rattle of the closing gate,
Nor are we free from terror and surmise
Till his last boot-creak in the gravel dies.

Now think you Mozart's blood had never run
Chill at the advancing step of bore or dun?
Had he not heard the million footsteps fall
Daily on pavements of the capital?
Was aught more common or outworn than this,
The hourly proof that man a biped is?
Yet how, in Don Giovanni, has he shed
Terror and mystery round the marble tread
That through the laughter strikes a chill and gloom,
Like the dull footfall of advancing Doom!
How in the overture we hear it sound,
No trivial step that falls on common ground,
But full of portent, as each clod that gave
Its echo back were hollow with a grave!
So Art can lift the meanest things that be
Up to the heaven of her felicity,
So can Imagination's touch sublime
Make things Eternal of the things of Time,
And so, as Music waves her baton round,
To shapes harmonious thrills the void of sound!

    Slow were the steps, the progress steep and long;
And Music's earliest stammer was in song;
No arduous notes, but such as idly rise
Unwilled, like tears of pleasure to the eyes;
Songs such as mothers o'er the cradle croon
At morn invented and forgot ere noon.
And might I guess who first with human words
Made measured cadence, simple as a bird's,
'Twas the world's mother, when, half joy, half awe,
Her image in her baby's eyes she saw,
And, as her first-born to her heart she strained,
Felt almost more than Paradise regained.
He, as he drew the pain of mortal breath,
Knew Eden lost, in life foretasted death,
And wailed aloud, while she rocked to and fro,
And to her motion sang, now fast, now slow,
As terror and delight by turns held sway
Within her heart and tempered all her lay:
So to her lips the laws of Time and Tune
Came up unasked, like violets in June:
"Sleep, darling, sleep," she softly sang, "in thee
"Our race renewed with fairer hope I see,

"Sleep, son of Adam, thou shalt never know,
"Like her who gave thee life, the utter woe
"Of giving death to others, but thy brow
"Shall still be fair and innocent as now!"
So sang she, feeling on her bosom stir
The rose-soft palms of that first murderer;
How many a mother since has sung as she,
And dreamed fair dreams with Cain upon her knee!

What need the advancing steps of song to trace
And all its changing moods of Age and Race?
Themes such as that, distinctions such as those,
Belong of right to science and to prose.
The light-winged Muse that Hippocrenë drinks
Recks not the weeds and pebbles on its brinks;
She clasps whole continents with gladdening eyes
Nor stays her footstep to geologize.
Yet must I linger! who untouched could leave
Those Hebrew songs that triumph, trust, or grieve?
Verses that smite the soul as with a sword,
And open all the abysses with a word?
How many a soul have David's tears washed white,
His wings borne upward to the Source of light!
How many his triumph nerved with martyr-will,
His faith from turmoil led to waters still!
They were his songs that rose to Heaven before
The surge of steel broke wild o'er Marston Moor,
When rough-shod workmen in their sober gear
Rode down in dust the long-haired Cavalier;
With these once more the Mayflower's cabin rang
From men who trusted in the God they sang,
And Plymouth heard them, poured on bended knees,
From wild Cathedrals arched with centuried trees.
They were grim men, unlovely,—yes, but great,
Who prayed around the cradle of our State;
Small room for light and sentimental strains
In those lean men with empires in their brains,
Who their young Israel saw in vision clasp
The mane of either sea with taming grasp,
Who pitched a State as other men pitch tents,
And led the march of Time to great events.
O strange New World that yet wast never young,[2]
Whose youth from thee by tyrannous need was wrung,

Brown foundling of the forests, with gaunt eyes,
Orphan and heir of all the centuries,
Who, on thy baby leaf-bed in the wood,
Grew'st frugal, plotting for to-morrow's food;
And thou, dear Bay-state, mother of us all,
Forget not in new cares thine ancient call,
Though all things else should perish in the sod,
Hold with firm clutch thy Puritan faith in God,
And the calm courage that deemed all things light
Whene'er the inward voice said, *This is right!*
If for the children there should come a time[3]
Like that which tried the fathers' faith sublime,
(Which God avert!), if Tyranny should strive
On limbs New-England-made to lock her gyve,
Let Kansas answer from her reddened fields,
" 'Tis bastard and not Pilgrim blood that yields!"

But lighter themes demand my wandering lay,
The Muse with gladness smoothes the frown away,
Content to follow down the ages long
The brooklike waywardness of gleaming song.

Music hath uses, nor of these the least
To be the inspiring handmaid of the priest,
To guide the soul to that serener air
Where praise, full-ripened, blossoms into prayer:
O ancient chants, O voice of chaste desires,
Tender with tears and warm with martyr-fires,
Blossom of saintly spirits, essence fine
Of all in human nature most divine,
Best aspirations, which we feel to be
Not one but every age's litany,
Who that has ever sorrowed, ever loved,
Can hear your ecstasies with soul unmoved?
Whether 'neath Sistine vaults, while twilight falls
O'er Michael's frescoes fading on the walls,
The Miserere trail its long despair,
And grief find solace in a pain more rare,—
Whether 'neath Peter's dome there swell the chant,
While Easter sunbeams through the incense slant,
And saints down-gleaming from the vaulted roof
Thrill in their golden Heaven so far aloof,
As with one burst of voice and instrument

He is arisen! down the nave is sent,—
Whether in England's hoary minster-piles,
The organ's thunders jar the quarried aisles,
Shaking the banners that had streamed of yore
In France's van at Creci and Agincourt,
And the long chant, with exultation flown,
Makes the carved leaves forget that they are stone,—
Or whether in some meeting-house which we
To call a Gothic edifice agree,
(Vandal were better,—all one, so we keep
Taste out of sight and do religion cheap),
Yet there, even there, within that bandbox shrine,
The soul may taste its sacramental wine,
May in Wachuset's place see Horeb stand,
As from the people, in a chorus grand,
"Old Hundred" rings, and memories dim for years
Rise up transfigured through a mist of tears!

If measured words man's nature so can move,
Song too must plead for Freedom, Joy, and Love:
How many a change the lyric Muse hath rung
Since all the woman burned on Sappho's tongue;
Since the mild Teian, innocently gay,
'Twixt wine and woman shared his genial lay;
Since fierce Tyrtaeus crashing o'er the lyre
For burning words found notes of kindred fire;
Since Horace sang in numbers clear and sweet
Life's social charm and friendship's Autumn heat!
Where'er man's heart with daring deed or hope
Hath felt its bounds, yet longed for wider scope,
The dumb emotion in the bosom pent
Hath found in song its solace and its vent.
When Luther roused to grapple with his foe,
Shaking all Europe with indignant *No!*
And moulding kingdoms in his peasant palms,
His doughtiest champions were a score of psalms;
On Music's wings and Memory's all abroad
They flew, the weaponed canticles of God,
Safe from the stake, the halter and the sword,
From the priest's guile, or Kaiser's broken word.

No easy task to frame the passionate lay
Whose force magnetic keeps old Time at bay,

To find the melody complex yet clear,
In no tongue alien, sweet to every ear,
Fresh still, though centuries old, as morning dew,
Familiar, though but yesterday 'twas new.
The artist knows not how within him sprung
The graceful marvel trembling on his tongue;
Dreams the brown Earth her mother-juices stir
In the rathe snowdrop that looks back on her,
Or that it stole from her dumb heart below
The tender secret of its perfumed snow?
Rare is the gift to marry to the chords
Words that are music, music that is words,
A perfect sympathy to ear and heart,
Nature made doubly natural by Art,
Words that across the yielding music fly
Like light winds gleaming o'er the scarce-bent rye,
Music that floats the thought unconscious up
As the lake swings the lily's argent cup,—
Such the true lyric, and the men how few
Who know the secret, or who ever knew!

Spirit of Song, by wandering breezes borne
Safe to the heart which thou wilt fill with morn,
Whether in some hushed hamlet 'mid the hills,
Or the smoked city loud with whirling mills,
Who knows what foundling's utterance thou lt unbind,
Take him from toil and give him to Mankind?
Thou foundest Burns a stripling at his plough,
The impatient genius lamping neath his brow;
Small need had he to mourn the lore of books,
The season's playmate, friend of fields and brooks,—
He sang as birds sing, and his joys and woes
Took beauty on as simply as a rose.
Thou foundest Moore a boy in amorous wars,
The lord's small toady, Cupid of boudoirs,—
Thou whispered'st him, and Erin's earth-bowed wrong
Sprang mailed with verse and falchion-girt with song,—
On "The Last Rose" there falls no winter blight,
The "Light of Other Days" is deathless light!
Where Paris' streets with million footsteps throb,
Child of the alley, pupil of the mob,
Thou found'st a bright-eyed boy, and sigh'dst "Come forth,"
"Alas!" he answered, "I am nothing worth,

"A shiftless creature, fit to be a king."
Thou spak'st once more, "And thou shalt be one,—Sing!"
Then gushed the lays, pathetic, tender, light,
Cheerful as sunshine, full of thought as night,
And France, that wept with him, and lent
Her choral tones to deepen all he meant,
Mourned (and 'twas long for France to mourn) a day,
Her greatest poet dead in Béranger.[4]

Have *we* no lyrics? Doth Euterpe scorn
To tread our prairies broad and woods unworn?
Answer, ye notes which shrilled o'er Yorktown's farms,
A country-jig, impressed to serve in arms,
When loath Cornwallis, scarlet-breasted, drew
His sword to yield it to the Buff and Blue;
Which shrilled again when, 'mid the war-clouds dun,
Yard locked with yard, hot gun-lip kissing gun,[5]
The English oak, long wont to spurn the seas,
Bent to the western pine its sturdy knees,
And the red cross, dread meteor of the wave,
Place to new stars in skies of empire gave!

Long as the sun beneath our hill-tops dips,
Ne'er may war set the trumpet to her lips,
And, with fierce summons, call from forge and field
Our youth that kindle slow and slowly yield;
But, oh! fair Freedom, if our choice must be
'Twixt war and craven recreance to thee,
Sooner, dear land, let each manchild of thine
Sleep death's red sleep within the enemy's line,
Let ocean whelm thy last ship's shattered trunk,
Her torn flag shaking challenge as she sunk,
To rot unconquered, all her thunders spent,[6]
Each rusting gun a brave man's monument,
Sooner than brook, what only slaves hold dear,
A suppliant peace that is not Peace, but Fear!

Poor though the air, and not of native growth,
The paltry words and music British both,
Yet Yankee Doodle's hurrying cadence suits
Our rapid Jonathan in seven-league boots.
And, mixed with glorious memories, can inspire
The heart with will and flood the veins with fire.

But have we nothing that is wholly ours?
No songs commensurate with our growing powers?
Answer, whose ears have felt the torturing blows
Of lays like "Jump Jim Crow" or "Coal-black Rose,"
The pioneers, from nightly lampblacked jaws,
Of all those tunes that set our teeth like saws!
Answer, ye patient victims, doomed to hear
The white man's Ethiop doggerel by the year,
Mothers, with industry of nursery choirs
Tired out,—because "Virginny *nebber* tires,"
Fathers, half-dead with hearing sons and heirs
Forever "gittin' up" those endless "stairs"
That led to empty rooms for Discord fit,
Not Attic, though,—*that* word we join with wit!

Music, thou keystone of Creation's arch,—
From morning stars that pealed Time's opening march,
From angels singing Christmas hymns of peace,
What a descent to banjo strains like these!
By these men enter not thy shrine, nor so
Thy springs of grace and solace learn to know;
Not so are oped those starry deeps of song
That make us weak to make us doubly strong;
O'er this grimed gate is carven deep and clear,
"Leave hope behind, all ye who enter here!"
No sin more base than thus to vulgarize
The Arts, which, rightly used, make great and wise,
By which the soul lives when the man is gone,
And Beauty's trophies mock oblivion;
These to degrade, through want of thought or pelf,
Is to debase the coin of God himself!

But I am preaching: ah me! what's the use,
Not they who teach please most, but who amuse,
Yet as we near our fortieth parallels[7]
We reach our temperate zone, if nothing else,
And threaten judgments less, because we find
Our own has not been always of one mind.
Who against music has not sinned? who not
In some vile chorus paid his vocal scot,
When all the letters of the scale to him
Were x's, unknown quantities and dim?

Long o'er the Lyric I have paused, but when
Was aught so dear, so eloquent, to men?
What like the human voice can soothe or stir,
The voice, and Music its interpreter?
Love softens it till every pleading tone
Seems shod with leaves of roses newly-blown;
Fear chokes it to a hoarse and husky breath
From some pale twilight realm 'twixt life and death;
Hate chills and hardens it until we feel
Under the civil sheath an edge of steel;
Courage rings through it like a trump that calls
"Havelock is nigh!" to Lucknow's trembling walls;[8]
And when beneath the torrid vault of brain
The eyes are dry and spent their futile rain,
It draws its pathos from profounder spheres,
Red heart-caves, far below the source of tears.
The voice it is that parts us from the brute,
The unfallen angels sing,—the fallen are mute.
Since God first spake, dividing day from night,
And in one act created speech and light,
Language hath been man's high prerogative,
Image express of Him by whom we live;
Unlanguaged Nature to the Earth is bound,
Yet speechward yearns in many a speechless sound,
For utterance longs, and finds at last in Man
The gift denied her in Creation's plan.
Yet by mere words the soul's but half released,
Nature had found, the spirit lacked her priest,
Who, as he offered for the adoring throng,
Could transubstantiate mortal words with song;
Then music came, and on the Poet's lips
Utterance full-orbed swam moonlike from eclipse:
As Man to Nature, so to Man is he
Who fledges words with wings of melody;
Through him the weary, weak, oppressed, and poor
Their stammering sorrow hear to rapture soar,
He by expression gives their hearts relief,
For a grief uttered is but half a grief.
O gift unequalled, by the spell of Tone
To make the aspirings of mankind his own!

But am I partial? Hath not Music flung
Her charm o'er other organs than the tongue?

O'er wood, and brass, and wire, insensate things,
She waves her wand, and each, enchanted, sings,
Takes Feeling's, Passion's, Thought's, or Fancy's hue
As pools grow deep with Heaven's reflected blue.

Than the Composer's art none more demands
The long-trained instinct of creative hands;
What breadth of brain, what tireless stretch of thought,
By which these miracles of sound are wrought!
What grasp of mind, what subtle tact of skill,
To wield the Orchestra with a single will,
The guiding thought and impulse to conceive
That Tone's ten thousand strands in one shall weave,
That in the Opera's gathering Fate shall suit
The tragic buskin to Euterpe's foot,
Endow the organ with a breathing soul
And like a moon its mutinous tides control!

Majestic Organ, in thy stops are blent
All Nature's tones, imperial instrument!
Thou canst wail plaintive like a soul in doubt
Or peal all Sinai's threatening thunders out,
Canst like a child entreat, or prophet warn,
Or hurl o'er kneeling hosts Jehovah's scorn!
Through Haarlem's aisles, or Freiburg's arches grand,
How thrill'st thou docile to the master's hand,
While through the forest of thy pipes there sweeps,
Like wind through pines, a storm from out the deeps!
In Bach's broad fugues the mid-sea waves, heaped high,
Roll on and on beneath a sunless sky,
Break on no shore, but endless rise and fall,
Till gradual silence drops like night o'er all;
Of if the player will, you seem to hear
Two choirs alternate, distant one, one near;
From mighty basses one to whispers dies,
Far off in heaven the treble clear replies;
So, till in distance lost, they seem to call
And answer still in chant antiphonal,
While like a golden censer, as they go,
They swing the choral incense to and fro.

Our fathers, large in faith and strong in heart,
Were bleak and northern on the side of Art,

And surely in the narrow path they trod,
When they shut organs from the house of God.
And when, with feuds like Ghibelline and Guelf,
Each parish did its music for itself.
A parson's son, through tree-arched country ways,
I rode exchanges oft in dear old days
Ere yet the boys forgot, with reverent eye,
To doff their hats as the black coat went by,
Ere skirts expanding in their apogee,
Turned girls to bells without the second *e*;
Still in my teens, I felt the various woes
Of volunteers, each singing as he chose,
Till much experience left me no desire
To learn new species of the Village choir.
Sometimes two ancient men, through glasses dim,
In age's treble deaconed off the hymn,
Paused o'er long words and then with breathless pace
Went down a slope of short ones at a race,
While who could sing and who could not, but would,
Rushed helter-skelter after as they could.
Well I remember how their faces shone,
Safe through some snare like *Re-sig-na-ti-on,*
And how some graceless youth would mock the tones
Of Deacon Jarvis or of Deacon Jones:
In towns ambitious of more cultured strains,
The gruff bass-viol told its inward pains
As some enthusiast, deaf to catgut's woe,
Rasped its bare nerves with torture-resined bow;
Hard-by another, with strained eyeballs set,
Blew devious discord through his clarinet,
And the one fiddle, that was wont to seek
In secular tunes its living all the week,
Blind to the leader's oft-repeated glance
Mixed up the psalm-tune with a country dance.

O, Muse, return, for somewhat nobler chords
Wait but thy touch to sing beneath the words;
Names crowd, of men that well deserved the bays,—
No chaplet frail of overhasty praise,
But sifted judgments, not of one or two,
Such as slow decades pass upon the few.
There Händel smiles, he who the song restored
That angel-choirs o'er Bethlehem's manger poured,

Who plucked great thoughts, with soul of mighty reach,
Easily as children pull a loosened peach,
And whose clear depth, and pure Arcadian tone,
Still, as the centuries pass, are all his own;
There Haydn towers, and, in his various strain,
Renews Creation's miracle again,
Poet and thinker, who to Music brought
The embracing range of astronomic thought;
There stands stout Glück, his seamed face glowing through
With the frank courage to its instincts true,
Who dared the bribes of Fashion to refuse
And rescued fallen Opera from the stews;
There Mozart rises, spirit ever young,
O'er whose charmed cradle murmuring Music hung,
That fresh, blithe nature, through whose veins we see
The ichor throb of innate Melody,
Whose artist hands so sweetly interwrought
Italian sunshine with Teutonic thought;
And there, majestic shade, with cliff-like brow,
Once scarred with stormy thought, but placid now,
The lion-head bent down with weight of mind,
The hair blown back with supernatural wind,
Beethoven passes,—what a soul was there
To wrench its triumphs from a life's despair!
A deaf musician! tell me, can there be
A man so stepmothered by Fate as he?
Not so: the Muse her little Ishmael found
Shut in his desert from the world of sound,
Showed him the rift whence living water sprang,
And in his brain all Nature's voices sang.
As, over Guido's fresco brightly borne,
His flaming coursers drives the god of morn,
So, with light grasp, yet strong, Beethoven strains
In glowing hands all Music's golden reins,
While, with resounding wheels, the car is driven
Through brightening spaces to the verge of Heaven!

I pass the living; say not I have set
Only round German brows the coronet;
O Italy, I love thee all too well
Not to have felt and loved thy music's spell!
Art will not leave thee; though the Bourbon brood
Stain thy fair streets, Parthenope, with blood,

Though Rome again within her broken walls
Hears with bowed head the tramp of barbarous Gauls
Spite French treachery and Teutonic wrong,
The land of Dante is the land of song,
Round the dead shell the soul of Music clings
And Passion only in Italian sings!

O Art divine, so strong to cheer and save,
Companion from the cradle to the grave,
Who know'st each stop, from thoughts whose lurid seams
Glow with Imagination's thund'rous gleams,
To airiest Fancies that like swallows skim
O'er the brain's surface with unceasing whim,—
Proteus! now gay as that auroral glance
That leads from Boreal skies its tireless dance,
Now sad as first earth on the coffin's lid,
Or yellowing letters after dear deaths hid,—
How shall my voice find art, or strike the key,
In fitting words to take her leave of thee?

Thou calm'st the infant on the mother's breast,—
Thou modulat'st aspiring youth's unrest,—
Thou sooth'st the mother pining for her boy,—
Pip'st to the bride to heighten joy with joy,—
O'er awestruck multitudes thou soar'st in praise,—
Wail'st for the dead gone forth through darkling ways,—
Thrillest the martyr with exultant hymn
From cloudy rows of waiting Cherubim,
Until the fiery cup, denied its power,
Folds its cool petals round him like a flower:
From the hushed edge of battle, when the breath
Chills 'neath the upas-shade of imminent Death,
The soldier hears thy clarion clangors come,
And the quick heart-beat of thy eager drum,
In airs home-breathing hears his country cry,
"Hath life such sweetness as for me to die?"
And mounts the breach, with eye as marble firm,
To crush the hailing battery like a worm.

Music, companion of Life's choicest hours,
Passion's best voice, spur of the manlier powers,
Fitly for thee to breathe a last farewell
The tones should fade, as, in the exiled shell,

Dies the faint murmur stolen from the sea,
The lifelong sigh of Love and Memory;—
Feeling should undulate each living line,
And the words match it, as across the brine,
Following the bark the stormy-petrel flies,
Sinks with the waves and rises as they rise;—
But, ah, to track the ideal Hope how vain!
The rainbow, caught, would be but icy rain,
And still before us glides the alluring bow
In its own heaven, and leaves us still below!

EPIGRAM ON J. M.

Said Fortune to a common spit,
"Your rust and grease I'll rid ye on,
And make ye in a twinkling fit
For Ireland's Sword of Gideon!"

In vain! what Nature meant for base
All chance for good refuses;
M. gave one gleam, then turned apace
To dirtiest kitchen uses.

THE TRUSTEE'S LAMENT

Per aspera ad astra

(Scene.—Outside the gate of the Astronomical Observatory at Albany.)

There was a time when I was blest;
The stars might rise in East or West
    With all their sines and wonders;
I cared for neither great nor small,
As pointedly unmoved by all
As, on the top of steeple tall,
    A lightning-rod at thunders.

What did I care for Science then?
I was a man with fellow-men,
    And called the Bear the Dipper;

Segment meant piece of pie,—no more;
Cosine, the parallelogram that bore
JOHN SMITH & CO. above a door;
 Arc, what called Noah skipper.

No axes weighed upon my mind,
(Unless I had a few to grind,)
 And as for my astronomy,
Had Hedgecock's quadrant then been known,
I might a lamp-post's height have shown
By gas-tronomic skill,—if none
 Find fault with the metonymy.

O hours of innocence! O ways
How far from these unhappy days
 When all is vicy-versy!
No flower more peaceful took its due
Than I, who then no difference knew
'Twixt Ursy Major and my true
 Old crony, Major Hersey.

Now in long broils and feuds we roast,
Like Strasburg geese that living toast
 To make a liver-*paté*,—
And all because we fondly strove
To set the city of our love
In scientific fame above
 Her sister Cincinnati!

We built our tower and furnished it
With everything folks said was fit,
 From coping-stone to grounsel;
And then, to give a knowing air,
Just nominally assigned its care
To that unmanageable affair,
 A Scientific Council.

We built it, not that one or two
Astronomers the stars might view
 And count the comets' hair-roots,
But that it might by all be said
How very freely we had bled,—
We were not laying out a bed
 To force their early square-roots.

The observations *we* wished made
Were on the spirit we'd displayed,
    Worthy of Athens' high days;
But *they*'ve put in a man who thinks
Only of planets' nodes and winks,
So full of astronomic kinks
    He eats star-fish on Fridays.

The instruments we did not mean
For seeing through, but to be seen
    At tap of Trustee's knuckle;
But the Director locks the gate,
And makes ourselves and strangers wait
While he is ciphering on a slate
    The rust of Saturn's buckle.

So on the wall's outside we stand,
Admire the keyhole's contour grand
    And gateposts' sturdy granite;—
But, ah, is Science safe, we say,
With one who treats Trustees this way?
Who knows but he may snub, some day,
    A well-conducted planet?

Who knows what mischief he may brew
With such a telescope brand-new
    At the four-hundredth power?
He may bring some new comet down
So near that it'll singe the town
And do the Burgess-Corps crisp-brown
    Ere they can storm his tower.

We wanted (having got our show)
Some man, that had a name or so,
    To be our public showman;
But this one shuts and locks the gate
Who'll answer but he'll peculate,
(And, faith, some stars are missed of late,)
    Now that he's watched by no man?

Our own discoveries he may steal,
Or put night's candles out, to deal
    At junkshops with the sockets:

Savants, in other lands or this,
If any theory you miss
Whereon your cipher graven is,
   Don't fail to search his pockets!

Lock up your comets: if that fails,
Then notch their ears and clip their tails,
   That you at need may swear to 'em;
And watch your nebulous flocks at night,
For, if your palings are not tight,
He may, to gratify his spite,
   Let in the Little Bear to 'em.

Then he's so quarrelsome, we've fears
He'll set the very Twins by the ears,—
   So mad, if you resist him,
He'd get Aquarius to play
A milkman's trick, some cloudy day,
And water all the Milky Way
   To starve some sucking system.

But plaints are vain! through wrath or pride,
The Council all espouse his side
   And will our missives con no more;
And who that knows what *savants* are,
Each snappish as a Leyden jar,
Will hope to soothe the wordy war
   'Twixt Ologist and Onomer?

Search a Reform Convention, where
He- and she-resiarchs prepare
   To get the world in *their* power,
You will not, when 'tis loudest, find
Such gifts to hug and snarl combined
As drive each astronomic mind
   With fifty-score Great-Bear-power!

No! put the Bootees on your foot,
Elope with Virgo, strive to shoot
   That arrow of O'Ryan's,
Drain Georgian Ciders to the lees,
Attempt what crackbrained thing you please,
But dream not you can e'er appease
   An angry man of science!

Ah, would I were, as I was once,
To fair Astronomy a dunce,
    Or launching *jeux d'esprit* at her,
Of light zodiacal making light,
Deaf to all tales of comets bright,
And knowing but such stars as might
    Roll r-rs at our theatre!

Then calm I drew my night-cap on,
Nor bondsman was for what went on
    Ere morning in the heavens;
'Twas no concern of mine to fix
The Pleiades at seven or six,—
But now the *omnium genitrix*
    Seems all at sixes and sevens.

Alas, 'twas in an evil hour
We signed the paper for the tower,
    With Mrs. D. to head it!
For, if the Council have their way,
We've merely had, as Frenchmen say,
The painful *maladie du* pay,
    While they get all the credit!

Boys, henceforth doomed to spell Trustees,
Think not it ends in double ease
    To those who hold the office;
Shun Science as you would Despair,
Sit not in Cassiopeia's chair,
Nor hope from Berenice's hair
    To bring away your trophies!

THE FATAL CURIOSITY

Some charm was round me, night and day,
    That made my life seem just begun;
A presence was it? Rather say
    The warning aureole of one.

And yet I felt it everywhere;
    Walked I the woodland isles along,

It brushed me with ambrosial hair;
    Bathed I, I heard a mermaid's song.

How sweet it was! a buttercup
    Could hold for me a day's delight,
A bird could lift my fancy up
    To ether free from cloud or blight.

What was the Nymph? Nay, I will see,
    Methought, and I will know her near;
If such, but guessed, her charm can be,
    Were not possession triply dear?

So every magic art I tried,
    And spells as numberless as sand,
Until one midnight by my side
    I saw her glowing fulness stand.

I turned to clasp her—but, "Farewell,"
    Fading, she sighed, "we meet no more;
Not by my hand the curtain fell
    That leaves you conscious, wise, and poor.

"Since you have found me out, I go;
    Another lover I must find
Content his happiness to know,
    Nor strive its secret to unwind."

BEFORE THE EMBERS

It is not far to the Macarian isles,
Nor to the gates of my enchanted palace;
There fountains rear their palpitating piles,
And Parian beauty gleams through twilight alleys.
There music, never heard in mortal air,
Swells and is hushed along the hillsides fair,
Or hides and seeks with echo in the valleys;
And in its pauses all the tree-tops sing,
And all the falling fountain-jewels ring,
And, with half-hushed emotion,
Up marble steps the unharmful billows swing,
Rimming with whispery pearls the sapphire ocean.

There are all things that soul or sense delight—
Imperial shapes that Phidias died conceiving,
Verses that musing poets meant to write,
And Raphael's dreams, at sunrise past retrieving;
Great windows open toward the western gold,
O'er hills on hills in amplest sunset rolled
To sharp snow-peaks, an opal chrism receiving,
And eastward over leagues of ocean stark,
Where, o'er the upheaving moon, some raven bark
With swift eclipse is stealing,
And there are walls cloistered with laurel dark,
To shut the senses round some chosen feeling.

But most my portrait-gallery I prize,
By memory reared, the artist wise and holy
From stainless quarries of deep-buried days;
There, as I muse in dainty melancholy,
Your faces glow in more than mortal youth,
Companions of my prime, now vanished wholly!
Though my dull soul refract Heaven's other rays,
Though truth, or what seemed truth, may feel decays,
Ye know not alteration,
But shine undimmed as when life's morning blaze
Flashed back from youth's white shield of expectation.

Ye glow serene through that celestial air
Which only fortunes passed are e'er arrayed in,
Secure from mist of doubt or blight of care,
The loud impetuous boy, the low-voiced maiden;
Ah, never master that drew mortal breath
Can match thy portraits, just and generous death,
Whose brush with sweet regretful tints is laden;
Thou paintest that which baffled here below,
Half understood, or understood for woe,
And, with a sweet forewarning,
Mak'st round the sacred front an aureole glow
Woven of that light which rose on Easter morning!

IL PESCEBALLO

OPERA SERIA: IN UN ATTO

Musica del Maestro Rossibelli-Donimozarti

PERSONAGGI

Lo STRANIERO   (Tenore)
IL CAMERIERE   (Basso)
LA PADRONA   (Soprano)
Un Corriere, Serve della Locanda, Studenti di Padova

La Scena è in Padova

[° *Il Pesceballo* (corruzione della voce inglese *Fish-ball*) è un prodotto della cucina americana, consistente in una combinazione di stoccofisso con patate, fatta nella forma di pallottole, simili alle nostre polpette, e poi fritta. Msgr. Bedini, nel suo *Viaggio negli Stati Uniti*, c' insegna che la detta pietanza si usa massimamente nella Nuova-Inghilterra, ove, secondo quel venerabile autore, viene specialmente mangiato a colazione nelle domeniche.]

SCENE I

Street in Padua. CHORUS of Students of the University,
first in the distance, then on the stage.

Hesper doth peer now,
Make we good cheer now,
With the new daylight
Back to the oar!

We're your true nightlarks!
Truce to all learning
Till, with the morning,
Comes the old bore!

Drinking and smoking,
Laughing and joking,
These are what students
Love to the core!

We have to study
Flossofies muddy,
'Ologies, 'Onomies,
    'Ics by the score!

All the strange lingoes,
Law, too, by jingoes!
Ever new sciences
    We must explore!

Drinking and smoking,
Laughing and joking,
These are the pleasures
    Night hath in store.

                    [*Exeunt.*

SCENE II

THE STRANGER

Cavatina

Behold thro' shadows lowering
The waning moon slinks cowering!
Dread Fate, my soul o'erpowering,
    No more my footsteps dog!
Ah! sweet, ecstatic vision,
Why leave me in derision?
I perish, dream Elysian,
    Unless I find some prog!
            [*He sinks upon a rock, weary, and almost
            desperate: after a pause, he begins again.*
Just Heaven, what splendor greets my aching eyes!
Methinks I see Hope's morning star arise!
Is it some sign transparent, or the moon?
Guide me, ye powers supreme, to some *Saloon!*
                    [*Exit.*

SCENE III

Dining-room of an Eating-House. THE LANDLADY, WAITER, MAIDS

L.   Pietro, say, are all things ordered right?
    There'll be a throng of customers to-night.

W. Bid them come on! we're ready and to spare:
    I hear the students singing in the square.
L. Yes, what a bore! sad customers are they!
W. Your pardon, Madam, good ones—when they pay.
L. Howe'er it is, submissive must we be: ⎫
    Go to the kitchen and the maids o'ersee, ⎬
    That everything be ready to a T. ⎭

                       [*Exit Waiter.*

SCENE IV

The Landlady, *sola*

Aria

How full is life of sorrow
   To one that keeps an hostel!
Doomed with each weary morrow
   To be upon the go still!
Send me, oh Heaven, some angel
   In answer to my moan!

In season and out of season,
   I wither here alone,
('Tis a shame, 'tis against all reason,)
   Wearing my hands to the bone!
My mind's made up! I'll seize on
   Some husband to share my moan!

SCENE V

Landlady, Waiter

W. *(aside).* Lo, she's alone! no better moment seek!
L. What is it, Pietro?
W.   Have I leave to speak?
L. Ah no! I see, the string you're always strumming; ⎫
    Don't waste your breath,—there's customers a-coming! ⎬
W. Yet hear me! I'm sincere.—D'ye call this humming? ⎭

Duet

L.   Alas, too well to me is known
      That hopeless song of love and woe.
W.   You cannot hush my anguished moan,
      Till you recall that fatal *"No!"*

L. ⌠ Thy importunings are in vain,
    │ Cease, cease, these sighs, 'tis wasted pain!
W. │ Though thou refuse me yet again,
    │ My love shall wax, but never wane!
L. ⌠ Again I say it cannot be;
    │ This hand, this heart, are not for thee!
W. ⌡ Again I swear, though cold to me,
    │ This hand, this heart, are thine in fee!

                              [*Exit Landlady.*

SCENE VI

In front of the Eating-House. The Stranger *knocks.*

Enter Waiter

W. Stranger of doubtful aspect, what make you at the door?
   Your face with Hunger's I O U's is written o'er and o'er;
   Yet much I do suspect me, you haven't *nary red;*
   Here but our clock hath leave to *tick!* make tracks! vamose! 'nough
       said!
S. O gentlemanly waiter, all day have I pursued
   A fleeting, fond illusion of broiled and roast and stewed;
   I am not Crœsus, 'tis too true, but I my scot can pay!
W. If that's the case, I ask no more; I pray you step this way,—
   Yet first (for I have sorrows, too,) your woeful tale impart!
S. Waiter of generous soul, I will, although it break my heart!

Cavatina

With love and hunger anguishing,
    As I in bed was tossing,
There passed a vision languishing,
    The murky midnight crossing!
"Arise!" it said, "and follow me!
    Follow with dauntless courage!
And find, ere darkness swallow me,
    For heart and stomach forage!"

W. And then?

                S. I followed, then, unterrified,
                    In hope (yet hope half-scorning)
                To see that promise verified,
                    All night and since this morning!

> At last the vision wonderful
> Stopped here before your portal,
> And then, like longings mortal,
> In cloud-wreaths disappeared!

W. O stranger, too, unfortunate, thy story starts a tear,
Step in, I prithee, and forget thy sorrows in some beer!

SCENE VII

The Eating-House. STUDENTS *seated.* WAITING-MAIDS.
To them enter the WAITER *and* STRANGER

CHORUS: *Popular Ballad*

There was a man went round the town
To hunt a supper up and down.

For he had been right far away,
And nothing found to eat that day.

He finds at last a right cheap place,
And stealeth in with modest pace ―――

S. Now, waiter, bring to me the bill of fare.
(aside) Ye pangs within, what will not hunger dare?

Aria

W. Here is the bill of fare, sir,
   Of what there is for supper,
   Long as the Proverbs of Tupper,―
   Command, then, *s'il vous plaît!*

     Soup, with nothing, twenty coppers,
     Roast spring-chicken, three-and-nine,
     Ditto biled, (but then they're whoppers!)
     Fish-balls, luscious, two a dime,
     Two a dime, sir, hot and prime, sir,
     Fried cod-fish balls, two a dime!
     There's the bill, and cash procures ye
     Any viand that allures ye;―
     Cutlet, pigeon, woodcock, widgeon,
     Canvas-backs, if you're a painter,
     Plover, rice-birds, (they're your nice birds!)
     And, to cut it short, there ain't a

Thing but you can play the lord in,
If you've got the brads accordin'.
Wines? We get 'em right from Jersey;—
Coffee? Our own beans we raise, sir;—
Ices? 'Cept we warmed 'em,—mercy,—
Freeze your tongue too stiff to praise, sir!
Best of all, though, 's the fish-ball, though,
We have made 'em all the fashion;
Come to try 'em as we fry 'em,—
Presto! liking turns to passion!
There we carry off the banner,
'Taint so easy, neither, that ain't,—
But, you see, we've got a patent,—
Do 'em in the Cape Cod manner,—
That's the way to make 'em flavorous!
Fried in butter, tongue can't utter
How they're brown, and crisp, and savorous!

S.   Peace, waiter, for I starve meanwhile,—but hold:
Bring me *one* fish-ball, ONE,—*(aside)* curst lack of gold!

SCENE VIII

The Stranger, Chorus

S.   Moment of horror! crisis of my doom!
Led by the dreadful Shape, I sought this room
With half a dime! A slender sum, and yet
'Twill buy one fish-ball! Down, weak pride, forget
Thy happier—but what prate I? Thought of dread,
If, with one fish-ball, they should *not* give bread!

Chorus

Beer here! beer here! hallo! waiter!
   Think ye *we* came here to wait?
Jupiter surnamed the Stator,
   Never had so slow a gait!
Beer here! beer here! brisk and foaming,
   Lager, Burton, Dublin stout!
If you take so long in coming,
   One would rather go without!

SCENE IX

Enter Waiter

W.   Here's your *one* fish-ball, sir—*(sarcastically)* you ordered *one?*
S.   Thanks,—and with bread to match, 'twere not ill done.

Duet and Chorus

W. *(with fury)*. With one single fish-ball, is't bread ye are after?
So wild a presumption provokes me to laughter!
So mad a suggestion proves, out of all question,
Howe'er you the test shun, you're mad as a hornet!
I trample it, scorn it, so mad a suggestion!
It fills me with fury, it dumbs me with rage!

S. With one dainty fish-ball do *you* bread refuse me?
It's *you* are the madman yourself, sir, excuse me!
My wish was immodest? Of men you're the oddest!
In strait-waistcoat bodiced, go hide ye in Bedlam!
Your fish-balls, *there,* peddle 'em! learn to be modest,
And tempt not a stranger half-starving to rage!

Chorus. O'er one paltry fish-ball d'ye make such a rumpus?
For gracious' sake, neighbors, we'd rather you'd thump us!
You make such a flare-up, such riot and rear-up,
Our comfort you tear up to rags and to tatters,
Come, settle your matters without such a flare-up,
Or soon you shall suffer a proof of our rage!

SCENE X

Enter Landlady

W. The Mistress comes, and I will all relate.
S. ⎰Oh, Heaven! my dream! *(aside)*
L. ⎱   Resistless stars! my Fate! *(aside)*
    What means, sirs, tell me, this unseemly riot?
    These twenty years my house has still been quiet.
All. Lady!
L.   Peace! Interesting stranger, tell
    The tumult's cause, and how it all befell.
S. I'll furnish voice, if thou'lt find ears as well!

Cavatina

With love and hunger anguishing,
   As I in bed was tossing,
There came a vision languishing,
   The murky midnight crossing!
"Arise!" it said, "and follow me!
   Press on with dauntless courage!
And find, ere darkness swallow me,
   For heart and stomach forage!"

L. What then!

S. I followed, then, unterrified,
    In hope (yet hope half scorning)
To see the vision verified,
    All night and all this morning.
At last the shape mysterious
    Stopped here before your portal,
    And then, like longings mortal,
    It vanished in a fog!

CHORUS and *Aria*

Chorus. Hurrah for the famous incognito!
    Here's marvels beyond exception!
I'd dance, though I had a mahog'ny toe,
    To give him a rousing reception!
Ah, if with Cupid's arrow
You tingle to the marrow,
    Yield to the sweet distraction
    Of instantaneous flame!

L. Much faith to joy- or sorrow-scopes
    My mind has never tendered,
Yet to a gypsy's horoscopes
    It instantly surrendered;—
"There comes a noble stranger
In mystery and danger,
    At once to seize the sceptre
    That sways thy bosom's throne!"

One of the Chorus. Pardon my rudeness, gentle stranger, do!
All. And ours!
S.   'Tis done!
Chorus.   Your vision, then?
S.   Proves true!

TRIO

W. Oh bah! confound his visions!
    'Twould be a tavern pretty,
    If *gratis* here the city
    Could all come in to dine,
    Consuming our provisions,
    Our fish-balls, and our wine!

L. O, if thou only knewest
To what a deed atrocious
Thou urgest me, ferocious,
My horror would be thine!
Aims such as thou pursuest,
A fiend would sure resign!

S. That she should prove benignant,
My wildest hope surpasses;
They are but dolts and asses
That doubt my dream divine!
Ah, do not be indignant,
If now I call thee mine!

SCENE XI

Enter a MESSENGER

Mess. Friends, was a stranger here of noble mien?
W. A stranger, yes.
Mess.   Half-starved? Of garments mean?
W. Precisely so, and coin of small amount!
Mess. 'Tis he I've sought for years, CARRARA'S COUNT!
L. Art speaking sooth?
Mess.   Of course; why this amaze?
A harsh stepfather turned him out to graze.
An exile long,—mark now the hand of Fate!
The old man's dead, and *his'n* the estate!
     (points to stranger.)
L. O, joy supreme!
Chorus.   I always told you so!
Mess. Are you a Paduan? *(To stranger.)*
S.   No, of Bergamo!
Mess. Then 'tis the Count!—Your memory recalls
Blithe days of childhood passed in marble halls?
S. Hanged if it does!
Mess.   'Tis *Hell*—One further test:
Wear you a locket with the fam'ly crest?
S. Not I!
Mess. 'TIS HE!!!—Yet, might I be so bold,—
Shows your left arm a roseate button-mould?
S. Not in the least!
Mess.   'TIS HE!!!! Conviction strong!
Salute him all!
Chorus.   I thought so all along.

Aria

L.   Yes, divine (ah, who can doubt it?)
      Was thy sweet ecstatic vision!
    Thrice divine, for how, without it,
      Had I known thy heart so true?
         Pietro slight thee? *I* invite thee;
    Order what you like,—I grant it;
    Eat up all, and, if you want it,
      Empty all the cellar too!

S.   Yes, divine (ah, who can doubt it?)
      Was my vision so Elysian!
    Thrice divine,—who dares to flout it,
      Now that I can call thee mine?
         Nought now frights me, *She* invites me,
    All the bill of fare's mine *gratis*,
    And if that should not be *satis*,
      There's the cellar full of wine!

W. No, a humbug (who can doubt it?)
      Was his lying, plund'ring vision!
    Take no pay? Give meals without it?
      Scorn, my soul, the base idear!
         Stuff ye, dead-heads, black-, gray-, red-heads,
    Eat whate'er you lay your eyes on!
    Gratis eat, and find it pison,
      Ending with unlooked-for *bier!*

L.   Sit down together, then, and eat away!
All. 'Tis sweet to eat and drink when others pay!

A WORTHY DITTY

Sung before the President His Excellency at Washington,
to a Barrel-Organ Accompaniment

    As I, one day, went on my way,
      A rowdy ill-conducted
    Growled, "You low whelp, I want your help
      To get me reconstructed;
    A gone-up man, I've (hic) a plan
      Of asking your assistance;

So give 's your cash at once, by dash!
    And keep your (hic) your distance!"

Said I, "You 're not precisely what
    I call a civil person;
You 're one I 'd list to use my fist
    Much sooner than my purse on;
However, come, give up your rum
    And all that 's been your ruin,
Drop your big airs, and your affairs
    I'll see what I can do in."

'T was plain my man from such a plan
    Of doing things relucted;
"I don't," said he, "(hic) want to be
    In your way reconstructed;
Not I, by dash! and you I'll thrash
    For treating me this fashion!"
With that he drew a knife, and flew
    Into a tearing passion.

Said I, "Heydey, why, that 's the way
    They do things in Timbuctoo;
And the police must keep the peace,
    And help you reconstruct, too:
Then (as I called, and wildly bawled
    "Take this man to the lock-up!")
Straight saw I come a giant glum,
    With blue close-buttoned frock, up.

Said he, "I think the man's in drink,
    You 'd better not molest him;
'T would only get him madder yet,
    If I should try arrest him."
"But don't you see," I cried, "that he
    Upon me run a muck did?"
Said he, "Mere play; it 's just his way
    Of getting reconstructed."

I turned to go; my rowdy, though,
    Was burning for the strife yet,
And muttered deep, "My grudge I'll keep,
    And have your dash-dashed life yet!"

"Is it not, then, just such vile men,"
I thought, "we 've bolts and keys for?"
And musing went, with eyebrows bent,
"What *do* we pay police for?"

MR. WORSLEY'S NIGHTMARE

[He having dedicated his translation of the "Iliad" to General R. E. Lee, late of the U. S. A., later of the C. S. A., "as the best living representative of its hero."]

Worsley *(Fallen into an uneasy after-dinner sleep)*

Bless my soul! here's a singular dream!
Can it be I am dead and don't know it?
That has happened ere now to a poet
Who thereafter wrote many a ream;
Is it certain to enter one's head,
When he *is* dead, to think that he's dead?
Here I am, or at any rate seem,
On the edge of a queer-looking stream
That would do very well for the Styx,
Or that one whom a nightmare fear eggeth on
Might imagine Cocytus or Phlegethon—
If it were, well, that would be a fix!
But perhaps an Homeric translator,
When he wakes up and sees that he's dead,
Would not feel any difference greater
Than the no-change that happened with lead
In the humbug they called transmutation:—
Is it death I've gone through or translation?
Or might all not result from the immersion
Of my wits for so long in my version?
If I'm dreaming, I'm mixing my classic-
al attainments in maddest confusion;
'T is like pouring in Chian with Massic:
Aristophanes jumbles with Lucian,
I can scarce tell my Greek from my Latin;
Only nonsense of all sorts comes pat in,
And the whole makes a mess of my own ideas
Worse than I did of poor old Maionides.

(He hears himself snore, and forthwith there enters his conception a)
Chorus of Frogs
Brekekex! Brekekex!

Worsley
Heavens! what's that?
Perhaps I had best be conning a prayer
To the maker's name inside my hat,
As we Britons are wont in despair
At services long and parsons flat.

Frogs
Brekekex! Brekekex! who goes there?

Worsley
Please your Frogships, Homer's last translator:
I've done it in metre that's called Spenserian.

Frogs
Which, used by a bore's a precious dreary one.
Onk! Onk! we wish you *might* be the last!
He's as like himself, when so recast,
As one of us to Jupiter Stator:
Why, because one can croak, d'ye think it follows
That one should set himself up to practise
A cavatina of Phœbus Apollo's,
With voice as rough as a nutmeg-grater?

Worsley
Ahem! well, my friends, you see the fact is,
We English are always taught to seek
For that inspiration in the Greek,
Which, when your literature was great, your
Authors could somehow find in nature:
Our whole scheme of training takes such pains
To make merest Attics of our brains,
That after all of our plague and fuss
Pure nature's all heathen Greek to us.

Frogs
Brekekex! Attic, eh? say Bœotian:
Scarce a grain of *that* salt in your ocean!
Some Greeks, friend, believed in transmigrations,
And get 'em, by Jove, in your translations!

Worsley

A theory downright Jacobinical!
Can it be that my brain, as it often is,
Is but brimful of old Aristophanes,
And, infect with his humor so cynical,
Is colored by what it doth brood on?
Why, I'm thinking as wildly as Proudhon!

Frogs

Brekekex! Coäx! don't fear a bit!
'T isn't infectious; *he* was a wit.
Brekekex! Coäx! This world is a hoäx,
Version poor of an excellent hit!

Worsley

Nay, this is profane: I'll hear no more on 't;
If a trick of my brain, I'll shut the door on 't.
  (Enter Bacchus, pretending tipsiness, in Charon's boat)

Bacchus

If I were to meet with old Silenus
We could n' tell which was which between us;
Cocktails and juleps! smashes and slings!
I've got so somehow with those Yankees
(They've such a talent at mixing things),
I can't make out where the gangway plank is;
It wavers and rises and falls and swings
Like one of my choruses dithyrambic,
Where you can't tell trochaic from iambic. *(He lands.)*
Well, the confounded rope-dance is past,
And here I am on the shore at last,
Safe escaped out of Erebus's low air,
With a kind of peristaltic motion,
A devious looseness in my knees,
A general tendency to nowhere,
That gives to firm earth the flux of ocean:
In such a case a gargle of—Bourbon,
I think they call it—will help to curb one: *(Drinking.)*
Good ferrers to le' me have a bottle,
For I am as dry as Aristotle!
Hallo! what's *your* name?

Worsley

My name is Worsley; *(Solemnly.)*
Translator, sir, of the last new Homer.

Bacchus

And, by this bottle, 't is no misnomer!
You could n' ha' made the statemen' terselier,
For nobody 'll ever translate him worselier;
He 's one o' those skinkers, as I divine, *(Aside.)*
That mixes water with rare old wine;
And, thus baptizing it by immersion,
Christens the puling result a version.
I say, my friend, do you chance to know
What *we* tempered our wine with, ages ago?
Put some *salt* in the water, and that
Saved the new product from tasting flat:
You 're surprised? Well, sure as my name's Lyæus,
You 'll find it so stated in Athenæus.

Worsley *(Aside)*

Ah, this comes of taking too much claret;
If 't was n't a dream I could n't bear it.

Bacchus

Well, Misser Worsley,
I warn you firs'ly
(Solemnly, too; you think I am merry),
As you seem meaning to cross the ferry,
Where Charon does *his* job of translation
In the true, legitimate, stolid way,
So many verses (or trips) every day,
Without depression, without elation,
And no more change in his rhythm of oars
Than in that contractor's measure of yours,
That metes its phrase like a soldier's ration,—
I say, Misser Worsley,
I warn you firs'ly,
That Hector is waiting you, mad as thunder,
As those Yankees say, at your dedication;
On the other side he 's taken station,
Vowing he 'll tear your ghost's limbs asunder,
Full of black bile as a theologian,

Cursing and swearing,
Ripping and tearing,
In the strongest phrase of ancient Trojan,
And I guess you 'd berrer stan' from under! *(Exit Bacchus)*

Frogs

Brekekex! Brekekex! look out, Worsley;
Heroes are apt to behave perversely;
If you meet Homer, we warn you, too,
Keep clear of *him*, whatever you do!

Worsley

I'm in for 't now, and have got to go,
Though the outlook's rather squally or so:
Here you, honest fellow, what's your fee? *(Hailing Charon)*

Charon

An obolus, mostly; but then, you see,
Sometimes there's special deductions made;
For when a man's been nothing on earth,
Nothing's as much as the job is worth;
It's *gratis* always for those in the trade,
And I understand, from Bacchus there,
Your business has been in the upper air
What my own down here is, more or less,—
Piloting folks to forgetfulness.
But what's that bundle under your arm?

Worsley

Why, nothing that *could* do any harm;
A few poor ghosts of my new translation;
I did up some half a dozen copies,
To have a few just for presentation.

Charon

Lethe once tasted, ghosts need no poppies:
Leave 'em behind you there on the levee,
And nobody 'll touch 'em, I 'll be bound:
What good in dying, if all the bevy
Of life's poor failures, and duns, and bores,
Could follow, to haunt us underground?
For a boat like mine, such verse as yours,
Though disembodied, were quite too heavy.

Come! in with you! I 've no time to wait;
I 've three more trips yet, and it 's getting late.
You 're English, eh? *(Talking as he rows)*

Worsley

Yes.

Charon

So I could swear!
You 've most of you such a stuck-up air,
And somehow look down on all creation
As if you were each the British nation;
Doer of everything under the sun,
From taking Troy to the last bad pun.
Once get your white chokers under your chins,
What conscience you *do* have for other folks' sins!

Worsley *(Aside)*

A most uncommonly vulgar hind!
We *have* done everything, time out of mind,
And so little boastful, modest elves,
That nobody knows it but ourselves.
If we should brag like the Yankees and French—

Charon

Come, be packing! Art grown to the bench?
Why, John Bull thinks e'en the lower regions
Must pay his comfort proper allegiance!

(Enter Hector and to him a crowd of American ghosts just landed)

Spirit of Smith *(Spits and speaks)*

General Hector, 't would make us proud,
If my friends and I might be allowed
To take so great a man by the hand,
And we 'd be grateful, if you 'n' your staff,
Would favor us each with an autograph:
My name is Smith, sir. I'll take my stand
And introduce 'em all as they land.
Gentlemen sperrits, you 'll step this way
And shake the general's hand, I say.

Hector *(After the presentation of three thousand)*

By Jove! I feel like an old town-pump;
I never was in such a scrape as this! *(Aside)*

Allow me, good sirs, to have the bliss
Of greeting the others in a lump;
And as for autographs, to my shame,
I never e'en learned to write my name;
I lived in the ages, you know, called dark,
When men had a way of making their mark.

Spirit of Smith *(Spits and speaks)*

Well, I hope you won't decide adversely
On one request I shall put to your vote—
That's to present my friend, Mister Worsley,
I made his acquaintance on the boat:
I rather guess it's likely you know him—
Author of "Homer," a first-class poem.

Worsley *(Aside)*

Confound his impudence! But for him,
I might have slipt by: my chance is slim.
Acquaintance, indeed! I'd like to know
If he makes 'em by treading on one's toe?
For no more, no less, that I could see,
Was all of his introduction to me!

Hector

Ah, here, then, I have you; come at last!
My staff has been longing, these three months' past,
To measure the back of that dedicator
Who likened me to the double traitor,
False to his country, false to his oath,
Me, who'd have given my life for both!
Me, who no omens could understand
But those that said, Fight for Fatherland!
Achilles dragged but my dust in dust;
You insult my soul without reason,
Coupling my name with a broken trust,
Dabbling my fame in the lees of treason.

Worsley *(Aside)*

That swelling nostril I hardly like,
Nor the look that makes me too mean to strike:
I never felt worselier since I was born,
Between my fears of his staff and scorn.

Hector

Did he war bravely? The more his shame;
And, once men take their side with wrong,
Their guilt stalks behind them, stern and strong,
And despair may win fair valor's name.
Courage is mostly a thing in the veins;
'Tis Valor that lives in the poet's strains,
Valor that stands for the right and true,
A thing unconceived by such as you!
Was *his*, then, your notion of the bravery
That swells in deathless echoes of song?
Forth from my presence, poor snob of slavery,
Herd with the dull souls where you belong!
Study that bible you call the Peerage,
Get what salvation therefrom you can,
Nor come near me, lest I pay the arrearage
Due to your ribs from an honest man.

(Mr. Worsley awakes in terror, but gradually composes himself by reading a few pages of his translation of Homer)

HOB GOBBLING'S SONG

Not from Titania's Court do I
Hither upon a night-moth fly;
I am not of those Fairies seen
Tripping[1] by moonlight on the green,
Whose dewdrop bumpers, nightly poured,
Befleck the mushroom's virgin[2] board,
And whose faint symbols[3] tinkling clear
Sometimes on[4] frosty nights[5] you hear.

No, I was born of lustier stock,
And all their puling night-sports mock:
My father was the Good Old Time,
Famous in many a noble rhyme,
Who reigned with such a royal cheer

[1] MS I: "Dancing."
[2] MS I: "silver."
[3] MS II: "cymbals."
[4] MS II: "in."
[5] MS II: "night."

He made one Christmas of the year,
And but a single edict passed,
Dooming it[6] instant death to fast.

I am that earthlier, fatter elf
That haunts the wood of pantry[7] shelf,
When minced-pies, ranged from end to end,
Up to the gladdened roof ascend;[8]
On a fat goose I hither rode,[9]
Using a skewer for a[10] goad,
From the rich region[11] of Cockayne,
And must ere morn be back again.

I am the plump sprite that[12] presides
O'er Thanksgiving and Christmas tides;[13]
I jig[14] it not in woods profound;
The barn-yard is my dancing-ground,[15]
Making me music as I can
By drumming on a pattypan;
Or if with songs your sleep I mar,
A gridiron serves me for guitar.[16]

When without touch the glasses clink,[17]
And dishes on the dresser wink
Back at the fire, whose jovial glance
Sets the grave pot-lids all adance;[18]
When tails of little pigs hang straight,

[6] MS II: "That made it."
[7] MS I rejects "closet."
[8] MS I: "From floor to roof in ranks ascend," and continues the stanza with the following lines:
> "And Charlie, as a glimpse he steals,
> Sees turkeys hanging by their heels,
> Portending vainly, as it seems,
> The next night's stomach-laden dreams."
[9] MS II: "On a fat goose's back I rode."
[10] MS II: "my."
[11] MS II: "far Country."
[12] MS I: "elf who."
[13] MS I: "O'er Xmas and Thanksgiving tides."
[14] MS I: "trip."
[15] MS I continues with the following lines:
> "When turkeys gobble in the night
> And geese reply with all their might."
[16] This line and the preceding are not found in either MS.
[17] MS II rejects "ring."
[18] MS II: "Makes all the merry potlids dance."

Unnerved by dreams of coming fate;
When from the poultry-house you hear
Midnight alarums,—I am near.[19]

While the pleased[20] housewife shuts her eyes,
I lift the crust of temperance pies,
And slip in slyly two or three
Spoonfuls of saving *eau de vie;*
And, while the cookmaid rests her thumbs,
I stone a score of choicer plums,
And hide[21] them in the pudding's corner,
In memory of the brave Jack Horner.[22]

I put the currants in the buns,
A task the frugal[23] baker shuns;
I for the youthful miner make
Nuggets of citron in the cake;
'T is I that down the chimney whip,
And presents in the stockings[24] slip,
Which Superstition's mumbling jaws[25]
Ascribe[26] to loutish Santa Claus.

'T is I that hang, as you may see,
With presents gay the Christmas-tree;[27]
But,[28] if some foolish girl or boy
Should chance to mar the common[29] joy
With[30] any sulky look or word,

[19] MS I: "Alarums shrill—then I am near."
[20] MS I: "good."
[21] MS I: "stuff."
[22] MS I: "That Willie may surpass Jack Horner. MS II reads "In memory of the brave." Following this line MS I begins a new stanza with these lines:
"Beside all this, I have prepared
Some gifts to be this evening shared,
Which grandpapa will please to see
Divided as decreed by me,
Who here inscribe the names of those
To whom each prize in order goes."
[23] MS I gives first reading "prudent"; then as an alternate gives the present reading.
[24] MS II: "stocking."
[25] MS II: "Which superstition without cause."
[26] MS II: "Ascribes."
[27] This line and the preceding are not found in either MS.
[28] MS I: "And."
[29] MS I: "general."
[30] MS I: "By."

By them[31] my anger is incurred,
And to[32] all such I give fair warning[33]
Of nightmares[34] ere to-morrow morning.

"POSEIDON FIELDS, WHO DOST THE ATLANTIC SWAY"

Poseidon[1] Fields, who dost the[2] Atlantic[3] sway,
Making it swell or flattening at thy will!
O, glaucous[4] one, be thou propitious still
To me, a minnum[5] dandled[*] on thy spray![6]
Eftsoons[7] a milkwhite porkerlet[8] we slay,
No sweeter e'er repaid Eumæus'[9] skill;
A blameless Lamb[10] thereon might feed his fill,
Deeming he cropped the new-sprung herb[11] of May:
Our board do thou and Amphitrite[12] grace;
Archbishop[13] of our literary sea,

[31] MS I: "Be sure."
[32] MS I rejects "that."
[33] MS I: "I now give warning."
[34] MS I: "cholics."

---

[1] [All numbered notes to this poem are Lowell's notes.] *Poseidon*, a fabulous deity, called by the Latins *Neptunus;* here applied to Fields as presiding over the issues of the Atlantic.

[2] "the Atlantic," to be read "th' Atlantic" in order to avoid the *hiatus* or gap where two vowels come together. Authority for this will be found in Milton and other poets.

[3] "Atlantic"—a well known literary magazine.

[4] "Glaucous"—between blue and green, an epithet of Poseidon, and an editor who shows greenness is sure to look blue in consequence.

[5] "Minnum"—vulgo pro *minnow*, utpote species *minima* piscium.

[6] "Dandled on thy spray." A striking figure. Horace has piscium genus summa hæsit ulmo, but the poverty of the Latin did not allow this sport of fancy with the double meaning of the word *spray*.

[7] "Eftsoons." This word (I *think*) may be found in Spenser. It means soon after i.e. before long.

[8] "Porkerlet." A pretty French diminutive, as in *roitelet*.

[9] "Eumæus." The swineherd of Ulysses, a character in Homer.

[10] "Lamb"—a well known literary character of the 17th century, chiefly remembered for having burnt his house to roast a favorite pig. He invented mint-sauce.

[11] "Herb"—grass. Borrow a bible, and you will find the word thus used in that once popular work.

[12] "Amphitrite." The beautiful spouse of Poseidon.

[13] "Archbishop." This is in the Elizabethan style. (N. B. the play is upon *sea* and *see*.) This term is beautifully, may I not say piously, appropriate, since the Grecian gods have all been replaced by Xtian saints and St. Anthony of Padua converted the finny nomads of the deep. He found a ready *herring*, I suppose.

[*] MS rejects "rocking."

Lay by thy trident-crozier for a space,
And try our forks: or, earless[14] to our plea,
Let this appease thee and the frown displace,—
The Gurneys come and John,[15]—then answer, *Oui!*[16]

CHARLES DICKENS[1]

A man of genius, simple, warm, sincere,
He left a world grown kindlier than he came;
His hand the needy[2] knew, but not his name;
Dumb creatures snuffed a friend when he drew near,
And the strange dog pricked one suspicious ear,
Then couched his head secure. Safe be this fame
From critics' measured praise or close-picked blame—
He loved God's gentler face, and made it dear.
Was then Stylites' post the better way,
Or mingling with his kind, a man with men,
Like Him that was and was not such as they?
I judge ye not, but to my simple ken,[3]
If on your guideboards the right name[4] be kept,
Some foe hath changed their places while ye slept.

TO MADAME DU CHATELET

If you would have me still a lover,
To me the age of love restore,
And let these twilight shades once more
The sunrise, if they can, recover.

---

[14] "Earless." This is not to be taken literally as in the case of Defoe, or as Hotspur misinterprets Glendower's bootless. It simply means *deaf.*
[15] "John." It is hardly necessary to say that there is but one John—to wit, J. Holmes Esq. of Holmes Place.
[16] "Oui." A neat transition to the French tongue, conveying at once a compliment to the learning of the person addressed and an allusion to his editorial position. Editors and Kings always say *We.*

---

[1] In MS the title reads "On some recent sermons," and is followed by the quotation: "His death eclipsed the gaiety of nations, and impoverished the public stock of harmless pleasure." Johnson on Garrick.
[2] MS: "hungry."
[3] In MS the first 12 lines were enclosed in a bracket beside which appeared the word "Bulldog" in the left margin. Similarly, the concluding couplet, lines 13 and 14, were bracketed with the word "Terrier."
[4] MS: "name" but bears a note: "I think *name* will do instead of *names,* which befogged the *their* in the next verse."

From spots[1] where shares the God of wine
With Love the sceptre of unreason,
Time, laying his chill hand on mine,
Warns me to steal away in season.

'Gainst his inflexible decree
Let us, at least, seek some assuaging;
He who hath not the wit[2] of aging
The victim of his years must be.

Leave to fair Youth the hours unreckoned
Of rapture wild, of dance and song;[3]
Since life is but two minutes long,
Let us on wisdom spend the second.

What, then, forever do ye leave me,
Illusion, folly, heedless waste,
Gifts of the gods, that could deceive me
To think life left no bitter taste!

Yes, one dies twice, I see it plain;
Ceasing to love or love to kindle
Is the worst death on Clotho's spindle;
Ceasing to live is little pain.

Thus with wet eyes did I require
The follies of my earlier days;
My soul bewailed the dancing fire
That led astray from beaten ways.

Then gentle Friendship deigned to bend her
Steps to my succor from above;
She was, it may be, quite as tender,
But not so full of life as Love.

Her beauty set my heart astir,
And, guided by her milder lustre,
I followed: but the tears would muster
That I must follow only her.

[1] MS: "haunts."
[2] MS: "art."
[3] MS: "Of rapture, wit, of dance and song."

AN EPITAPH

World, Flesh, and Devil gave him all they could,
Wealth, harlots, wine and disbelief in good;
Fame, too, he bought, our modern kind of fame,
The morning-column reeking with his name;
Lifelong he never did his lusts deny
One pleasure sin could give, or money buy.
The halter bilked, a pandar's coward shot
Sent him to where he—nay, I had forgot;
That's *passé*, so they tell us who should know,
Put out with milk and water years ago:
No retribution, then? Yes, something worse
Than angry justice e'er distilled in verse;
He had (could shame or vengeance this exceed?)
Living, Gould's friendship, dead, the tears of Tweed!

THE WORLD'S FAIR, 1876

Columbia, puzzled what she should display
Of true home-make on her Centennial Day,
Asked Brother Jonathan: he scratched his head,
Whittled a while reflectively, and said,
"You're own invention and own making, too?
Why, any child could tell ye what to do:
Show 'em your Civil Service, and explain
How all men's loss is everybody's gain;
Show your new patent to increase your rents
By paying quarters for collecting cents;
Show your short cut to cure financial ills
By making paper-collars current bills;
Show your new bleaching-process, cheap and brief,
To wit: a jury chosen by the thief;
Show your State Legislatures; show your Rings;
And challenge Europe to produce such things
As high officials sitting half in sight
To share the plunder and to fix things right;
If that don't fetch her, why, you only need
To show your latest style in martyrs—Tweed:
She'll find it hard to hide her spiteful tears
At such advance in one poor hundred years."

CAMPAIGN EPIGRAMS

A Coincidence

Banks made a speech and sate; the band full soon,
As if by instinct, struck up Bonnie Doon;
O strong enchantment of those Scottish lays!
That make us still associate Banks and brays.

The Widow's Mite

When currency's debased, all coins will pass.
Ask[1] you for proof? The Widow's might is brass.

Moieties

A Widow? Yes, and not of one but twain,
The worser half of Sanborn and of Jayne;
She helped their dubious profits, and, they gone,
At the old stand the business carries on.

The Astronomer Misplaced

Boutwell could find a big hole in the sky,
Blind to the small ones in the Treasury.
Tell him of leaks, he doesn't care a pin;
Can't they be stopped by sticking sponges in?

[1] MS rejects false start "What."

THREE SCENES IN THE LIFE OF A PORTRAIT

Scene I: 1879

I

Your portrait? Charming! And for me!
    And such a capital resemblance!
'T will serve when you 're beyond the sea—
Crayon? Ah, no; lithography—
    To keep you freshly in remembrance.

II

Where shall we hang it? Juan,[1] my dear,
  Make yourself useful this *once*, pray do!
Yes, there 's some empty wall-space here;
But, then, 't would hardly do so near
  That dark oil-picture of Quevedo.

III

No hurry, say you? We can wait?
  We 've got the rest of life before us?
Poor women! It is still our fate
To hear such wisdom. How I hate
  That universal husband's chorus!

IV

Myself I 'll hang it where I reign
  Like our old kings sans Constitution:
In my boudoir. Since here in Spain
Men talked of rights, the only gain
  Has been high taxes and confusion.

Scene II: 1889

I

Juan, I must need contrive some space
  To hang this bit of old *repoussé*;
One's gatherings grow at such a pace!
Ah, to be sure, there 's just the place—
  Why not have said so sooner, goosie?

II

That portrait of poor What'shisname—
  What *was* his name? Well, I can spare it;
It really has no sense of shame,
To stare so! It can do the same,
  Without offending, in the garret.

III

One's memory plays such tricks perverse!
  But I recall his story now well;
He used to bore me with his verse

---

[1] Mr. Riaño. (See Notes p. 273)

And prose—I don't know which was worse.
A Yankee, and his name was Powell.

IV

What tiresome notes he used to write
    To his *Querida Doña Emilia!*
Some in *such* Spanish! My delight
Was in the blunders. Well, good night;
    A bore should like the *Boardilla.*[2]

SCENE III: 1899

I

Ten years; and I, an aimless ghost,
    Dim as Assisi's vanished frescos,
Glide where shrill minstrels deafen most
And blessed *prenderos*[3] keep their post,
    Along the Calle de Tudescos.

II

The same old reckless odds and ends,
    Pistols, coins, lace, unholy clutter!
Life's castaways that have no friends,
Dead lovers' gifts—who knows? So ends
    A poet sometimes in the gutter!

III

And there, beside the selfsame door
    (How many years they must have kept him, oh!),
With the same seasick look he wore,
But faded out a trifle more,
    Hangs my old friend Fernando Septimo.[4]

IV

I—but what portrait 's that below?
    Oh, Doña Emil—wast thou, too, shoddy?
Yes, 't is the face I used to know
Seen in a mirror long ago,
    When this poor shadow had a body.

[2] The garret.
[3] Dealers in bric-à-brac.
[4] The king.

CUIVISCUNQUE

On earth Columbus wrote his name,
Montgolfier on its circling air;
Lesseps in water did the same;
Franklin traced his in living flame,
Newton on space's desert bare.

Safe with the primal elements
Their signatures august remain;
While the fierce hurtle of events
Whirls us and our ephemeral tents
Beyond oblivion's mere distain.

Our names, as what we write on, frail,
Time spunges out like hopeless scores,
Unless for mine it should prevail
To turn awhile the faltering scale
Of memory, thus to make it yours.

VERSES

(Written in a Copy of "Fireside Travels" for P. G. S.)

If to my fireside I return,
And, as Life's embers fainter burn,
No travels plan save that last post
To the low inn where Death is host,
Yet when my thoughts an outing seek,
Bowed pilgrims and with footing weak,
No spots to all men's memories known
Shall lure them forth; one path alone
Will they with constant faith retread,
Brightening 'neath Memory's sunset red.
Across the muffled course of steeds
Through the sheep-dotted park it leads
By water silvered in the breeze
With the swan's shattered images,
By sun-steeped elms where not the rush
And rapture of the embowered thrush
Detain them—that could once detain

Those feet more light than summer rain
That sang beside me:—Sure 'tis I,
And not my lumpish thoughts, that fly
To lay my tribute at those feet
Of gratitude forever sweet
For comfort given when great the lack,
For sunshine, when my heaven was black,
Poured through my dull and sullen mood
From skies of purest womanhood.

This path lifelong my feet shall bless
With sense of dear indebtedness;—
Yet what avails it her or me,
Myself a dream, a vision she?

VERSES WRITTEN IN A COPY OF SHAKSPEARE

Here Music fledges thought as leaves the pine
Whose strong stem lightward lifts those minstrels fine,
And in this symphony no voice is mute
Of kindling trump or meditative flute,
For 't is the high prerogative of song
To nerve the weak and mitigate the strong:
Here passion is sublimed until its throes,
Seen in reflection, feed the mind's repose;
Here life is shown as only he could see
Who found in Man the World's epitome
And knew the pygmy-giant, idiot-sage,
The same in every clime and every age,
While, as the motley throng goes by, we scan
Mask after mask to find beneath the man,
Matchless in all, the circuit of whose soul
Girt human nature round from pole to pole.
Here is Truth's well, and this its constant law,
That still and still it deepens as we draw;
Bring larger vessels, larger yet, and more;
Fill them to running-over; still there's store;
Get all experience, and at last it is
But as a key to part decypher his;
Observe, think, morals draw, part false from true,
He did all long ago, and better too;

Go, seek of Thought some yet unsullied strand,
His footprint there confronts you as you land;
What need for help on many words to call?
When I say Shakspeare, I have said it all.

"My Shakspeare" Milton called him, echoing Ben;
"My Shakspeare" he to all the sons of men;
'T is the world's common field and each man's share
To just what treasure he first buried there,
And he shall bring mere fairy-gold away
Who finds here but the matter of a play.
Those inbred fates that shadow, under wings
With lightnings seamed, the stormy fates of kings,
Measure to *us* as to ourselves we mete,
Drag *us* before the unerring judgment-seat,
Sow in our passions the same seeds of death
As in Othello, Hamlet, Lear, Macbeth,
And fairy vanities our fortunes mix,
Play with our baffled sense the selfsame tricks
As Ariel did, or, like sly Puck deride,
With ears all see but us, the brains inside.

STREET DOORS

I have no doubt that Bluebeard's chamber door
The features of a guiltless portal wore;
Its keyhole whispered not; its handle made
No sign that all the crime within betrayed;
And the smooth panels could their secret keep
As calm pools do that o'er drowned wretches sleep.

So smooth, so calm, the city's front doors close
On lives laid waste and more than Theban woes;
The indifferent wood without grimace shuts in
The mother's anguish or the husband's sin;
Perhaps the hand, from whose familiar thrill
The latch just fallen scarcely yet is still,
[I]n vain appeases, with beseeching sign,
The lawful tyrant crimson—hot with wine,
Or idly strives, beside the fluttering breath,
To push away immitigable Death.

Who knows or dreams? Men so demurely can
Confront their God, much more their fellow man.

[B]ut now and then some portal left ajar
Gives glimpses swift of what our neighbors are;
Or, flung back suddenly, lets forth the shriek
Of some lone anguish, pent for many a week,
Tow'rd which the passers eddy, and incline
A moment's ear, then hurry on to dine.
And it so oft hath happened that, whene'er
A chink has gaped through which my eye could peer
Into one cell of those still murmuring hives
Where we gregarious men lead lonely lives,
So much of sin and sorrow have I seen,
So many scars yet raw where both have been,
So little happiness, but in its stead,
A base content, unhopeful, callous, dead,
That I have cried, "Fate, show me, then, the home
Where Death or worse hath not this morning come,
The one safe sanctuary, whither Sorrow
Came not to-day or will not come tomorrow!"

And so a line of street doors standing white,
Stiff and respectable from morn till night,
Oft as strong to fill my mind with glooms
As a dumb city of unwindowed tombs,
Where my roused fancy, deft in such grim tricks,
Strives with a shuddering eagerness to fix
In which uncertain one of them may strive
Some coffined horror dungeoned there alive:
Nay, worse than doors of sepulchers are these
That close o'er all of Death except his peace!

HIS SHIP

"O watcher on the Minster[1] Hill,
    Look out o'er the sloping sea;
Of the tall ships coming, coming still,
    Is never one for me?[2]

[1] MS: "Beacon."
[2] MS: "Is there never a one for me?"

"I have waited and watched (the weary years!)
　When I to the shore could win,
Till now I cannot see for tears
　If my ship be coming in.

"Eyes shut, I see her night and day,
　No inch of canvas furled,[3]
As a swan full-breasted push her way
　Up out of the underworld.[4]

" 'Tis but her wraith![5] And all the time
　These cheated eyes grow dim.
Will her tardy topmasts never climb
　Above the ocean's rim?[6]

"The minster tower is goldener grown[7]
　With lichens the sea winds feed,
Since first I came; each bleak head-stone[8]
　Grows hard and harder to read.[9]

"Think![10] There's a dearer[11] heart that waits,
　And eyes[12] that suffer wrong,
As the fruitless seasons join[13] their mates
　While[14] my ship delays so long!"

"From among so many pennons bright
　On which the sunshine pours,
From among so many wings of white,
　Say, how shall I single yours?"

"By her mast that's all of the beaten[15] gold,
　By her gear of the silk so fine,

[3] MS read "With no inch of canvas"; then rejects "With."
[4] MS rejects "To light from the underworld."
[5] MS rejects "Still fades the vision."
[6] MS: "From under the ocean's rim?"
[7] MS: "The tower you watch from is yellower grown."
[8] MS: "grave-stone."
[9] MS: "The names grow harder to read." This whole stanza is an interpolation probably written at a later time, on the margin of the MS.
[10] MS read "Think"; then substituted "And think."
[11] MS: "softer."
[12] MS: "Dearer eyes."
[13] MS: "follow."
[14] MS: "And my ship."
[15] MS: "yellow."

By the smell of spices in her hold,
  Full well may you know mine."[16]

"O some go west and some go east;
  Their shadows lighten all the sea;[17]
'Tis a blessing of God to see the least,
  So stately as they be.

"Their high-heaped sails with the wind are round;
  The sleek waves past[18] them swirl;
As they stoop and straighten without a sound,
  They crush the sea to pearl.

"Wind-curved[19] the rainbow signals stream,[20]
  Green, yellow, blue, and red,
But never a ship with the glory and gleam
  Of the tokens you have said."[21]

"My ship of dreams I may never see
  Slide swan-like to her berth,
With her lading of sandal and spicery
  Such as never grew on earth.

"But from peril of storm and reef and shoal,
  From ocean's[22] tumult and din,
My ship, her freight a living soul,[23]
  Shall surely erelong come in[24]

"With toll of bells to a storm-proof shore,[25]
  To a haven landlocked and still,
Where she[26] shall lie with so many more
  In the lee of the Minster[27] Hill.

[16] MS: "You well may single mine."
[17] MS: "Their shadows light the sea."
[18] MS: "round."
[19] MS: "Aloft."
[20] MS rejects "gleam."
[21] MS: "Of the tokens that you have said."
[22] MS: "From the ocean's."
[23] MS read "My ship, with her freight of a living soul"; then the words "with" and "of" were deleted.
[24] MS: "In God's good time shall come in."
[25] MS read "Come in where there's never change of sky"; then substituted "Come in to a halcyon-hearted shore"; and finally substituted "With sound of bells to a stormproof shore."
[26] MS: "we."
[27] MS: "Beacon."

"In God's good time she shall 'scape at last
From the waves' and the[28] weather's wrong,
And the rattle of her anchor cast[29]
There's a heart shall hear life-long."[30]

THE INFANT PRODIGY

A veteran entered at my gate
    With locks as cherry-blossoms white;
His clothes proclaimed a prosperous fate,
    His boots were arrogantly bright.

The hat was glossy on his head,
    Gold-rimmed his eye-glass, gold his chain,
In genial curves his waistcoat spread,
    And golden-headed was his cane.

Without a preface thus he spoke,
    "I've called to get my annual due";
Whereat I too the silence broke
    With, "Who, respected sir, are you?

"What is your claim against me, pray?
    A many-childed man am I,
Hard-pinched my monthly bills to pay,
    And prices rule perversely high."

"Not know me? Everybody knows
    And gladly gives his mite," quoth he,
"Why, I'm a babe in swaddling clo'es,
    I am an Infant Industry."

"Forgive me, Reverend Shape," I cried,
    "You set my faith a heavy task;
This infancy which seems your pride,
    Is it your *second*, may I ask?

[28] MS omits "the."
[29] MS: "And the sudden crash of her anchor-cast."
[30] It is only in this last line that MS II differs from the final reading of MS I, to which all the variants in former notes refer. In MS II the line was at first written as in the present text, then altered to read "Shall din in one heart life long."

"Or have you, where so many failed,
   The key to life's Elixir found?
You look like one who never ailed,
   In wind and limb sedately sound."

"You doubt my word? (Excuse these tears,
   They flow for you and not for me;)
Young man, for more than seventy years
   I've been an Infant Industry.

"Your father rued my helpless lot,
   Lifelong he handed me his fee
Nor ever asked himself for what;
   He *loved* an Infant Industry."

Quoth I, "He paid my ransom then
   From further tribute, small or great;
Besides, if I can judge of men,
   Since that, you've grown to man's estate."

He murmured, as I bowed him out,
   "The world is getting worse and worse;
This fellow almost makes me doubt
   Whether I've not been changed at nurse.

"But no, this hat, this cane, these boots,
   This suit in London made by P.,
Convince me to the very roots
   I am an Infant Industry."

Until he vanished from my sight
   These words came floating back to me:
"Yes, 'spite of Time, in Reason's spite,
   I *am* an Infant Industry!"

MY BROOK

It was far up the valley[1] we first plighted troth,
   When the hours[2] were so many, the duties so few;

[1] MS I read "Far in the forest"; then added "It was far . . ."
   MS II: " 'Twas deep in the woodland."
[2] MS I rejects "days."

Earth's burthen weighs wearily now on us both—[3]
But I've not forgotten those dear days; have you?[4]

Each was first-born of Eden, a morn without mate,
    And the bees and the birds and the butterflies thought
'Twas the one perfect day ever fashioned by fate,
    Nor dreamed the sweet wonder for us two was wrought.[5]

I loitered beside you the whole summer long,[6]
    I gave you a life from the waste-flow of mine;
And whether you babbled or crooned me a song,
    I listened and looked till my pulses ran wine.[7]

'Twas but shutting my eyes; I could see, I could hear,
    How you danced there, my nautch-girl, 'mid flag-root and fern,
While[8] the flashing tomauns tinkled joyous and clear
    On the slim wrists and ankles that flashed in their turn.

Ah, that was so long ago! Ages it seems,
    And, now I return[9] sad with life and its lore,
Will they flee my gray presence,[10] the light-footed dreams,
    And Will-o'-wisp light me his lantern[11] no more?

Where the bee's hum seemed noisy once, all was so still,
    And the hermit-thrush nested secure of her lease,
Now whirr the world's millstones and clacks the world's mill—
    No fairy-gold passes, the oracles cease![12]

The life that I dreamed of[13] was never to be,
    For I with my tribe into bondage was sold,[14]

[3] MS I read "Life's burthen is heavy today on us both"; then substituted "lies" for "is." MS II: "Life's burthen lies wearily now on us both."
[4] MS I rejects "those days, dear, have you?" MS II: "But I've never forgotten . . ."
[5] MS I omits this stanza.
[6] MSS I and II: "the summer day long."
[7] MS I: "till methought you ran wine."
[8] MS I: "And."
[9] MS I: "And now I come back."
[10] MS I: "Will they flee from my presence."
[11] MS I: "And good Will o' wisp offers his lantern." MS II: "And Will o' Wisps offer their lanterns."
[12] MS I omits this stanza.
[13] MS II: "The life I then dreamed of."
[14] MS I read "For I like the rest the world's livery donned"; then substituted "For I like the rest into bondage was sold."

And the sungleams and moongleams,[15] your[16] elf-gifts to me,
    The miller transmutes into work-a-day[17] gold.

What you mint for the miller will soon melt away;
    It is earthy, and earthy good only it buys,[18]
But the shekels you tost me are safe from decay;
    They were coined of the sun and the moment that flies.

Break loose from your thralldom! 'Tis only a leap;
    Your eyes 'tis but shutting, just[19] holding your breath;
Escape[20] to the old days, the days that will keep.
    If there's peace in the mill-pond, so is there in death.[21]

Leap down to me, down to me! Be, as you were,
    My nautch-girl, my singer; again let them glance,[22]
Your tomauns, the sun's largess, that wink and are there,[23]
    And gone again, still keeping time as you dance.

Make haste, or it may be I wander again;[24]
    It is[25] I, dear, that call you; Youth beckons with me;
Come back[26] to us both, for,[27] in breaking your chain,
    You set the old summers and fantasies free.

You are mine and no other's;[28] with life of my life
    I made you a Naiad, that were but a stream;
In the moon are brave dreams yet, and chances are rife
    For the passion that ventures its all on a dream.[29]

Leapt bravely! Now down through the meadows we'll go
    To the Land of Lost Days, whither all the birds wing,[30]

[15] MS I: "And your singing and dancing." MS II: "And your sungleams . . ."
[16] MS II: "gay."
[17] MSS I and II: "everyday."
[18] MS I rejects " 'Tis earthy, and earthy good only can buy."
[19] MS I: "but."
[20] MSS I and II: "Come back."
[21] MS II: "there's better in death!"
[22] MS I rejects "sing."
[23] MS I: "The tomauns, my own bridegift, that flash and are there."
[24] MS I: "Make haste, for I wait my blithe playmate again."
    MS II reverses the order of this and the following stanza.
[25] MSS I and II: " 'Tis."
[26] MS I: "Escape."
[27] MS II: "dear."
[28] MS II: "You are mine; fly with me, then."
[29] MS I omits this stanza.
[30] MS I: ". . . where it always is spring."

Where the dials move backward and asphodels blow;[31]
Come flash your tomauns again, dance again, sing!

Yes, flash them and clash them on ankle[32] and wrist,
    For we're pilgrims to Dreamland, O Daughter of Dream!
There[33] we find again all that we wasted or mist,
    And Fancy—poor fool!—with her bauble's supreme.

As the Moors in their exile the keys treasured still[34]
    Of their castles in Spain, so have I; and no fear[35]
But[36] the doors will fly open, whenever we will,[37]
    To the prime[38] of the Past and the sweet[39] of the year.

IN A VOLUME OF SIR THOMAS BROWNE

Strange spoil from this weird garden Memory brings;
Here, hard by Flower de Luce, the night-blast sows
Moonstruck Thessalian herbs; o'erhead (who knows?)
Or from beneath, a sough of missioned wings;
The soil, enriched with mould of Coptic kings,
Bears, intertwining, substances and shows,
And in the midst about their mystic rose
The Muses dance, while rapt Apollo sings.
All-potent Phantasy, the spell is thine;
Thou lay'st thy careless finger on a word,
And there forever shall thine effluence shine,
The witchery of thy rhythmic pulse be heard;
Yea, where thy foot hath left its pressure fine,
Though but in passing, haunts the Attic bird.

[31] MS I: ". . . move back and the asphodels blow."
[32] MS I: "anklet."
[33] MSS I and II: "Where."
[34] MS I rejects ". . . exile took with them the keys."
[35] MS I read "so had I those of mine"; then substituted "so have I; never fear."
[36] MS I omits this word.
[37] MS I rejects "please."
[38] MSS I and II: "heart."
[39] MS I: "prime."

INSCRIPTION FOR A MEMORIAL BUST OF FIELDING

He looked on naked Nature unashamed,
And saw the Sphinx, now bestial, now divine,[1]
In change and rechange;[2] he nor praised nor blamed,
But drew her as he saw with fearless line.
Did he good service? God must judge, not we;[3]
Manly he was, and generous and sincere;[4]
English in all, of genius blithely free:[5]
Who loves a Man may see his image here.

FOR A BIRTHDAY

How many years have subtly wrought,
  With patient art and loving care,
To rear this pleasurehouse of thought,
  This fabric of a woman fair?

'Twere vain to guess: years leave no trace
  On that soft cheek's translucent swell;
Time, lingering to behold that face,
  Is cheated of his purpose fell.

Why ask how many, when I find
  Her charm with every morrow new?
How be so stupid? Was I blind?
  Next birthday I shall ask how few.

[1] MS: "Saw her half bestial, saw her half divine."
[2] MS read "With both content, he neither praised nor blamed"; then substituted "Accepting both . . ."
[3] MS: "Was he not fashioned in her image, too."
[4] MS read "And should he revive the Mighty Master's plan?" then omitted the initial "And."
[5] MS: "Let others palliate, he would dare be true."

"I AM DRIVEN BY MY LONGING"

I am driven by my longing,
Of my thought I hear the summons
That to singing I betake me,
That I give myself to speaking,
That our race's lay I utter,
Song for ages handed downward.
Words upon my lips are melting,
And the eager tones escaping
Will my very tongue outhasten,
Will my teeth, despite me, open.

Golden friend, belovèd brother,
Dear one that grew up beside me,
Join thee with me now in singing,
Join thee with me now in speaking,
Since we here have come together,
Journeying by divers pathways;
Seldom do we come together,
One comes seldom to the other,
In the barren fields far-lying,
On the hard breast of the Northland.

Hand in hand together clasping,
Finger fast with finger clasping,
Gladly we our song will utter,
Of our lays will give the choicest—
So that friends may understand it,
And the kindly ones may hear it,
In their youth which now is waxing,
Climbing upward into manhood:
These our words of old tradition,
These our lays that we have borrowed
From the belt of Wainamoinen,
From the forge of Ilmarinen,
From the sword of Kaukomeli,
From the bow of Jonkahainen,
From the borders of the ice-fields,
From the plains of Kalevala.
These my father sang before me,
As the ax's helve he fashioned;

These were taught me by my mother,
As she sat and twirled her spindle,
While I on the floor was lying,
At her feet, a child was rolling;
Never songs of Sampo failed her,
Magic songs of Lonhi never;
Sampo in her song grew agèd,
Lonhi with her magic vanished,
In her singing died Wipunen,
As I played, died Lunminkainen.
Other words there are a many,
Magic words that I have taught me,
Which I picked up from the pathway,
Which I gathered from the forest,
Which I snapped from wayside bushes,
Which I gleaned from slender grass-blades,
Which I found upon the foot-bridge,
When I wandered as a herd-boy,
As a child into the pastures,
To the meadows rich in honey,
To the sun-begoldened hilltops,
Following the black Maurikki
By the side of brindled Kimmo.

Lays the winter gave me also,
Song was given me by the rain-storm,
Other lays the wind-gusts blew me,
And the waves of ocean brought them;
Words I borrowed of the song-birds,
And wise sayings from the tree-tops.

Then into a skein I wound them,
Bound them fast into a bundle,
Laid upon my ledge the burthen,
Bore them with me to my dwelling,
On the garret beams I stored them,
In the great chest bound with copper.

Long time in the cold they lay there,
Under lock and key a long time;
From the cold shall I forth bring them?
Bring my lays from out the frost there
'Neath this roof so wide-renownèd?

Here my song-chest shall I open,
Chest with runic lays o'errunning?
Shall I here untie my bundle,
And begin my skein unwinding?

.   .   .   .

Now my lips at last must close them
And my tongue at last be fettered;
I must leave my lay unfinished,
And must cease from cheerful singing;
Even the horses must repose them
When all day they have been running;
Even the iron's self grows weary
Mowing down the summer grasses;
Even the water sinks to quiet
From its rushing in the river;
Even the fire seeks rest in ashes
That all night hath roared and crackled;
Wherefore should not music also,
Song itself, at last grow weary
After the long eve's contentment
And the fading of the twilight?
I have also heard say often,
Heard it many times repeated,
That the cataract swift-rushing
Not in one gush spends its waters,
And in like sort cunning singers
Do not spend their utmost secret,
Yea, to end betimes is better
Than to break the thread abruptly.

Ending, then, as I began them,
Closing thus and thus completing,
I fold up my pack of ballads,
Roll them closely in a bundle,
Lay them safely in the storeroom,
In the strong bone-castle's chamber,
That they never thence be stolen,
Never in all time be lost thence,
Though the castle's wall be broken,
Though the bones be rent asunder,
Though the teeth may be pried open,
And the tongue be set in motion.

How, then, were it sang I always
Till my songs grew poor and poorer,
Till the dells alone would hear me,
Only the deaf fir-trees listen?
Not in life is she, my mother,
She no longer is aboveground;
She, the golden, cannot hear me,
'Tis the fir-trees now that hear me,
'Tis the pine-tops understand me,
And the birch-crowns full of goodness,
And the ash-trees now that love me!
Small and weak my mother left me,
Like a lark upon the cliff-top,
Like a young thrush 'mid the flintstones,
In the guardianship of strangers,
In the keeping of the stepdame.
She would drive the little orphan,
Drive the child with none to love him,
To the cold side of the chimney,
To the north side of the cottage,
Where the wind that felt no pity,
Bit the boy with none to shield him.
Larklike, then, I forth betook me,
Like a little bird to wander,
Silent, o'er the country straying
Yon and hither, full of sadness.
With the winds I made acquaintance,
Felt the will of every tempest,
Learned of bitter frost to shiver,
Learned too well to weep of winter.
Yet there be full many people
Who with evil voice assail me,
And with tongue of poison sting me,
Saying that my lips are skilless,
That the ways of song I know not,
Nor the ballad's pleasant turnings.
Ah, you should not, kindly people,
Therein seek a cause to blame me,
That, a child, I sang too often,
That, unfledged, I twittered only.
I have never had a teacher,
Never heard the speech of great men,
Never learned a word unhomely,

Nor fine phrases of the stranger.
Others to the school were going,
I alone at home must keep me,
Could not leave my mother's elbow,
In the wide world had her only;
In the house had I my schooling,
From the rafters of the chamber,
From the spindle of my mother,
From the axehelve of my father,
In the early days of childhood;
But for this it does not matter,
I have shown the way to singers,
Shown the way, and blazed the tree-bark,
Snapped the twigs, and marked the footpath;
Here shall be the way in future,
Here the track at last be opened
For the singers better-gifted,
For the songs more rich than mine are,
Of the youth that now are waxing,
In the good time that is coming!

VERSES

(To P. G. S. Written in a Gift Copy of Mr. Lowell's Poems.)

If here, sweet friend, no verse you find
To wake far echoes in the mind,
No reach of passion that can stir
Your chords of deeper character,
Let it suffice if here and there
You seem to snuff New England air,
And give a kindly thought to one
Who in our ampler Western sun
Finds no such sunshine as he drew
In London's dreariest fogs from you.

VERSES

(Written in a Copy of "Among My Books" for P. G. S.)

Last year I brought you verses,
This year with prose make bold;
I know not which the worse is;
Both are but empty purses
For your superfluous gold.
Put in your sunny fancies,
Your feeling quick and fine,
Your mirth that sings and dances,
Your nature's graver glances,
And think they all are mine.

COLLEGE VERSE

GRAND OPERA;

FOR THE BENEFIT OF

THE PEOPLE OF EAST TENNESSEE.

SIGNORA FIORRANCIO!!!

SIGNORA LAVALLETTA!!!

SIGNOR LUNGOPRATO!!

SIGNOR SOTTOBOSCO!!

SIGNOR SILESIANO!!

On Tuesday, Thursday, and Saturday Evenings,
May 10th, 12th, and 14th,

Will be produced, with a powerful chorus, new and brilliant scenery, and magnificent appointments,

THE GRAND ROMANTIC OPERA

IL PESCEBALLO.

Music by the CHEVALIER ROSSIBELLI-DONIMOZARTI.

La Padrona,..........................SIGNORA FIORRANCIO.
La Serva, ...SIGNORA LAVALLETTA.
Lo Straniero, ...SIGNOR LUNGOPRATO.
Il Cameriere,........................SIGNOR SOTTOBOSCO.
Il Corriere, ...SIGNOR SILESIANO.

Leader of the Chorus, SIGNOR TOCCAMANO.

☞ In order to give éclat to the performance, SIGNOR SILESIANO has consented to accept the comparatively small part of the Corriere.

Conductor and Leader of the Orchestra, SIGNOR PARCHERO, assisted by SIG. GUGLIGALLI.

N. B. The Pianos used by this Company are from the celebrated manufactory of Chickering & Sons.

Ἡ ΣΦΑΙΡΗΠΟΥΣ *Homer's neu Heldengedicht, von Diog: Teufels-dröckh herausgegeben.* Weissnichtwo, Stillschwiegen und Cg^le. 1837.

The critics of Germany, always distinguished in the pursuits of litera-ture, have lately made a discovery, brilliant enough to reflect even addi-tional lustre on a land which has already given birth to a Faust and a Luther. It is to one of their number that we are indebted for having brought to light the before unknown poem of Homer, which has furnished us with a subject for this article.

In the Weissnichtwo Gazette of January, 1836, it was announced, that the learned professor Teufelsdröckh had accidentally lit upon this gem which for more than twenty centuries had been lost to learning and the world. "This inestimable treasure," continues the Gazette, "which, when given to the public, will add another leaf to the distinguished professor's already acquired laurels, this gem beyond all price (*edelstein über aus trefflich*) dropped from the folds of an ancient garment which the pro-fessor was examining when laying the foundations of his everywhere-celebrated clothes philosophy." To worthier hands so distinguished a fortune could not have fallen!

This long-expected and eagerly-desired volume has at length appeared in Germany, under the personal superintendence of the immortal Teufels-dröckh. The poem in question was probably composed (I had nearly said written) like the Pygmæogeranomachia, to while away the leisure hours of the blind old man of no particular birthplace.

The subject of the epic is the game of Football, an amusement as popu-lar among the students of the Greek universities as it is in our own in these degenerate days. The manuscript is peculiarly interesting, as it throws additional light upon the manners and customs of ancient Greece, and proves that the character and discipline of their universities has descended in an almost unaltered state to us, in spite of time, and the thick darkness which brooded over the earth during the midnight of the middle ages.

How delightful, how touching is it to follow the steps of the Father of Poesy through the lowly walks of common life, and to read in the actions of the unsophisticated Freshmen of Athens and Lacedæmon that inno-cent simplicity and unassuming merit which characterizes their name-sakes of our own enlightened Republic!

We have ventured to attempt a few translations of some of the finest passages, in order to let our readers judge for themselves of the beauties of the poem. The first book is taken up by the invocation and introduction to the subject; in the beginning of the second book the action of the poem

181

commences, and the following beautiful extract occurs. We think that even in its present state the reader will find enough to compensate for the poorness of the translation.

> Now after dinner Jove in silence strode,
> (Stepping full slowly 'neath th' ambrosial load,*)
> To where, inviting with its outspread arms,
> His easy chair displayed its cushion'd charms.
> Arrived at length, he sits him down in state;
> The polish'd arm-chair roaring† with the weight,
> Received the corpus of the well-fill'd god,
> Who lit his pipe, and soon began to nod.
> At ev'ry bob of his macassared poll
> Outrageous thunders down Olympus roll,
> The staring sun looks blue; the trembling earth
> From Ætna's jaws gives 'hot-press'd volumes' birth.
> So when fierce Mars his blazing sword waves round,
> "The rage of jumping chariots shakes the ground!"

After this description, which, for force and aptness of expression, and for sweetness of sentiment, is scarcely equalled by the most admired passages in our author's other, and long celebrated productions, Fame enters. She, having succeeded in attracting the drowsy attention of Jupiter, by a severe tweak on the organ of olfactory sensation, informs him, in one hundred and twenty as finished verses as we ever perused, that the telegraph, on the highest summit of the most elevated portion of many-peaked Olympus, announces the near approach of the dreadful battle at Football between the hosts of opposing Sophomores and Freshmen. Jove, having scratched his head and relighted his pipe, rings the bell for his scales. Into one side he throws the ambition to sustain the novel honors of the 'toga virilis'; while Juno places in the other the acknowledged superiority and importance conferred by the long and arduous experience of one year's seniority.

The painfully anxious expectations of the lookers-on is ended by the slow, but obstinate depression of the Sophomoric side of the balance. Jupiter, who had privately determined to give the victory to the Fresh-

---

* "Βραδέως," κ.τ.λ. Even under so quaint an expression as that in the text, the poet impresses us with an idea of the majesty of Jupiter. It would require an endless commentary to point out all the peculiar beauties of this delightful poem. T. (The notes marked 'T.' are by professor T. himself.) [Lowell's note.]

† "Βρέμονδα καθέδρα," κ.τ.λ. 'Roaring with the weight'; mark the peculiar beauty and force of this expression, which Homer must have penned in his happiest mood. We read in the Iliad and Odyssey of tables 'groaning' beneath the load of superincumbent edibles; but the poet here tells us, that so great was the postmeridian weight of Jupiter, that the agonized chair actually 'roared' with the pain of the pressure. T. [Lowell's note.]

men, finding it impossible, throws down the golden scales in a huff, and saunters off, in vain endeavoring to assume an air of independence, with his hands in his pockets, alternately puffing diligently at his pipe, and humming the highly popular Spartan war-song, called "Yankee Doodle." Juno trips lightly to her piano, and, while the accomplished Apollo turns the leaves of her music, 'executes'* the grand national anthem of "Settin' on a Rail."

The bard now carries us back to earth, and the description of the battle, (by far the most thrilling episode in the poem,) commences. The football is slowly dragged to the ground by two panting Freshmen, selected for that arduous service. It was of such enormous size, that twelve Freshmen of our degenerate days could scarce lift it; for even in Homer's time, he tells us that

> "A ball like this, so monstrous and so hard,
> Six eager Freshmen scarce could kick a yard!"

The gods next descend to the conflict, with the exception of Jupiter, who disliked a long walk after dinner, and Minerva, who was engaged in an earnest discussion with one of the professors on the culture of the Olive. Apollo also was absent, being unable by whip or spur to force the obstinate Pegasus down from the many-peaked Olympus. The cause of this refractoriness on the part of his steed, he afterwards stated, was, that on a former visit to the University, having tied his horse to the post at the gate, five or six of the students tackled him into a wagon, and drove with such furious haste up the neighboring mount Parnassus, as materially injured the wind of the beast.

We shall commence our second translation with some extracts from the account of the combat, which is written in our author's best manner, and, from its style, gives additional proof of the genuineness of the poem. The struggle has already commenced, and our interest in the event is scarcely lessened by the assurance given us beforehand by the scales of Justice, to which party the victory will incline. The following is a passage of intense interest; a Freshman has caught the ball, and

> Then, the sole centre of admiring eyes,
> He grabs with both his hands the splendid prize,
> Stands on his utmost toes to seem more tall,
> And with stentorian voice addresses all.
> "From distant realms to learning's shrine I come,
> Far from my nurse's arms and peaceful home,
> And that dear maiden whom behind I left,

---

* This 'execution,' as the golden-haired Phœbus Apollo wittily remarked afterwards, at a soirée given by Venus, amounts in many cases to little more than "legal murder." [Lowell's note.]

Of seven senses by my loss bereft!
Blest in my talents, and remote from strife,
In raising calves my father spends his life;
His name in Ajax GRIPES—and ditto mine,
In me are plac'd the hopes of all my line!
Of me my friends all 'feel,' (or ought to,) 'great,'
Search through the globe you would not find my mate!
And here I stand in arms my father wore,
(What time the brunt of raging war he bore,)
Two boots of cowhide, fram'd of 'sterner stuff'
Than would make twenty Sophs cry 'hold! enough!' "
Thus having said, the cowhide-booted youth
Call'd Jove to witness that he spoke the truth,
And cocking fiercely one cerulean eye
With glance triumphant waited a reply.

Nor waited long: a Soph with look of fire
Straightway pull'd out the stopple of his ire:
"Rush you on death, vain boy, that vaunting thus,
With voice exalt you strive to make a fuss?
'Far better were it: better were it far'
You ne'er had tried the fate of cruel war;
Far better were it on your nurse's lap
To suck your thumb and gulp diurnal pap;
Better to face the prowling panther's path,
Than meet the storm of Sophomoric wrath!
Thy father raises calves? egad, 'tis true,
And never reared a greater one than you!"
He said: the frantic Freshman fiercely frown'd,
Then hurl'd the pond'rous football to the ground;
"Fair lick!" he cried, and rais'd his dreadful foot
Arm'd at all points with the ancestral boot;
Like a huge comet, cheated of his tail,
The ball flew swifter than the steamboat mail,
High in the air it wings its hasty flight,
And, (if't were dark,) had whizzed quite out of sight.

Alas poor GRIPES! he had but scanty space
To boast the fame thus added to his race,
Swift as Jove's lightnings from the storm-clouds shoot,
Full on his shins descends the hostile boot.
No Ethiop he: and yet his ghastly grin
Spoke the keen anguish of the injured shin;

Prone in the dust his stately form he threw
A corpse gigantic—*nearly* four feet two!*
The victor rush'd to grab the costly spoil,
The hard-earned "summat" for his warlike toil;
Two boots and those *two* tails, with which we see
Freshmen feel large as fierce bashaws with three.
But, as he stoop'd the well greas'd greaves to find,
Great Jupiter crept slyly up behind,
Involved the Freshman in a cloud of smoke, ⎤
And dealt the Sophomore so hard a stroke, ⎥
(With a good staff of Constitution oak,) ⎦
As made him more bright Constellations view,
Than ever gemm'd night's spangled arch of blue!

Minerva, who, as well as Jupiter, has now entered the combat, conveys
the Freshman to his room, where his cries make such a disturbance, that
a proctor enters and commands the blue-eyed goddess "to disperse."
This order she reluctantly obeys.

On the battle field, in the mean time, the assistance of the Seniors and
Juniors is called in, and the poet describes some of the principal com-
batants. The leader of the Juniors we are told was

A kingly form, as *Polyphemus* tall,
By head and hat he far o'ertops them all,
Firm as a rock he stems the raging fight,
Flinging his mighty fists from left to right,†
Like mountain torrent rushes on the foe,
And wields the terrors of his dreadful toe!

After many exploits on both sides, the armies retire with no decided
advantage on either part. Or, as our author expresses it,

Like crews of *geese* who seek the frozen pole,
Where falling icebergs fright the fearful soul,
And 'expeditions' waste both time and men
In working up and working back agen.

The gods withdraw to Olympus and Jupiter despatches Esculapius,

---

* Virgil must have seen this poem, we think, from his palpable imitation of the
above passage, in the 6th book of the Æneid; where he says,
"per tota novem cui jugera corpus
Porrigitur."
If he never had read the line in the text it is, as Walter Savage Landor would say, "a
remarkable coincidence." [Lowell's note.]
† "From left to right." We usually say from "right to left"; but the poet, with
the boldness always attendant on true genius, has here reversed the order, thereby
rendering his hero far more grand and peculiar. [Lowell's note.]

(with a jug of opodeldoc, a syringe, and the unmentionable part of a linen shirt,) to the assistance of the wounded. Esculapius, (poor fellow!), having probably drunk a little too deeply of his favorite nectar, was persuaded by some valorous Sophomores to go with his squirt to "visit" a Freshman. But here, the sport was not wholly on one side; for the unfortunate Esculapius was obliged to return precipitately to Olympus, having lost his syringe, (valued at one drachma,) besides being assisted down stairs by the toe of the indignant Freshman.

The concluding lines of the poem are so fine, that we cannot refrain from giving them entire.

> Now Jove with nightcap *on* or *in* his head
> Saw, (wondrous sight,) two moons their lustre shed°!
> But striding on, to reach his 'polished couch,'
> He took his snuff-box from his ample pouch;
> Thrice tapp'd the cover with his kingly hand,
> Took two vast pinches, and pronounced it 'grand.'
> He sneez'd; the Thund'rer sneezed; the stars
> Trembled like volunteers pursued by Mars,
> Ten thousand comets whisk their endless tails,
> Ten thousand dittoes load the startled gales,
> And fast as legs can wag, the storm-king flies,
> "Coruscant lightnings darting from his eyes!"
> But Jove, meanwhile, quite used to such a din,
> Climb'd up his bed and huddled snugly in,
> Put an extinguisher upon the moon,
> And ordered breakfast to be serv'd at noon.

"Finis coronat opus!" exclaims the immortal Teufelsdröckh, as he lays down his pen, after his editorial labors; and "finis coronat opus" is reëchoed by the voice of thousands from this side of the Atlantic. Yes, such an ending as the above is indeed worthy to cap the climax of the noble work before us!

But amid the universal plaudits called forth by the professor's publication, one jarring note is heard,

——"argutos inter anser olores."

And whose voice is this which is thus raised to blacken the fair fame of

---

° " Ἐγκέφαλος," κ.τ.λ. On this passage the critics are divided. Some assert that 'nightcap' is used in the cant sense of 'evening dram'; and support the theory by the fact of the Thunderer's seeing two 'queens of night.' Others on the other hand, and with them I am proud to rank myself, say that this second sight, as it were, was meant by the poet to express a peculiar privilege of the immortals, and to show Jupiter's *elevation* above the inhabitants of earth. T.

In the translation, we have endeavored to combine the two expressions, so as to satisfy all readers. [Lowell's note.]

the glorious Teufelsdröckh? Truly that of a nameless critic, who, speaking of the poem, writes thus: "in the first place, I deny that such a man as Homer ever existed; and secondly, I affirm that he did not write the epic in question."

To his first proposition I shall not condescend to reply; and concerning his second I shall merely remark, that it is scarcely less flimsy than his first. I leave it to the decision of my readers whether the hand of Homer is not discernible throughout; a hand, which, like that of Midas, transforms all it touches into gold!

One thing yet remains to be spoken of, viz., our author makes "the father of the gods" a smoker. This has been pitched upon, by the enemies of Teufelsdröckh, to prove the German origin of the poem. But even the most prejudiced will allow the genuineness of Virgil's Bucolics, and does he not there say

"Incipe Mænalios mecum mea *tibia* versus,"
"Begin with me my *pipe* Mænalian strains."*

With regard to our versions into English, we trust no harsh critic will apply to Homer, the exclamation which Quince with so much pathos addresses to the unfortunate Bottom;

"Bless thee, Bottom! Bless thee! thou art *translated!*"

IN IMITATION OF BURNS

I

Those liquid een o' winsome blue,
Like sparklin' draps o' heav'n's ain dew,
Those modest cheeks o' changin' hue
        Are aye before me;
Where'er I turn they meet my view,
        An' hover owre me.

II

Fu' aft I've talked o' laughin' girls,
An' sparklin' een, an' auburn curls,
An' smiles disclosin' rows o' pearls,
        Wi' mickle glee;
But *she*, alas! my heart strings dirls
        In spite o' me!

* Warton. [Lowell's note.]

III

Na, ne'er till now I've felt the sway
Of een that mock'd pure Hesper's ray,
An' voice mair sweet than when, in May,
 The playfu' breeze
Sighs aft, as if it long'd to stay
 Amang the trees.

IV

Oh had I but *ae* lock o' hair
That now sae fandly nestles there
Just peepin' out, (her smiles to share),
 Frae 'neath her bonnet,
For a' life's ills I wad na care
 While gazin' on it!

DRAMATIC SKETCH

"De omnibus rebus et quibusdam aliis."

Scene; *a college room.* Time; *evening. The Editors of Harvardiana sitting
round a table.*

First Editor *(snatching a paper from one of his brethren.)*

Is this a sonnet that I see before me,
Its title towards mine eyes? or is it but
An outward semblance of a sonnet, shaped,
By the vain dreamings of my tortured brain,
From "airy nothing" but to cheat my sense?
I see thee still, and, from thy smiling front,
Large scrawls of ink look meekly in my face,
In silent eloquence, as if to say
"Regard me well; I am a CONTRIBUTION!"

Second Editor

Yes, *'tis* a contribution, and myself
I took it with these hands from out our box,
As I returned, with circular, by names
Unsullied, sadly to my room to weep!
Oh! I have passed a miserable day!
So full of honied "nays" and soft refusals—

I would not pass another such a day
Though 't were to smoke, (Oh best of earthly joys!),
The nicest *"real Spanish,"* ever made
By Yankee ingenuity and art.
'T was but an hour ago, that wreathed in smiles,
I placed "the paper" 'neath a Freshman's nose,
And asked, in accents bland, "Will you subscribe?
We need a few great names to head the list;
To sign or not to sign; *that* is the question."
Then with my ready pencil poised between
My thumb and finger, waited a reply.
He started back as if his nostrils snuffed
Contamination, "grinned a ghastly grin,"
And cried, "I've *seen* the work!" It was enough;
I opened not my mouth, for "I liked not
The grinning" humor which that Freshman had!
Oh 'tis a grievous thing to be an Editor!
Men look askance and say, "He hath the 'LIST,'
The foul subscription list within his pocket!"
Nor this the worst; "the *little* dogs and all,
Tray, Blanch and Sweetheart, see, they bark at me!"

Third Editor

Well, less than this we could not much expect;

"He who ascends the mountain tops, shall find
    The loftiest peaks most wrapt in clouds and snow;
He who surpasses or subdues mankind,
    Must look down on the hate of those below!"*

But gained you not one name?

Second Editor

Alas! not one.

Third Editor

Gods! can a single student long debate
Which of the two to choose, subscribe or not?
"Oh I could weep; save that I may not stain
With grief" this hour made sacred to the nine.
Hast a cigar?

* Childe Harold. [Lowell's note.]

FOURTH EDITOR (*abstractedly*)

No, and alas! no cash
To buy them with. I had a fourpence once,
A treasured *one;* there was the look
Of pureness on its venerable cheek,
Such as the coiners love to give to their
Debased metal. How I loved that coin!
It left my purse, and never to return.
A saddened smile lit its round face, a tear
Seemed almost trickling down that long loved cheek;
I saw it slide, slide gently, through the fingers
Of the glad Herald boy; then sternly wiped
The woman from my eye, and cried, "I'm penniless!"

FIFTH EDITOR

" 'T was strange, 't was passing strange, 't was pitiful,
'T was wondrous pitiful!" But listen, hark!
(*a voice is heard in the street.*)

DEVIL (*sings*)

Where the types are, there are I;
And on costly *sheets* I lie;
There I couch when cats do cry
In the murk night lovingly;
On my bare feet do I fly
After "Copy" merrily!
"Merrily, merrily shall I live now"
And pick up a living the *devil* knows how!

FIFTH EDITOR

Didst mark that song? "it had a dying fall,
Oh! it came o'er my ear" like a sweet fife—
But here's the devil!

(*Enter*) DEVIL

COPY! Copy! *ho!*

FIFTH EDITOR (*gives him a bag*)

"I tax not you, poor devil, with unkindness!"

DEVIL

If you did, it would be "werry annoying," as the gemman said ven he
vos hung by mistake.   [*Exit*

THE SERENADE

I

Hark! o'er the lake rings
  My lover's guitar;
Hush my fond heart—Lord!
  He'll wake up Papa!

II

Nearer! Oh now he'll
  His fond suit renew—
My hair's all in papers—
  Oh! what shall I do?

III

Hist! to his voice chimes
  The gondolier's oar—
Heavens! my Pa wakes!
  No! 't was but a snore!

IV

"Waken, my Anna!
  Oh list to my song,
As, on the night breeze,
  It hastens along!

V

"See! the moon trembles
  In light on the lake,
So trembles my fond heart,
  Oh wake, dearest, wake!"

VI

"Throw up the ladder
  Mine own dearest love!
But oh! wake not father,
  Who sleeps just above!"

VII

Lightly the true lover
  Leaped to the land,

Gently he crept up,
With ladder in hand.

VIII

Softly a casement
Oped over his head,
And a gruff voice thus
Most savagely said—

IX

"Seek you for me, Sir?"
"Ah no! for your daughter!"
"Do you? take this then—
This tub of cold water!"

X

Sadly the lover sneaked
To his canoe—
Wet to the skin, he
Thus sighed his adieu—

XI

"Farewell! I tinkle
No more my guitar,
But my heart beats true
As ——— d——n your Papa!"

WHAT IS IT?

I

Oh! it flashes and beams in the eloquent eye,
And beats thick in the heart when that *one* form is nigh;
It gleams forth through the glow of the unbidden blush,
Like the mild star of eve in the sunset's last flush.

II

It burns warm in each whisper, it melts in each tear,
And its half-formed words falter—but oh! not with fear;
It appeals to the soul in the ill-suppressed sigh,
Which, unconscious, we utter, and then wonder why.

III

It communes in a voice far too thrilling for speech,
In a mystical language, which *words* cannot reach,
Like the breath of the Zephyr, the harpstrings along,
When it sighs forth its love-notes and dies with the song.

IV

If 't is checked, like the torrent, it swells but more high,
Or returns to its home, like the hurt dove—to die!—
Ask your heart what this fairy-like vision may seem,
And it throbs as it answers—" 'T is LOVE'S youthful dream!"

SARATOGA LAKE

"There is an Indian superstition attached to this lake, which probably
had its source in its remarkable loneliness and tranquillity. The Mohawks
believed that its stillness was sacred to the Great Spirit, and that, if a
human voice uttered a sound upon its waters, the canoe of the offender
would instantly sink."

Willis—American Scenery, v. 1, p. 19

It was an Autumn evening and the lake,
(Save when some light breeze ruffled it,
In dalliance with a blushing water lily,)
Lay tranquil as a spotless maiden in her rest,
Whose sleep is peace itself—except some gleam
Of newborn love flit o'er her dream—and then
Her pulse beats quicker, and her traitor lips
Tremble, as they reveal the only secret
Her breast e'er knew.

Skimming the quiet waters,
Like the scared wild-fowl whom the hunter's foot
Has startled from her solitary nook,
Out shot a light canoe upon the lake.
Two only forms it held, and they were lovers—
A pale-face and his bride.—His practised arm,
Which, until now, had urged the little bark
With speed well nigh as swift, as would the shaft,
Winged with destruction, leave the Indian's bow,
Relaxed its efforts; and they floated on

O'er the still bosom of the lake, now rosy
With that mild tint which blushes o'er the sky,
When the last autumn sunshine fades to twilight.

It was a lovely scene, and they, (his arm
Was thrown unwittingly around her waist,)
In silence listened to the voice of nature
As, clothed in beauty, she discoursed, in tones
Which language knows not, to their spirit's ear,
Of HIM who made this glorious world, from which,
As from one vast Cathedral, all things raise
An everlasting anthem of Thanksgiving.

The scene was lovely—but to those two lovers
'T was more, far more; it almost seemed as if,
(So to the holy Prophets once 't was given,)
The scales had left their eyes, and they beheld
The present glories of a better world.
Oh love! thou art the sunshine of the soul,
Gilding with thine own hues whate'er thou touchest,
And warming into life the spirit's currents,
(Before dull icebound streams,) until they gush
In the wild music of untutored Poetry!

Their hearts were full; they gazed upon the scene,
And then upon each other. Oh that gaze!
If but to speak be death, why sank they not?
For worlds of speech were crowded in that gaze.
A tear shone trembling in that eye which oft
Had met the fearful glance of Death and quailed not.
He clasped her to his breast, and, as his lips,
(Scarce consciously,) met hers, murmured "my love!"
The spirit of the lake was wroth—calmly,
(How awful was that calm!) yet suddenly,
The charmed waves yawned wide and overwhelmed them
In life and love, as in their death, united.

.   .   .   .   .

No sound is heard except the mournful note
Of the lone whippoorwill, who tells his love
To the deceitful echo, which, from far,
Like a fond mate, makes answer, cry for cry—
But the glad ears, which one short moment since,

Drank in the wailing melody, heed not.
The evening star still throws his trembling glance
In silver lustre on the lake below,
But they, who gazed so oft upon his beams
And wondered, in their love, if he contained
Beings one half as happy—where are they?
Dead—and what's Death that we should fear him so?
It is not Nature's prompting; for the babe
Who knows not Death, sinks, at his beck, to rest
Calmly as on a fond mother's bosom—
Like children, we have drest a phantom up,
And fear to look on what ourselves have made.

.   .   .   .   .

In pity of the lovers' mournful fate,
The merciful Great Spirit broke the spell
That bound those quiet waters; but e'en now,
So says the Mohawk hunter, at that hour,
That loveliest hour of Autumn twilight,
The light canoe still skims the lake, and still
Those two float for a moment round the spot
They loved so well on earth, and then are gone.

SCENES FROM AN UNPUBLISHED DRAMA

By the late G. A. Slimton, Esq.

Act I—Scene I

SCENE.—*Oystershop.* TIME.—*10 o'clock, P. M. Room brilliantly illumin-
ated by two tallow candles.* OYSTERMAN *in the background
brandishing his knife with a tragic air over a prostrate oyster.
Enter* TOM *and* DICK.

Thomas (*loquitur*)

This hour is big with fate, and must decide,
As Shakspeare well remarks—

Richardus

I like 'em fried,
They suit me rather better; and I think
That, (as you pay,) we'll have a little drink.

I'm not at all particular, but fain
Would—*(to Oysterman)*—hand that bottle—taste of
   this Champagne.
   (To Oysterman)
Just file the wires or break them with a fork,
And, when I'm ready, liberate the cork.

THOMAS

Say, gentle Oysterman, old Neptune's son,
Oh say and soothe me! are the shellfish done?

OYSTERMAN

That warn't my father's name! I've no idee
Of having fun nor nothing poked at me!
But to add rubbing in to poking—yes,
That's most too hard for any one I guess,
And as for me—young man I tell you what⎤
I am—no matter what I am—I'm hot,   ⎬
Ay, in my wrath a very mustard pot!   ⎦
A curse is on me, wander where I will
That dreadful ban, by jingoes! dogs me still!
E'en so some puppy, to whose harmless tail
Some urchin's hand has tied an old tin pail,
Flees to escape it, yet forever feels
The cumbrous pendent dangling at his heels,
And finds the only method left to take
Is—for his heart, or tail, or both, to break!
   I once was gentle as my own sweet Sam,
But perfidy has made me what I am!
I have been cheated, and have suffered wrong
Not to be sneezed at, I have borne long, long,
That pay deferred that makes the full heart ache—
Oh trebly cursed be they who coldly take
The poor man's oysters, eat them up and say
"Trust us, good Oysterman"—and never pay!!

THOMAS *(aside)*

I've heard of second-sight, but can it be
That fate's dark book is conned by such as he?
If it be so, perhaps he may not trust—
We'll eat the oysters though, and then he must!

OYSTERMAN

'Tis hard, at best, to keep a wife and child
And grievous when the last, last tatur's biled!
When the wide world is wrapt in slumbers all
And only Sammy wakes, and wakes to squall,*
Then on my restless couch I sleepless turn.

RICHARDUS

I say! old cock, these oysters here will burn!

OYSTERMAN

Let me alone for that—I scratch my head
To think the morrow brings no loaf of bread.
All this is sad enough, but sadder far,
When I pass by the tavern's well-stocked bar,
See rum o'er rum, o'er whiskey, whiskey placed,
And my mouth waters for one *leetle* taste
To warm the blood that curdles round my heart,
And add fresh vigor to my baser part,—
Often I've told the bar-keeper how slick
'T would be for both, if he would only "tick,"
Just tick this once, I'd never ask again,
'T would *so* relieve an intermittent pain,
A sort of daily cholic that *would* come,
And only yielded to New England Rum.
  (Aside)
Take that junk bottle, Samuel, my son,
(It stands up in the corner there,) and run
Round to the grocer's; get it filled with—stuff
And hasten back again—Begone! Enough!

THOMAS

Much like the frightful colds which students tell,
Just reach their crisis at the matin bell,
Sudden they come and sudden disappear
When the loud breakfast peal salutes the ear.
The symptoms are a deep lethargic snore
Till much-loved prayers and more-loved Locke are o'er,
At morning meal an appetite diseased,
Which, like poor Rachel, will not be appeased.

* "And only sorrow wakes, and wakes to weep."—*Rogers*. [Lowell's note.]

The danger then subsides, but oftentimes
Returns more dreadful by next morning's chimes—
In former days they had a funny cure,
Which, though severe, was almost always sure;
The President in person used to pick
In Craigie's woods full many a walnut stick
Of toughest quality, and having got 'em
Applied the same unto the patient's ● ● ● ● ● ●.†
But now-a-days the country air is thought
To cure such maladies of every sort.
 But are the oysters fried? I cannot wait
Much longer, Oysterman, it's getting late.
I hear sad accents which you cannot hear,
Ventriloquistic voices meet my ear,
My mental ear, and weeping, seem to say
"Our Commons dinner was but poor to-day."
And when I strive to put the tempter down,
They moan again, "Do have them fried quite brown!"
Dick, if Fate's hand were ever shown in aught,
These dreadful omens are not meant for nought.
So ghosts, when Cæsar fell, wrapt up in sheets,
"Did squeak and gibber in the Roman streets,"
As Shakspeare says—

RICHARDUS

Dear Tom, the oysters wait,
Don't stand and moralize, but fill your plate.

THOMAS

Fill! I'll do more, I'll empty it as fast
As what is "present" hastens to be "past;"
For verily my nose, most mighty Dick,
Informs my bowels that the treat is slick!
E'en so some grunter, monarch of the stye,
Lifts o'er the new-brought swill his nostrils high,
Keeps all the other rev'rent piglings off
As he inhales the incense of the trough,
And while his very tail for rapture curls,
Prefers his banquet to a feast of pearls.‡

† Manuscript illegible. [Lowell's note.]
 ‡ "Cast your pearls before swine," &c. Every one has heard of Cleopatra's
pearl. After her example, pearls dissolved in vinegar became almost a standing article
of dessert among the luxurious Romans. [Lowell's note.]

RICHARDUS

Bring on the bottle, Oysterman, this knife
Shall bring its prisoned energies to life,
See how it foams and fizzles to be free,—
   (Cuts the cork loose.)
Pop! that's a sounder! how it sparkles! See!

THOMAS

E'en so my spirit, Richard, scorns the rules
Of College order, made to shackle fools!
What are all laws in fact but galling chains,
The empty work of still more empty brains;
A poor device, if history tell us true,
To make the many buckle to the few?
Laws! shame that such frail gossamer should bind
The God-like powers of the mighty mind!
   (Dick, in the mean while, keeps alternately tipping the
      bottle towards his glass, and his glass towards his
      mouth, with a dexterity which Sancho Panza himself
      might have been proud to imitate.)
Oh how my spirit struggles to be loose
And strives in vain! alas it ain't no use!
Oh Dick! Dick! Dick! if you but had a soul
Like mine, to grasp the world from pole to pole,
And, in its universal charity take in
Each fellow mortal of whatever skin;
Brown Indian, roasted by the eccentric sun,
And ebon Ethiop, rather overdone,
(What time poor Phaëton in Sol's bright car,
"Shot from the zenith like a falling star,")
Had you a soul, I say, as vast as that,
You'd say—these things are fried in too much fat—
You'd say, What are the laws to me, to any one,
If but approving conscience say, "Well done!"

RICHARDUS

Well done, forsooth! Well done! I do not care
What conscience likes, but *I* prefer things *rare!*
   (With this he pours down the last glass of Champagne)

THOMAS

Yet why this eloquence? he heeds me not,
Far better eat my oysters while they're hot.

Besides, this speech, if husbanded with care,
May one day make the Harvard Union stare,
And bellowed forth with more than Stentor's lungs
Call thundering plaudits from a dozen tongues! ! !
So some huge Freshman, hero of a *tail*,
Delights to feel it fluttering in the gale,
But more delights to save it nicely brushed,
Till Sophs' fell ire by Sunday's calm is hushed,
Then proudly does his young ambition soar,⎤
As he struts sternly to the chapel door,   ⎬
In all but age and size, a Sophomore!   ⎦

RICHARDUS

Oh nature's noblest gift, New York Champagne!
Light of the sense! Elysium of the brain!
Who cast aside the grape, and mixed instead
With one part brandy, four of pure white lead,
And thus our country's freedom did enhance,
No more dependent on the vines of France?
A leather medal his reward should be,
A leather medal and an LL. D.!   *(after a pause, sings)*

> "Come hey down derry
> Let's drink and be merry
> In spite of Mahomet's law!"

But stop! oh sight of horrors! by the stove
Stand two twin oystermen! they do, by Jove!
Glaring at me, with look intent, they stand,
And knives, for murder thirsty, in their hand,
Oh men of oysters! men of oysters oh!
What can possess ye to regard me so?
And Thomas! long loved, honored Thomas too, ⎤
Why have you thus transformed yourself to two? ⎬
I ne'er expected such a thing of you!   ⎦

THOMAS

Richard, thou 'rt drunk! you're fuddled Dick, I say,
Here, take my arm, and let us haste away.

RICHARDUS

Believe me, Tom, I really am not high,
This seeing double's wholly "in my eye"—
And really, (hiccup,) Tom, I cannot see

Why you should thus insinuate at me.
E'en so the pot behind the kettle's back,
As history tells us, called his cousin black.
A meddling saucepan to the kettle told
The whole affair, before the words were cold.
The latter *boiled* with wrath, 'called out' the pot,
And shot the luckless slanderer on the spot!!
So prithee, Thomas, do not make a fuss,
And let the pot's sad fate take one of us.

THOMAS

I will not, dearest Dick—but let us go,
We've something else to do to-night, you know;
And though some proctor, on his evening scout,
Led by his nose, should chance to find us out,
And peeping through night's blanket cry hold! hold!
I'd try his courage, Dick, I feel so bold!!

RICHARDUS

Yes, Tom, if courage dwelleth in the *feet,*
I think you'd stand the fairest chance to beat.
                    [*Exeunt Tom and Dick singing*

        "We won't go home till morning!"

(A proctor comes out from the other cell in the shop)

PROCTOR

Now will I keep a very strict look out,
And, (if thou'rt faithful to thy charge, my snout,
And guid'st me truly yet this one time more
As thou, unerring, oft hast done before,)
I hope to nip in time this budding scrape,
Nor let the actors or the act escape!
Then in all future proctors' mouths my name
Shall be synonymous with deathless fame.
Guy Fawkes was nothing to this horrid plot,—
But I must strike while yet the iron's hot!
            [*Exit Proctor, in his haste forgetting to pay.*

Manet OYSTERMAN

Now by the terrors of this mighty fist
Which rival oystermen could ne'er resist,
I'll *pay* that rascal who forgot to pay,

E'er yet the sun proclaims another day.
Nor sword nor horrid oysterknife will sheathe
Until I make him banquet on his teeth!!°
  (Takes a swallow from the bottle.)
To seal the oath I take one leetle drop—
Sam! while I'm gone, do you attend the shop!†
        [*Exit.*

   END OF ACT FIRST

SKILLYGOLIANA. No. II

 "O most lame and impotent *conclusion!*"

Readers! if those there be that ever read
Our sleepy page and bid the work "God speed!"
To each and all we wish a happy year
Unsullied by one doubt or care or tear,
Save those bright drops at parting, rendered sweet
By the found thought that we again shall meet,
And those of joy, that virtue only knows,
When our cup filled with gladness overflows.
And ye, fair readers, if indeed one glance
Of sunshine on our foggy pages dance,
From eyes so soft they seem of heaven's own blue,
Like violets sparkling in the morning dew—
And thou, almost ideal! whose pure face
Beauty and innocence combine to grace,
Whose voice is music and whose glance is love,
Whose smile like what we dream of joy above,
Whose eyes—but whew-ew! what's bewitched our pen?
The seventh heaven is beyond your ken;
Come back again, and wish our readers fair
An hundred happy new years for their share.
*(Here followeth a vision "that caused our bones to shake and made the
very hair of our flesh to stand up.")*

   PENNA *(interloquitur)*

An hundred to a lady! bless your eyes
They would n't thank you for the "soft surprise!"
Wish 'em all matrimony, love, or fat,

° A poetical expression for knocking his teeth down his throat. [Lowell's note.]
† "Tityre dum redeo, brevis est via, para capellas." [Lowell's note.]

Or death, or any other bore than *that;*
Wish 'em long noses, mouths,—nay, even ears,
But never, never wish 'em length of years!

POETASTER

Well, call it fifty.

PENNA

Where alas! would be
Those eyes that sparkle now with girlish glee?
Peering through spectacles with vacant look
They spell the sentences of some worn book;
Where that fair hand, that tiny hand of snow,
Whose taper fingers have bewitched you so?
Why, knitting stockings with absorbing care
And always trembling o'er the self same pair.
And where the voice whose music makes you start,
Sending the warm blood quicker to the heart?
Garrulous with age it tells you, day by day,
What such and such an one were wont to say
In days gone by—pauses for breath—and then
Repeats the same old story o'er again,
Look on the picture—have not fifty years
Made mournful changes in their long careers?

POETASTER

What! is that spectacled old lady there
The maiden whom I once esteemed so fair?

PENNA

"That spectacled old lady!" cast your eyes
Upon that glass—nay stifle your surprise—
Those are not crowsfeet, they are dimples—nay
Don't look so blank, those curled locks are not grey;
Come, hasten! fly! get down upon your knees
At that young lady's feet, and pray and teaze
To print one kiss upon that lily hand,
Which owns no lovely rival in the land.—

POETASTER

Now I look closer, why I think I *do*
See that she's not so *very* old—don't you?
But call it twenty.

PENNA

Where the deuse might be
This venerable university?
Just think of buildings flying round the yard
On the swift pinions of a hand-grenade!
Imagine five and forty thousand tomes.
Torn from companions dear and long loved homes,
Darting about, here, there, and everywhere,
Scattering the dust of ages in the air,
And breezes turning those vast pages o'er,
Which, save their writers, none e'er turned before!
Lo! monstrous Polyglotts and sermons rise
Jostling with plays and novels to the skies,
And getting higher in the public view
Than e'en their authors would have wished them to!
The janitor beginning to perceive
Through his dim specs, that all were taking leave,
Would think 't was one, and give a farewell shout,
"One o'clock, gentlemen! you must go out!"
Then, on some cherished tome he'd take his flight,
And, coat-tails flying, vanish out of sight.
Perhaps to some bright planet-realm he'd soar
Where DUCKS* are sacred, and all toils are o'er,
Perhaps to Erin green he'd wing his way,
"O'er the glad waters of the dark blue *say!*"
Then too the Philosophic "things" below,
(Put there to catch the dust and make a show,
And twice a week, for lecturers to take
To show their audience how "slick" they break,)
Just think how quick the orreries would be,
With all their suns and stars, in apogee;
How "transit instruments" and all would change
To *exit* instruments,—'t would be as strange
As some men's politics, which oft obtain
The name of weathercock, they are so *vain.*
How "FUTTERBUNKS" would streak it through the air
With so much "*emphasis*" his very hair,
His auburn hair, that stands too proudly straight
Would sink in terror from its high estate!

* "*There* you're too hard for me!" [Lowell's note.]

SKILLYGOLIANA.   No. III

"O most lame and impotent *conclusion!*"
Since Friday morning, on each busy tongue,
"Shameful!" "Outrageous!" has incessant rung.
But what's the matter? why should words like these,
Of dreadful omen hang on every breeze?
Has our Bank failed, and shown, to cash her notes,
Not cents enough to buy three Irish votes?
Or worse than that, and worst of human ills,
Will not the lordly Suffolk take her bills?
Sooner expect, than see her credit die,
Proud Bunker's pile to creep an inch more high.
Has want of patronage, or payments lean,
Put out the rush-light of our Magazine?
No, though Penumbra swears "the thing is flat,"
Thank Heaven, taste has not sunk so low as that!
Can no cigars be bought in all the town,
Of Marshall, Ramsay, Wood & Hall, or Brown?
Though other crops were small, and grain is dear,
Oak-leaves were very plentiful last year.
Has Texas, freed by Samuel the great,
Entered the Union as another state?
No, still she trades in slaves as free as air,
And Sam still fills the Presidential chair,
Rules o'er the realm, the freeman's proudest hope,
In dread of naught but bailiffs and a rope.
Has then the hero of the claret coat
Swamped General Arcularius* and boat;
When, paddling out, he boldly draws his sword
Against great Navy Island's conquering horde,
And as he fiercely shakes the thirsty blade,
Demands the "captured" cannon, undismayed
Though met by heroes who might well defy
The maids of Billingsgate in sharp reply?
Oh no! Columbia's angel stretched her arm
To shield her bravest son from every harm,
And still he lives to see on muster field

* General A. was the "force" despatched to preserve neutrality, and to retake the cannon from the "ragged regiment" on Navy Island. Troy was taken by a wooden horse, but such has been the improvement in military tactics, that the Navy Islanders were too wise to be deceived into anything but Billingsgate by a living jackass. [Lowell's note.]

The bristling squadrons bloodless charge and yield.
What *is* the matter then? Why Thursday night
Some chap or other strove to vent his spite
By blowing up the chapel with a shell,°
But unsuccessfully,—he might as well
With popgun threat the noble bird of Jove,
Or warm his fingers at a patent stove,
As try to shake old Harvard's deep foundations,
With such poor despicable machinations.
Our Alma Mater laughs such plots to scorn,—
Her glory yet is but the early dawn,
Which shall, as every shadow melts away,
Grow bright and more bright to the perfect day.
Long may she live, and Harvard's morning star
Light learning's weary pilgrims from afar!
And long may 'Star-eyed Science' love to twine
Her greenest wreaths for this her fairest shrine!
Long may the chapel echo to the sound
Of sermon lengthy and of part profound,
Long may it stand to hear young stentors pour
Latin and Greek in one continued roar,
And long may Dana's gowns survive to grace
Each future runner in the learned race!

UHLAND'S "DES KNABEN BERGLIED"

I

The mountain shepherd boy am I ,
No Baron boasts a hold so high,
The sun's first morning rays I see,
He lingers longest here with me,—
I am the mountain herd boy!

II

My cup is hollowed by the spring,
Ere it begins its wandering,

° This attempt would be scarce worth noticing but for its enormity. While a few glasses were broken by the explosion of a petard or so, it might be called thoughtlessness, but the character of this offense stamps it as deliberate villany. This Erostratian method of being "damned to endless fame," is, after all, but a small way of gaining a reputation. [Lowell's note.]

Forth from the rock it leaps amain,
In sport I toss it back again,—
I am the mountain herd boy!

III

My heritage is this bare peak;
The mountain tempests round it shriek,
From north and south their hosts they call,
But my glad song outsounds them all,—
I am the mountain herd boy!

IV

My home is ay 'mid sunshine sweet;
The thunder growls beneath my feet;
I know full well his surly tone,
And cry, "Let Father's house alone!"
I am the mountain herd boy!

V

When peals the tocsin's warning dread,
The mountain beacon answers red,
Then down I rush and march along,
And swing my sword and sing my song,—
I am the mountain herd boy!

A DEAD LETTER

"My heart is sair, I darena tell,—
My heart is sair for somebody."

I joined the crowd, and I thought of *thee* only,
And thy bright smile,—
Thou wast not there, oh! how heartsick and lonely
I felt the while!

To many maidens I have sent gay letters,
Yet dared not tell
One hope to her, who all my heartstrings fetters
As with a spell.

'T was weary work to flatter unknown beauties
All o'er and o'er,

While there was *one*—my heart thou know'st how true 't is,
  Deserved far more.

But, though I feared to *write*, I ceased not thinking,
  Fairest, of thee!
And Fancy still thy gentle tones was drinking,
  Thy glance of glee.

And oh! when round thee lovely forms are glancing
  'Mid feast and song,
When happy hearts and fairy feet go dancing
  In joy along;—

When, 'mid bright eyes, *thine* eyes of blue are brightest,
  Then condescend,
To waste one little thought, though but the lightest,
  Upon
                                        A FRIEND.
Cambridge, May-day Evening, 1838.*

EXTRACTS FROM A "HASTY PUDDING POEM"

Does College life feel no ambitious cares?
Are students only free from all her snares?
Fancy, for one short fraction of an hour,
That we are gifted with Asmodeus' power,
Then snugly seated on old Harvard's cap,
We'll take a look, or if you please, a nap,—
If it may chance that my unworthy strain
Bring rest to one, I have not sung in vain.
Now then, you must n't mind the chilly breeze,
We're seated, look around you, if you please.

Mark yon enthusiast, his lamp grows dim,
His pale fire smoulders, but 't is nought to him!
What 's paltry coal compared with endless fame,
Or wasting tapers to the muses' flame?
His gilt-edged superfine devoted lies

* The above letter was left in the Post-Office and never called for. It was, by a lucky chance, saved from being sent on to Washington, to be opened by the unfeeling hands of government clerks. [Lowell's note.]

In virgin purity before his eyes,
Save where, (sole token of poetic rage,)
"Sonnet" stands staring from the modest page.
Poor guiltless word! long doomed to pine alone,
Like aged toad imbedded deep in stone!
Harvardiana's pages bid him seek
"An immortality of near a week."
Ambition lends him industry, and she,—
May one day make a bard of even me!
Methinks e'en now the poet's eye may look
With prophet vision on the future's book,
And see, like Dædalus, the minstrel rise
On self-invented pinions to the skies,
Spur his racked hobby in the muses' teeth,
And snatch in triumph at the deathless wreath!
And as stout Vulcan's axe impetuous clove
The blue-eyed Goddess from the scull of Jove,
So labor beats from dulness' brain ideas
While each more brilliant than the last appears,
Until at length, his patent wings full spread,
Enormous epics blossom round his head!
Perchance improvement, in some future time,
May soften down the rugged path of rhyme,
Build a nice railroad to the sacred mount,
And run a steamboat to the muses' fount!
O happy days! when "steaming" to renown,
Each bard shall rise, the wonder of his town!
O happy days! when every well-filled car,
With stubborn rhymes in rugged strife shall jar,
And every scribbler's tuneless lyre shall squeak,
When whizzing swiftly up Parnassus' Peak!

Stop! hear you not that concourse of sweet notes,
Thrilling the soul as on the breeze it floats?
Ah music's votaries! full well ye know
To win the senses from dull study's woe,
To lull the mind to quiet, yet to keep
Your drowsy neighbors from too sound a sleep.
'T is sweet to hear, when sinking to a doze,
Some tuneful neighbor chanting through his nose.
Just when, oblivious of sublunar things,
Free fancy soars away on dreamy wings,
When, themes well finished or postponed awhile,

Light Somnus greets one with Pickwickian smile,—
'T is sweet to be awakened, though 't is true
There's pleasure in a calm siesta too.
But ah, much sweeter, when the night has thrown
Her sable mantle round her starlit throne,
When the day's weariness has given zest
To the soft pillow and the soothing rest,
To be awakened by the mingled sound
Of many laboring instruments around,
Far more melodious than the startling call,
That shattered Jericho's embattled wall.
"Ah!" one exclaims, "this music is a bore,
They might have let me sleep a little more,
With windows closed, I think they well might spare
'To waste their sweetness on the desert air!' "
No! what were music, if it were not known
Who pealed the loudest, who the sweetest tone?
Ambition fills them all, they all aspire
To get on string of Phœbus' silver lyre.
Full many such "oft in the stilly night"
Exert their voices with stentorian might,
"From morn till night, from night till startled morn,"
Twang loud alarums on the groaning horn,
Or when they should be chewing learning's root,
Wring heartfelt moanings from the tortured flute.
All, all, have ears; though some more highly blest
Have ears much longer than the luckless rest;
Yet amidst sizes of near every sort,
None, (I must say it,) are at all too short!

.   .   .   .   .

Fain would I more;—but could my muse aspire
To praise in fitting strains our College choir?
Ah, happy band! securely hid from sight,
Ye pour your melting strains with all your might;—
And, as the prince, on Prosper's magic isle,
Stood spell-bound, listening with a raptured smile
To Ariel's witching notes, as through the trees
They stole like angel voices on the breeze,—
So when some strange divine the hymn gives out,
Pleased with the strains he casts his eyes about,
All round the chapel gives an earnest stare,
And wonders where the deuce the singers are,

Nor dreams that o'er his own bewildered pate,
There hangs suspended such a tuneful weight!

TRANSLATIONS FROM UHLAND

I

"DAS STÄNDCHEN"

THE SERENADE

"What gentle music from my sleep
    Awaketh me?
Oh mother look! at this late hour,
    Who can it be?"
"Nought can I hear, nought can I see,—
    Oh slumber on!
They bring no serenade to thee,
    My poor sick son!"
"These are no earthly tones that make
    My heart so light,
The angels call me with their songs,—
    Mother, good night!"

II

"DER WEISSE HIRSCH"

THE WHITE STAG

Three huntsmen into the greenwood went,
To hunt down the white stag they were bent;
They laid them down 'neath a green fir-tree,
And there dreamed the selfsame dream all three.

FIRST HUNTSMAN

I dreamed that as I was beating the brush,
The white stag swiftly leapt out, rush! rush!

SECOND HUNTSMAN

And as from the yelping hounds he sprang,
I thought that I peppered his hide, flash! bang!

THIRD HUNTSMAN

And when the white stag on the ground I saw,
I lustily winded my horn trara!

Now while the three huntsmen a talking lie,
The white stag boundeth merrily by,
And, ere the three huntsmen had seen him fair,
O'er valley and hill he had sped like air.
    Rush! Rush! Flash bang! Trara!

TO MOUNT WASHINGTON

On a Second Visit

How are you, mine ancient hoary headed friend?
 How have you been since I saw you last?
Hast any more[1] wild Indian legends to tell,
 Sturdy old chronicler of the past?[2]

What, mum? poor old fellow! I see how it is,—
 You're berhymed and betravelled too much!
You can scarcely peep out with your storm-beaten phiz,
 But you fall in some viewhunter's clutch.[3]

I suppose you remember when Time was young,
 Say, what makes[4] him so crabbed and cross?
Did he speculate largely in Eastern lands,
 Which the deluge made all a dead loss?[5]

Did he lose his affianced, (poor soul!) in the flood?
 Or write a small poem or two,
And turn misanthropic on reading a squib
 In some acid præ-Adam review?[6]

---

[1] MS: "Have you any more."

[2] In MS a marginal gloss appears beside stanza 1: "The poet addresseth the mountain and kindly enquireth after his health."

[3] In MS a marginal gloss appears beside stanza 2: "Receiveth no answer and supposeth a reason therefor."

[4] MS: "made."

[5] In MS a marginal gloss appears beside stanza 3: "Asketh after Time, whether he *sunk* all his fortune in the flood ('There is a tide in the affairs of men/ Which, taken at the *flood,* may lead to fortune.')"

[6] In MS a marginal gloss appears beside stanza 4: "Enquireth whether he was snubbed in some review, perhaps edited by Ishmael for his hand was against every man &c."

He must be your friend;—why you're not changed at all,
  Save some wrinkles the torrents have made,
When you wrung out the water from some stray[7] cloud
  To replenish a dried-up cascade.

You're a pious old chap to stand pointing there still,
  With admonishing finger on high,—
'T is a pity your visitors don't[8] improve
  By your lofty, silent homily.

Did you ever (you must live next door to the spheres)
  Enjoy a nice[9] spherical serenade?
If so, do relax that unsociable frown,
  And tell on what pieces they each of 'em played.[10]

Come, speak,—does the carbuncle light its old spot?
  Is the lake of the clouds too still there,
Which served for a looking-glass when you were young,
  To arrange your then plentiful hair?

And now that I think of it, try Ward's hair oil,
  'T will resist age, misfortune, and weather;
And, make your locks long as when you and old Time
  Began life's rugged journey together.

Nay, never look cross, for you know you *are* bald,
  And have been so these two thousand years,
And scarce take a look in your truth-telling glass,
  Without shedding a river[11] of tears.

You won't say a word? hey, old vinegar face?
  Hold your tongue then, I don't care a bit,—
If you open your clamshells you'll only show,[12]
  That you've lost both your grinders and wit.

Good bye! milestone huge on eternity's road,
  Stand there proudly till earth's latest[13] day,

[7] MS: "straggling."
[8] MS: "wouldn't."
[9] MS omits "nice."
[10] MS: "And tell on what instruments they played?"
[11] In MS a marginal gloss appears upon this word: "The Saco rises on the summit of one of the Mts. (Munroe I think) and runs down from the lake of clouds."
[12] MS: "you'll only just show."
[13] MS: "dying."

May you powder your head with old winter's last snow,
And smile back on the sun's latest ray.[14]

SONG

"Their tricks and craft hae put me daft,
  They've ta'en me in, and a' that;
But clear your decks, and 'Here's the sex!'
  I like the jades for a' that."
               BURNS, *Jolly Beggars.*

I

A pair of black eyes,
  Of a charming size,
And a lip so prettily curled O!
  Are enough to capsize
  The intentions wise
Of any young man in the world O!

II

For a pretty smile
  Is a grievous[1] wile
For a heart, for a heart that is light O!
  And a spirit[2] like a dove
  Draws one slily into love,[3]
Though he knows that it is n't right O!

III

Oh a gentle heart
  Is the better part
Of the loveliest woman's wealth O![4]
  And I totter on the brink
  Of love when I think,
When I think how our eyes met by stealth O![5]

[14] In MS a marginal gloss appears beside stanza 12: "Repenteth his reviling and liketh not to leave his old friend in anger. Ergo blesseth him."
  [1] MS: "mighty."
  [2] MS: "girl."
  [3] MS: "Makes a man fall in love."
  [4] MS: "Of a lovely woman's looks O!"
  [5] MS: "When I think, when I think of Miss B—— O!"

IV

For a thousand girls
Have hair that curls,
And a sort of expressive face O!
But it is n't the hair,
Nor the genteelish[6] air,—
'T is the heart that looks bright and gives grace O!

V

Ay, lasses there[7] are many
With the devil a penny,[8]
But with hearts worth their weight in gold O!
Who would sooner win my heart
Than the richest in the mart,
Whose prudent love may be bought and sold O![9]

VI

No bee e'er yet sucked honey
From gold or silver money,
But he does from the lowly[10] flower O!
Then give me a spouse
Without fortune,[11] land or house,
And her charming self for a dower O!

VII

For love it is a thing
That will quit the lonely king,
To make sunny the cot[12] of the peasant O!
And it folds its gauzy wing,—
In short it is a thing,
'T is[13] a thing—that is deuced pleasant O!

VIII

Though Platonism will do
For the verd-antique blue,
Who no portion has but her tongue O!

6 MS: "genteel."
7 MS omits "there."
8 MS: "Without e'en a penny."
9 In MS the last three lines of this stanza read
　　　　"Whom I'd sooner wed,
　　　　　Yea, and sooner bed
　　　　Than a princess rich ugly and old O!"
10 MS: "lovely."
11 MS rejects "silver" and substitutes "fortune."
12 MS rejects "heart" and substitutes "cot."
13 MS omits " 'Tis."

Yet that is rather tame,
And a little hotter flame
Is the thing for the heartsome young O![14]

TO THE CLASS OF '38,
BY THEIR OSTRACIZED POET, (SO CALLED,)
J. R. L.

I

Classmates, farewell! our journey's done,
Our mimic life is ended,
The last long year of study's run,
Our prayers their last have blended!

CHORUS

Then fill the cup! fill high! fill high!
Nor spare the rosy wine!
If Death be in the cup, we'll die!
Such death would be divine!

II

Now forward! onward! let the past
In private claim its tear,
For while *one* drop of wine shall last,
We'll have no sadness here!

CHORUS

Then fill the cup! fill high! fill high!
Although the hour be late,
We'll hob and nob with Destiny,
And drink the health of Fate!

III

What though Ill-luck may shake his fist,
We heed not him or his,
We've booked our names on Fortune's list,
So d——n his grouty phiz!

CHORUS

Then fill the cup! fill high! fill high!
Let joy our goblets crown,

[14] This entire stanza is omitted in MS.

We'll bung Misfortune's scowling eye,
   And knock Foreboding down!

IV

Fling out youth's broad and snowy sail,
   Life's sea is bright before us!
Alike to us the breeze or gale,
   So hope shine cheerly o'er us!

CHORUS

Then fill the cup! fill high! fill high!
   And drink to future joy,
Let thought of sorrow cloud no eye,
   Here's to our eldest boy!

V

Hurrah! Hurrah! we're launched at last,
   To tempt the billows' strife!
We'll nail our pennon to the mast,
   And DARE the storms of life!

CHORUS

Then fill the cup! fill high once more!
   There's joy on time's dark wave;
Welcome the tempest's angry roar!
   'Tis music to the brave.

CLASS POEM

"Some said, John, print it; others said, Not so:
Some said, It might do good; others said, No."
                                        BUNYAN.

DEDICATION[1]

TO THE CLASS OF 1838,

Some of Whom He Loves, None of Whom He Hates.
This "Poem" is Dedicated

by

Their Classmate

[1] By the advice of friends the original dedication of this performance is suppressed, so that now, gentle reader, as Grumio says, "it shall die in oblivion, and thou return unexperienced to thy grave." [Lowell's note.]

PREFACE

Many of my readers, and all my friends know that it was not by any desire of mine that this rather slim production is printed. Circumstances, known to all my readers, and which I need not dilate on here, considerably cooled my interest in the performance. Many of the lines, though in fact they would even then be indifferent good, I should prefer if possible to see in prose. *Sed Dis aliter.* Many were written merely as rough draughts, which I intended to have altered and revised, but the change of feeling, mentioned above, has prevented, and rough draughts they are still. There are a few grains of gold, or at least tinsel, in the composition, but the lead—oh word infaust to poets!—will I fear, far outweigh them. A few passages have been omitted, whose place is sufficiently well supplied by asterisks.

Paltry, however, as it is, I submit it (at their desire) to my readers, confident

"That never anything can be amiss,
When simpleness and duty tender it."
Concord, Mass., August, 1838.

CLASS POEM

I

Brothers! you know that every passing year,
    When it has dug enough in learning's mine,
Each class still meets to take its parting here,
    To Alma Mater gives one farewell line,
And throws, perchance made fresher by a tear,
    Its wreath of tribute blossoms on her shrine,—
Pray Heaven! she be not smothered by the flowers
That visit her with such perennial showers!

II

And eloquence and song are called to swell,
    With music's dreamlike witchery and prayer,
The faltering cadence of the sad farewell,
    And beauty's heart-inspiring smile is there,
And brilliant eyes more softly beam to tell,
    That in the moment's sadness they too share,
Like stars, seen fainter through some filmy veil,
Which makes their light seem purer, though more pale.

III

Long years we've trod our dusty path together,
　　Years duller e'en than when retraced in rhyme,
Sharing alike Fate's storms and sunny weather,—
　　Three silently have floated through the void of time,
The fourth still stays his ruffled plumes to feather,
　　And make his last record of sin and crime,—
Fancy e'en now can hear his dusky wing
Flutter and flap at parting, while I sing.

IV

Oh! would I had a better voice for singing!
　　That I might plunge into a tide of song,
And, to some little plank of reason clinging,
　　Float gaily on the rushing waves along,
From side to side the glittering foam-drops flinging,
　　Bresting the yesty waves with purpose strong,
Until at last, far, far from either shore,
I sank in bathos-depths to rise no more!

V

Or, heavenward striking on unwearied wing,
　　Seek the star-broidered empyrean, thence,
Leaving to earth's dull clods each *common* thing,
　　As common metre, words, and common sense,
Soar on and upward, till each cracking string
　　Of feeling vibrate with a thrill intense,
And, wandering on, far out of mortal view,
Quite lose myself, alas! and hearers too!

VI

To those who understand me not, I'd say
　　" 'Haud tibi spiro,' we want sympathy,
If you don't like me turn another way;"
　　Or else I'd grow pathetic, rub my eye,
And snivel out in half-choked words, "My day
　　Of triumph yet will come before I die;
So 't was with Milton, Shakspeare, and a host,
Unhonored all, till they gave up the ghost!"

VII

I might,—but I'm like one who turns a glass
　　Among those heavenly melodists the stars,

Nor knows while o'er his raptured gaze they pass,
  Wheeling and turning in their golden cars,
Which fairest one to single from the mass,
  Minerva, Venus, Juno, Vesta, Mars,
So lovely are they all to gaze upon,
Sweet, modest shunners of the garish sun.

VIII

Or more like one who makes his choice among
  Some dozen garments in their latest stage,
Whose gaping mouths, could they have found a tongue,
  Had told full many a tale of fortune's rage,—
So I,—for all things have been said or sung
  In this long-winded pathobathic age,
Who let philosophers (God wot!) command 'em,
Because they (honest souls!) can't understand 'em.

IX

What they can't comprehend must be profound,
And so they toil along the same blind round,
Admiring all who talk in tropes and rant,
From heaven-high Fichte up to viewless Kant.
Kant! happy name! change but the K to C,[2]
And I will wring my poem out of thee.
Thanks, vast Immanuel! thy name has given
The thing for which my brains so long have striven.
Who ever thought that *thou* could'st be of use
To give a subject to a puzzled muse?
Spread, Pegasus, thy wings! for thou and I
In one short hour have many leagues to fly,
Cant be my theme, and when she fails my song,
Her sister Humbug shall the lay prolong.

X

Dim realm of shades! ere yet I take my flight,
To pierce the gloom of thy eternal night,
Where Cant, sublime upon her throne of brass,
Feeds every knave and feeds on every ass,
Oh let me breathe one last, one parting prayer,
To be my talisman of safety there.

[2] The subject was literally hit upon in the way stated, or rather hinted at, in the text. [Lowell's note.]

Oh thou! to whom, where'er my footsteps roam,
My restless soul would spread its pinions home,—
Reality! more fair than any seeming
E'er blest the fancy of an angel's dreaming,—
Be thou my muse, in whose blue eye I see
The heaven of my heart's eternity!
Oh hover like a spirit at my side,
In all my wanderings a heavenly guide,
Then, if in Cant's dim mists I lose my way,
Thy blessed smile shall lead me back to day,
And, when I turn me from the land of night,
Thou, morning star of love, shalt herald light!

XI

Hail Cant's great watchword, quickstep march of mind!
   Whose gallant leaders hurry on so fast,
They have no time to cast a look behind,
   And take a lesson from the hoary past;
On, like a torrent in their pauseless course,
They rush, to bring Millennium by force,
And in the holy warfare growing warm,
Would take the New Jerusalem by storm!
Thee first I sing. Not mine the poet's fire,
Or hand that deftly strikes the sacred lyre,
Not mine the bays, and yet a muse like mine
Might wreath a rainbow round the dullest line.

Hail progress days! Farewell! thou good old age,
When talking nonsense did not make a sage,
Bacon and Locke, your day of empire's o'er,
To dust and bookworms sink for evermore!
The march of mind is going on too fast,—
So half the world run mad with some one's last,
(Would that it were indeed his last!) and then
With Teufelsdröckh run full as mad agen.
"Look! look!" they cry, "upon this book, and see
What a philosopher this man must be!
What quaint-mouthed sentences! and how profound!
You'll grant there's bathos in the very sound;
Such long and lofty nouns and verbs had well
Graced the *high* words between those giants fell,
Whom Scripture tells us poured out so much blood,

As nearly drowned the earth before the flood.[3]
Johnson to this man was a fool 't is plain,—
In his great work you'll seek such words in vain.
Then too those other saints, this side the sea,
Already write as crooked words as he;
Now, as all arguments of words consist,
And everything is magnified by mist,
In all debates of course he gets the best
Who brings more words and mistier than the rest."

Thus they, infatuate as the Jews of old,
Worship a calf, though not a calf of gold,
And on their godship's heads take monstrous pains
With laurel wreaths to hide the want of brains.
"Omne ignotum pro mirifico,"
They *know* that's grand whose sense they cannot know;
And, proving thus that bombast is profound,
Through works of deepest mist they grope around,
Staring at sentences so vastly high,
That all their meaning quite escapes the eye,
So lengthy too, that rhyme must own it fears,
Nothing can match them but their author's ears,
So strange, that Murray would have wept to hear,
Unless indeed while writhing through his ear,
They put the good old grammatist to sleep,
Ere he could pull his kerchief out to weep,—
And so immensely deep—the reader's head
In vain tries soundings with its native lead.
Thus they wade on, now measuring some word
Of which no other Christian ever heard,
Now toiling slowly up some premise steep
To pitch, half-drowned, in some conclusion deep,
Until at length they end their march in nought,
Or break their shins by stumbling on a thought.

XII

Hail too great drummer in the mental march,
Teufelsdröckh! worthy a triumphal arch,
Who send'st forth prose encumbered with jackboots,
To hobble round and pick up raw recruits,
And, able both to battle and to teach,

[3] "And there were giants in those days and after." *Genesis.* [Lowell's note.]

Mountest thy silent kettledrum to preach.
Great conqueror of the English language hail!
How Caledonia's goddess must turn pale
To hear thy German-Greeco-Latin flung
In *Revolutions* from a Scottish tongue!

Yet here the muse would fold her wing to weep[4]
O'er genius buried in lethargic sleep,
O'er talents misapplied, o'er heavenly fire
Smothered beneath a mass of wordy mire,
And only bursting forth at times to show
How much still lies to sorrow for below.
Oh! better that the sombre cypress wave
Its mourning branches o'er a fameless grave,
Than gain a name by talents thus applied
To a base intellectual suicide.
Burst, prisoned eagle, burst thy chains and soar
Where soulless eye can track thy flight no more;
Where shafts of satire, feathered from thy wing,
No more can gall thee with their insect sting!
Proud bird of Jove! seek Heaven's purest air,
And dwell forever with thy compeers there;
Go sit at Shakspeare's sainted feet, and see
How man can trample on mortality!

.   .   .   .   .

Ah, Clothes Philosophers, you'd better try
     To make the garments you but mar in prose,
You'd find a tailor's wages much more high
     And profitable too, as this world goes;
No doubt the balance on your printer's book
Will add its counsel—if you dare but look;
Those winged words, of which you prate so much,
Cannot be yours, and had you any such,
Off from your pens they'd spread their wings and fly
To seek, elsewhere, for better company.
Lay down the goosequill then—take up the goose,
And put your talents to their proper use.

    4 No one admires Mr. Carlyle's genius more than I do; but his style is execrable,
though, for a change, entertaining. His tying himself down to such a diction, &c.
reminds one of a punishment still practised in China, chaining a living criminal to a
dead body. Of course the ridicule is meant for his imitators—the "servum pecus," as
Horace calls them. [Lowell's note.]

XIII

Alas for poor Philosophy! that she
In her old age should come to beggary
And turn a tailoress, who from her throne
Once ruled fair Greece, and called the world her own.
Those days are gone, when poet, hero, sage
In rapture brooded o'er her speaking page,
And fixed in breathless wonder, silent hung
On the proud lessons swelling from her tongue,
Then spread her truths to earth's remotest bound
Till haughty Error trembled at the sound.
Those days are gone, and now her only friends[5]
Are misty rhapsodists, whom Heaven sends
To form a contrast with the blessed light,
And make Truth's holy lustre seem more bright.
Who, blessed with souls scarce larger than a broker's,
Would furnish them to pots and pans and pokers,
And, having made a "universal soul,"
Forget their own in thinking of the whole;
Who, seeking nothing, wander on through space,
Flapping their half-fledged wings in Reason's face,
And if they chance the vestal flame to find,
That burns a beacon to the storm-tost mind,
Like senseless insects dish within the fire,
And sink forgotten in their funeral pyre.
Few ever meet with such a glorious end,
Or towards the light their aimless ramblings bend;
But, having fretted out their little age,
Sink into chaos, and their sleepy page,
Lining some trunk, shall be the only note
That what's-his-name their author lived and wrote.

Woe for Religion too,when men, who claim
To place a "Reverend" before their name,
Ascend the Lord's own holy place to preach
In strains that Kneeland had been proud to reach,
And which, if measured by judge Thatcher's scale,
Had doomed their author to the county jail!
When men just girding for the holy strife,

---

[5] The "most melancholy Jaques" seems to have had a prophetic voice, when he said,
        "My lungs began to crow like Chanticleer
          That fools should be so deep-contemplative." [Lowell's note.]

Their hands just cleansed to break the bread of life,
Whose souls, made whole, should never count it loss
With their own blood to witness for the cross,
Invite a man their Christian zeal to crown
By preaching earnestly the gospel—down,
Applaud him when he calls of earthy make
That ONE who spake as never yet man spake,
And tamely hear the anointed Son of God
Made like themselves an animated clod!

They call such doctrines startling, strange, and new,
But then they're *his*, you know, and must be true;
The universal mind requires a change,
Its insect wings must have a wider range,
It wants no mediator—it can face
In its own littleness the Throne of Grace;
For miracles and "such things" 't is too late,
To trust in them is now quite out of date,
They're all explainable by nature's laws—
Ay! if you only could find out their CAUSE!
I know in these wise days 't is very flat
To ask for any thing so small as that,
But all mankind are not transparent eyes,
They only see things of their usual size,
And, when the very grass beneath their feet
Grows by a law that only God can mete,
Strive not to analyze that mighty will
Which raised the dead, and made the tempest still.
Such doctrines new! they've been repeated oft
Since first the Jews at their Redeemer scoffed,
Stained their vile hands with the Messiah's gore,
And filled the bitter cup to running o'er!
Alas! that *Christian ministers* should dare
To preach the views of Gibbon and Voltaire!
Alas! that one whose life, and gentle ways,
E'en hate could find it in its heart to praise,
Whose intellect is equalled but by few,
Should strive for what he'd weep to find were true!

XIV

Alas for Poesy! her brightness gone,
With draggled plume she flutters lamely on,
Pelted and scoffed at by the rabble rout,

Who mock her heartfelt shame with ribald shout,
And, at each turn their illmatched verses pour,
   Struggling to get apart, (when not too weak,)
While grammar, sense, and taste for mercy roar,
   And metre howls a supplicating shriek,
Buried alive beneath the weight of lead
That pours in masses from the poet's head.
Apollo! crush this milk-and-water school,
Rhymesters by rote and rhapsodists by rule,
Who boldly plagiarize from Mother Goose,
And never grant poor common sense a truce;
Who hunt one little, frightened thought to death,
(At least till they themselves are out of breath,)
And, when recovered from the fruitless chase,
Too stupid e'en to play the fool with grace,
Exclaim, "There's not the slightest use for thought,
If poets would but rhyme as poets ought!"
Fools! in the duck-pond at their kitchen door,
As muddy as their own dull brains or more,
A Hippocrene they discern, and count
Their duly fingered feet beside their fount!
Poor hapless bards! misfortune's eldest sons,
Whose only real followers are duns,
Whose "highest heaven of invention" is
The garret where they spin their quiddities!

XV

Farewell, great Shakspeare! nature's second self,
Compose thyself with care to grace a shelf,
The world now worships bards of that new school
Who show us Nature duly squared by rule,
Who give the length and breadth of every tree
That shades the desert of their poetry,
And sound each brook, whose music as it flows,
Draws notes in concert from the reader's nose.
So in the gardens in Queen Bess's time,
The streams did all that's natural but climb,
And every rock, shrub, flower, tree, and limb,
Was nature bettered by the owner's whim.

Yet memory with mournful smile would turn
Where earth still weeps o'er Shakspeare's sacred urn,
Where Freedom twines fresh wreaths around the bust

Whose sightless orbs watch Milton's holy dust,
And Nature still with drooping eyelid mourns
Her nurseling buried in the tomb of Burns.
Oh Poetry! best gift to mortals given
To color earth with hues that rival Heaven,
Thou hast breathed life in all created things,
And clothed bright Fancy with her roaming wings;
There's not a leaf that frolics on the tree
But has it its tiny cherisher from thee,
There's not a breeze that dances through the air
But thou hast placed some sweet musician there,
And not a flower in whose honeyed mine
Dwells not some sylphid pensioner of thine.
Thine are the fays that trip the verdant ring,
And the sweet spirits of the crystal spring,
Where the worn pilgrim, ere he bend to drink,
Blesses the shape that loves its mossy brink;
Thine are the Peris nursed with rich perfume
Of India's blossoms in their freshest bloom,
Who in the fleeting tints of heaven's bow
Find fitting shelter for their limbs of snow;
Thine are the forms that haunt the ocean cave
Gemmed with the dewdrops of the restless wave;
Thine are the witches, and the elves are thine
Who guard the treasures of the sunless mine;
Thine are the gay processions yearly seen
In fairy carnival at Hallowe'en;[6]
Thine are the legends round the old hall fire
That made young hearts for knightly deeds beat higher,
As the shrill tones of some old withered crone
Told deeds of sin that well might seem her own.
Thine are they all—Oh let us cherish still
The hallowed sprites of fountain, dell, and hill!
Cling fondly to these lovely dreams of eld,
Nor fling away the faith our fathers held
For all that now for deepest pathos passes,
For fifty Peter Bells and half-starved asses![7]

[6] See Burns's "Hallowe'en":—
  "Upon that night, when fairies light,
  ——————————————dance," &c. [Lowell's note.]
  [7] The day has long past when any one would think of ridiculing Wordsworth. As Carlyle says of Fichte, "What is the wit of a thousand wits to him? The cry of a thousand choughs assaulting that old cliff of granite." But his fame as a poet does not rest on Peter Bell, (though it contains passages as beautiful as almost any in the

Long may the wave-worn sailor love to tell
Of maids that bless old ocean's dreary swell,
And long the plaided shepherd thrill to hear
The gude folks' silver bridles ringing clear,
And elfin music stealing through the trees,
Borne on the pinions of the listening breeze!
Lives there a man so cold, that has not felt
With song too deep for words his bosom melt,
When reading something in a woman's eye,
Might tell a skeptic soul could never die,—
Or when his spirit wings its way afar,
To dwell with Fancy in some heavenlit star,—
Or when he sees the demon of the storm
Folding the clouds about his giant form,
Flapping his raven pinions in the west,
The thunder brooding o'er his wind-tost crest,
Nursing the lightnings 'neath his shaggy wing,
Like startled serpents coiled and prompt to spring?
Whose soul so dead but hears in hours like these
A more than common music in the breeze?
Oh! pure as Venus rising from the foam,
Or thoughts that call my muse's bosom home,
Bright as the tear of thanks for comfort spoken,
Or memory's falling on some cherished token,
Fair Poesy, from all thy foes seek rest,
Within the cell of each whole-hearted breast!

XVI

Farewell, bright realm of Poesy! I grieve,
With downward wing, thy purer air to leave;

---

language,) nor on any of his "Nursery" poetry, as it has been termed. A man may be a great genius and yet be mistaken, and so apparently Wordsworth thought himself, for he gradually shook off the style of his younger poetry. He probably saw that what was silly in prose no verse would ever make wiser.

And yet we have floods of verses with *all* the childishness and none of the redeeming points of Wordsworth's earlier style. For instance, Tennyson's "Oh darling Room!" of which one verse will be a sufficient speciman.

"Oh darling room, my heart's delight,
Dear room, the apple of my sight,
With thy two couches soft and white,
There is no room so exquisite,
No little room so warm and bright,
Wherein to read, wherein to write."

The last four lines are considered "so exquisite," that they are repeated in the course of the piece. Some men seem to think, to use Byron's words,

"That Christmas stories tortured into rhyme
Contain the essence of the true sublime." [Lowell's note.]

But canting fanatics next pour along,
Claiming a tribute from my halting song,
And first and greatest, those who roar and rave[8]
O'er the exaggerate tortures of the slave.
Not mine the heart that would not keenly feel
A fellow's moans 'neath slavery's iron heel,
Nor mine the eye which could unquivering see
Oppression grind the weak that clasp his knee,
But still I own no sympathy with those
Whose stony hearts can count the falling blows,
Who, standing at safe distance, boldly gnash
Their teeth in concert with the whistling lash,
And make a sermon on each purple drop,
Which shrill invectives strive in vain to stop.
Shall Britain too ship saintly cargoes o'er,[9]
To add their whinings to the general roar,
(With maids who, finding flattery too tame,
Mistake their eartrumps for the trump of fame,)
And stop her ears to Erin's mournful cry[10]
Of babes and mothers in their agony,
Where blood of hue as crimson as her own
Cries from the ground to the Almighty's throne,
And famine grinning o'er each cheerless hearth
Mocks shrinking misery with her fiendish mirth?
Oh, England! England! while thy snowy sails
Swell to the kiss of earth's remotest gales,
And all beneath thy meteor flag is free,[11]
As the wild wave that wafts it o'er the sea,
When 't is thy pride that chains can gall no more,
The wretch whose fettered foot hath touched thy shore,
When every Briton, be he ne'er so mean,

[8] It is too late in the day now to *sneer* at Abolitionists. Even their enemies have come to that conclusion. For I suppose there is not a man in New England who is not an abolitionist at heart. But those fanatics who try to get up an excitement, and especially the females (if I may be allowed to call them so) who go round ranting, when they ought to be at home educating their children, are deserving of more than ridicule. For those who have reached what Dante calls the "mezzo cammin de nostra vita," "In *maiden* meditation, fancy free," there is more apology perhaps. Hamlet's advice to Polonius, not to let his daughter "walk i' the sun," might be a great deal benefited by.
   " 'T is a pity when charming women
    Talk about what they don't understand." [Lowell's note.]
[9] George Thomson, being in dread of the bailiffs in Glasgow, hit upon the ingenious plan of drawing a revenue from, by blackguarding, us. [Lowell's note.]
[10] See the "Report on the Irish Poor Laws," &c. [Lowell's note.]
[11] "The meteor flag of England
    Shall yet terrific burn," &c.—CAMPBELL. [Lowell's note.]

Claims rights as sacred as thy virgin queen,
Shall it be whispered to thy endless shame,
Thy bounds held worse than slaves without the name?
Slaves whom no duller current in their veins,[12]
Or different skin had doomed to scourge and chains?
And dost thou talk of mercy? dread the rod
In the red hand of an offended God!

But to my theme,—I would not call him knave,
Who breaks the hated fetters of the slave,
But I *do* blame that man who takes his place
The self-made benefactor of his race,
Who in his zeal his neighbor's eye to free
From motes that calumny can hardly see,
Dreams not that aught can shadow *his* clear sight,
Showing him all things in a jaundiced light,
And in his care about another's sins,
On Satan's threshold breaks his own sweet shins.
Bold saints! why tell us here of those who scoff
At law and reason thousands of miles off?
Why punish us with your infernal din,
For what you tell us is the planter's sin?
Why on the North commence the fierce crusade,
And war on them for ills the South has made?

"What! would you have them run the risk to mar
Their saintly sleekness with a coat of tar?
When they can gain the name of martyrs here
With half the breath they'd gasp for there with fear?
Did blest St. Paul e'er turn his footsteps south,
Or in the slave-states even ope his mouth?
We do not find he risked his life at all,
Pray why should our saints go beyond St. Paul?"

Gone are those days when Christians held it grace,
To treat like Christians all the human race;
But lives there one whose calm and manly pen
Can lash the vice, yet scorn to wound the men,
Whose temperate zeal would liberate the slave,

---

[12] Cowper says,
                    "He finds
His fellow creature guilty of a skin
Not colored like his own"—
and dooms him to chains, &c. I forget his precise words. [Lowell's note.]

Yet shrink to desecrate the master's grave,
Whose heart, with Christian mildness running o'er,
Disdains to curse whom God has cursed before,
Whose mind like purest crystal gives to view
Each ray of truth adorned with rainbow hue,
And in whose broad philanthropy find place,
Not slaves alone, but all the human race?
Yes! still thank God! some pilgrim blood remains
To stir the lazy current of our veins,
Thank God! that stout New England's rocky earth
To men of simple virtue yet gives birth!
And Truth may point to where no breath of blame
Can wilt the wreaths that circle CHANNING's name!

XVII

But most of all my maiden muse would scorn[13]
That hybrid race, nor man nor woman born,
Whose misplaced petticoats are all the claim
They have upon the latter hallowed name;
Who leave their zero husbands in the lurch,
To raise a riot at some new free church,
Who wish to prove by force of arms that they
With man should hold at least divided sway,
And so without regard to where or when,
They play the fool as wisely as the men.
Oh woman! gentle woman! given to show
How much man has to struggle for below,
Whose smile can well reward each action high,
And kindle courage in the quailing eye,
Who know'st untaught so well the minstrel's art,
To touch the strings of music in the heart,
And in whose spirit's calmer, purer tone,
There breathes a spell to harmonize our own,
Who that has ever read in almost trance
The soul's full language speaking in thy glance,
Who that has seen thy modest eyes just dare
To meet his own and read thine image there,
Who that has ever knelt before thy shrine

13 I would remind the advocates of the "Rights" of Women of the ingenious expedient of a king of the Longobards, to get rid of the teazings of his wife and other ladies of his court for a share in the government of the state. There is another story extant in which the women actually raised the standard of revolt, and were only saved from bloodshed by an expedient as ingenious, though not quite so printable, as the other. [Lowell's note.]

And murmured vows that only can be thine,
Would render up those magic master keys
That ope the inmost heart to claims like these?
Like stars, thy sphere is far above the strife
And petty turmoils of our work-day life,
Shrinking from public noisiness, as they
Fade from the glances of the "eye of day,"
Yet still, as old astrologers divined,
With all our fortune's windings close entwined.

XVIII

Nor this the worst, the groves of academe
Have echoed to the Negroes' fancied scream,
And youths, the down upon whose cultured chins
Scarce lifts its head to blame the razor's sins,
Take up the cry in treble, tenor, bass,
To mourn the woes of Afric's fallen race.
Freshmen, just set at liberty from school,
Their palms still tingling for some broken rule,
Who stand quite speechless when they strive to scan,
Leave Zumpt, to squabble o'er the rights of man;
Nor need the prophet's eye look far to see,
In the dim vista of futurity,
Little enthusiasts mounting on their stools,
To curse the slave-states in our infant schools.
E'en where Religion mildly strives to teach
Her ward, the graver graduate, to preach,
Men, though forbidden, break the college laws
To meet and show their zeal in virtue's cause,
And fierce invectives in the chapel there
Jar with the music of the rising prayer.

XIX

Oh abolitionists, both men and maids,
Who leave your desks, your parlors, and your trades,
To wander restless through the land and shout,
But few of you could tell us what about!
Can ye not hear where on the Southern breeze
Swells the last wailing of the Cherokees?
Hark! the sad Indian sighs a last adieu
To scenes which memory gilds with brighter hue,
The giant trees whose hoary branches keep
Their quiet vigil where his fathers sleep,

'Neath the green sod upon whose peaceful breast
He too had hoped to lay him down to rest—
The woods through whose dark shades, unknown to fear,
He roamed as freely as the bounding deer,
The streams so well his boyish footsteps knew
Pleased with the tossings of the mock canoe,
And the vast mountains, round whose foreheads proud,
Curled the dark grandeur of the roaming cloud,
From whose unfathomed breast he oft has heard
In thunder tones the good Great Spirit's word.
Lo where he stands upon yon towering peak
That echoes with the startled eagle's shriek,
His scalptuft floating wildly to the gale
Which howls an answer to his mournful wail,
Leaning his arm upon an unbent bow,
He thus begins in accents sad and low—

1

"We must go! for already more near and more near
The tramp of the paleface falls thick on the ear—
Like the roar of the blast when the storm-spirit comes
Is the clang of the trumps and the death-rolling drums.
Farewell to the spot where the pine trees are sighing
O'er the flowery turf where our fathers are lying!
Farewell to the forests our young hunters love,
We shall soon chase the deer with our fathers above!

2

"We must go! and no more shall our council-fires glance
On the senate of chiefs or the warriors' dance,
No more in its light shall youth's eagle eye gleam,
Or the glazed sight of age become young in its beam.
Wail! wail! for our nation; its glory is o'er,
These hills with our war-songs shall echo no more,
And the eyes of our bravest no more shall look bright,
As they hear of the deeds of their fathers in fight!

3

"In the home of our sires we have lingered our last,
Our death-song is swelling the moan of the blast,
Yet to each hallowed spot clings fond memory still,
Like the mist that makes lovely yon far distant hill.
The eyes of our maidens are heavy with weeping,

The fire 'neath the brow of our young men is sleeping,
And the half-broken hearts of the aged are swelling,
As the smoke curls its last round their desolate dwelling!

4

"We must go! but the wailings ye wring from us here
Shall crowd your foul prayers from the Great Spirit's ear,
And when *ye* pray for mercy, remember that Heaven
Will forgive (so ye taught us) as *ye* have forgiven![14]
Ay slay! and our souls on the pinions of prayer
Shall mount freely to Heaven and seek justice there,
For the flame of our wigwams points sadly on high
To the sole path of mercy ye've left us—to die!

5

"God's glad sun shone as warm on our once peaceful homes
As when gilding the pomp of your proud swelling domes,
And his wind sang a pleasanter song to the trees
Than when rustling the silk in your temples of ease;
For He judges not souls by their flesh-garment's hue,
And his heart is as open for us as for you;
Though he fashioned the Redman of duskier skin,
Yet the Paleface's breast is far darker within!

6

"We are gone! the proud Redman hath melted like snow
From the soil that is tracked by the foot of his foe;
Like a summer cloud spreading its sails to the wind,
We shall vanish and leave not a shadow behind.

[14] Our policy towards the Indians has never been equalled, except by the Saracen disciples of Mahomet. We give them the Bible with one hand and the sword with the other. The Indian's remarks on this point in the text appear to me just and sensible. Here is a speciman of our humane policy. General Jesup writes to Mr. Poinsett, Secretary of War, as follows. "The villages of the Indians have all been destroyed; and their cattle, horses, and other stock, with nearly all their other property, taken or destroyed. . . . They have nothing of value left but their rifles.

"These results, trifling as they are compared with those of the Creek campaign," &c. Vide *Boston Daily Advertiser*, Aug. 2, 1838.

This man's heart must be of a very peculiar texture—"these results, trifling as they are"! How well prepared these poor fellows must be to "emigrate" into the Pacific Ocean! The coolness with which the General talks of burning and destroying is only to be equalled by that of the boys pelting frogs. Why,

                       "The common executioner,
Whose heart the accustomed sight of death makes hard,
Falls not the axe upon the humbled neck,
But first begs pardon."—[Lowell's note.]

The blue old Pacific roars loud for his prey,
As he taunts the tall cliffs with his glittering spray,
And the sun of our glory sinks fast to his rest
All darkly and dim in the clouds of the west!"

The cadence ends, and where the Indian stood[15]
The rock looks calmly down on lake and wood,
Meet emblem of that lone and haughty race,
Whose strength hath passed in sorrow from its place.

XX

Oppression, Famine, Pestilence, and Steam[16]
Have done their worst upon this fated race—
They fade in silence, as a morning dream,
Before Improvement's forest-levelling pace;
And soon by mountain, valley, wood, and stream,
The stranger scarce shall find the Indian's trace:
The Whiteman's avarice asks a rood of earth—
And lo! the ploughshare rends the Redman's hearth!

XXI

And yet his heart, though wilder, beats as warm,
And clings as fondly to his wigwam's hearth
As if its case were whiter, and his form
Steps nobler o'er the soil that gave him birth,
Ay, manlier bears the peltings of the storm—
And shall we grudge him six poor feet of earth
(His own by birthright) where to lay his head,
And sleep in quiet with the happier dead?

XXII

Has conscience never whispered in our ear,
The untutored Redman too has had a mother,
His brow is holy with a mother's tear—
Baptismal font more pure than any other—

---

[15] My readers may think that I have kept the poor savage exposed rather too long on his elevated position. Those, who had the pleasure of seeing our Pawnee visitors last autumn, will not think much of their dread of exposure. The knight of the rueful countenance, when his gambols excited the holy horror of his faithful esquire, was nothing to them. Besides, his indignation would not allow him to think of cold or colds. [Lowell's note.]

[16] The sinking of a steamboat, and drowning of *"about* three hundred" (for our government talks of them as if they were cattle) "emigrants,"—for such is the soft expression,—is probably fresh in every one's mind. "Emigrants," good lack! a man might as well be called an "emigrant," who was kicked out of his own door by some impudent interloper. [Lowell's note.]

He too has held some dark-eyed maiden dear,
　　His wayward heart has yearned towards a brother—
Nay, more—perchance the pure, undying light
Of sister's love has made his wigwam bright?

XXIII

Some thirst of vengeance slakes this side the tomb,
　　And ceases with the mournful bell's long toll
That calls the victim to his cell of gloom—
　　But we—oh deepest bloodspot on the scroll
Of God's recording angel! *we* would doom
　　Alike the Redman's body and his soul:
We sell him *first* our whiskey, then the Word,
Then punish Gospel-breaking with the sword!

XXIV

I've often wondered, and I often wonder
　　If God has ceased to look with wrath on crime,
If lifted hands, fresh from unholy plunder,
　　All red and reeking with their bloody slime,
Can rise in prayer, nor dread his angry thunder—
　　Our nation seems to think so—but will Time
Be of the same opinion? What will be
The juster verdict of Futurity?

XXV

Has the warm blood of seventy-six grown cold?
　　Has Freedom left her Cradle to rush in
And join the general scramble after gold?
　　One heart hath plead against a nation's sin;
Where Liberty's first blood was dearly sold,[17]
　　One voice hath risen o'er the work-day din,
And told far better than my heavy song
Our Country's baseness and the Indian's wrong.

[17] Rev. R. W. Emerson's letter—which does equal honor to his head and heart. There was a peculiar fitness in its being dated at Concord, where the first blood of the Revolution flowed.

Speaking of Concord—having spent most of my "vacation" in that town, I can recommend it as a residence for any student, whose precarious state of health requires a change of air. Though the situation is low, the air is salubrious.

The inhabitants (to whom I return my heartfelt thanks for their kind attention to a stranger) are hospitable and pleasant. Moreover, I can bestow the still higher commendation on them, that (which is rare in country towns) they mind their own business wonderfully. P.S. I have been informed that this last is only at *one end* of the town. [Lowell's note.]

XXVI

That voice pealed out where first the Heavenly fire
  Came down to light the altar of the free—
'T is fit the blaze should thus be kindled higher,
  And spread its holy light from sea to sea;
Oh may it still descend from hoary sire
  To son—a heritage of Liberty;
And may our maidens, as in ancient Rome,
Still nurse this vestal flame, whose shrine is—home!

XXVII

Oh for a voice of pleading like the roar
  Of many waters—that its tones might sweep
In mournful deepness on from shore to shore,
  And wake the heart of mercy from its sleep!
Rouse! Rouse ye! ere the hour for right is o'er,
  Ere justice shall have nought to do but weep!
Rouse, ere the bloody vintage yet be trod[18]
To fill the wine-cup of the wrath of God!

XXVIII

When the last dreaded trump of doom shall sound,
  That calls us from our narrow place of rest
To meet our Judge—shall we be spotless found?
  Will not the earth lie heavy on our breast,
Where cries our brother's heart's blood from the ground?
  Will not the gold we've wrung from the opprest,
Though now it buy us friends and fools and power,
Weigh like a mountain on us in that hour?

XXIX

Oh ye who ship supplies to struggling Greece,
  Or furnish flannel waistcoats for the slave,
And get a fraction of a thank apiece,
  Telling the public just how much ye gave—
Do all your tender pricks of conscience cease,
  Because there's none to *call* you "good" or "brave"?

[18] "The same shall drink the wine of the wrath of God, which is poured out without mixture into the cup of his indignation.

"And the angel thrust in his sickle into the earth, and gathered the vine of the earth, and cast it into the great winepress of the wrath of God.

"And the winepress was trodden . . . and blood ran out of the winepress."—Rev. xiv. 10, 19, 20. [Lowell's note.]

Will not your hearts grow warm unless your name
Gain in the Newspapers a half-hour's "fame"?

.   .   .   .   .

XXX

'T is true our army didn't shed much blood,[19]
    (Unless beneath some cunning flag of truce,
When they nipt all our honor in the bud,)
    In fact they were not of important use,
Except to lose the nation's shoes in mud,
    And blackguard foes (when distant) like the deuce—
It would have spared the Treasury a groan,
Had General Jesup waded round alone.

XXXI

He might have killed as many as he chose—
    On paper[20]—without losing e'en a man;
He might have brought the campaign to a close
    (Had he but tried this economic plan)
Ere Brother Jonathan could blow his nose;
    As 't was, indeed, the little blood that ran
Was shed with ink—which saved more lives than pence,
Since *that* was furnished at the State's expense.

XXXII

Time was when men were wont to show their scars,[21]
    When standing candidate for any place,

[19] General Hermandez is already so essentially damned to fame, that it is impossible that my voice should add at all to his unenviable celebrity. If I thought that my small voice could add at all to the greenness of his laurels, I would exert it most cheerfully.—With regard to the brave conduct of our army, I shall speak in the words of Falstaff. "I call thee coward! I'll see thee damned ere I call thee coward: but I would give a thousand pound I could run as fast as thou canst. You are straight enough in your shoulders, you care not who sees your back." Most of the battles were fought, I suspect, "by Shrewsbury clock," and more pains were taken by our army to *save* their own scalps than to *take* those of the enemy, who, most unfortunately, had a habit of carrying off their dead, much in the same way as their invaders always made it a principle to convey away their *living*. This they did with a "quick dexterity," that "honest Jack" might have envied. [Lowell's note.]

[20] This was the method of the "deep-contemplative" Touchstone—"Oh sir, we quarrel in print, by the book." Perhaps Uncle Toby's plan of fighting his battles o'er again would be as cheap and more amusing. [Lowell's note.]

[21]
>   "MENENIUS.
>   It then remains,
>   That you do speak to the people.
>   CORIOLANUS.
>   I do beseech you,

Telling of battles "quorum magna pars"
And so forth—*now* that's not the case,
Our heroes *talk* in tones might frighten Mars—
    Should chance e'er bring them but before his face—
As yet they've never met him, though they saw
During the last campaign—one living Squaw!

.   .   .   .   .   .

XXXIII

Immortal Cant! beneath thy sheltering wing
The ultra temperance men their pæans sing,
Inspired, as any man of sense would think,
By no peculiarly inspiring drink;
At least quite guiltless of those sparkling waters,
Which flow for all Apollo's sons and daughters,
Where Pegasus struck out with hoof of fire
That spring which ends its winding course in mire.
Full many poets seek this wondrous fount,
Where it rolls brightly down the muse's mount,
But getting wearied ere they reach its source,
Drink,—strive to sing,—and find their voices hoarse,
And oft when verse just spreads its opening bud,
Stick fast, and flounder in the fertile mud.
So 't is I fear with you, poor bards, who shape
Your couplets dull to hack the harmless grape,
Pray cease to shame fair water with your praise,
But pour it on your self-created bays,
Drown yourselves in 't,—do any foolish thing,
('T will be quite natural,) but do *not* sing![22]

"Be temperate in *all* things," Scripture saith,
And there, there only, will I pin my faith.

    Let me o'erleap that custom; for I cannot
    Put on the gown, stand naked, and entreat them,
    For my wounds' sake to give me suffrage."
If any of our soldiers *should* take up this plan, though it is scarce possible, they
might use the same address that Coriolanus thought of—
                            "Look, sir!—my wounds!
    I got them in my country's service, when
    Some certain of your brethren roared, and ran
    From the noise of our own drums." [Lowell's note.]
[22] Their verses put one in mind of Touchstone's remark: "I'll rhyme you so eight
years together; dinners, and suppers, and sleeping hours excepted."
    "For God's sake stop, my friend! 't were best—
    Non Di, non homines—you know the rest."
                            BYRON'S *Vision of Judgment*. [Lowell's note.]

Who damns another in the world to come
Because he drinks no dearer drink than rum,
While his own feet avoid a rectiline,
Led by the costlier blandishments of wine;—
Or loads his duller neighbor with abuse,
To show him poison in the grape's bright juice,
And runs stark mad in his indecent haste
To cure these sinners of their wretched taste,
Sins much as he who reeling through the street
Tramples his reason 'neath his drunken feet.
The worst intoxication man can feel
Is that which drains the burning cup of zeal;
This lights the fagots of the martyr's pile,
And eyes his writhings with a pious smile,
This fired the madness of that bloody train,
Who erewhile made a slaughter-house of Spain,
This mewed the heretic in dungeons damp,
Which knew no cheering but the jailor's lamp,
Tried mild conversion on his shrinking back,
Or used the Christian pleadings of the rack,
And strove with flame and carnage to increase
The holy army of the Prince of Peace!

Oh world-philanthropy! Oh cant and stuff!
Of thy blest influence we've seen enough,
Whether you prove war's ills by force of fist,
Make your own ends seem public good by mist,
In zeal to spread your temperance pledges wider
Fell apple-trees to stop the use of cider,
Or fill your purse and show your moral bravery
By suffering eggdom in abusing slavery.
Time was (dark age) ere men had oped their eyes
To see the good of being pennywise;[23]
When women, men, yea, families might eat
Just what they pleased, or prudence thought most meet,
And did n't know (poor fools!) that half the time
They swallowed poison and committed crime.
'T is truly shocking to the feeling breast,
To think what nightmares must have broke their rest,
Turtles in aldermanic gowns and wigs

[23] "Penny wise and pound foolish."—*Old proverb.*
Mr. Buckingham's advice on the subject of diet contains sound doctrine,—"Eat your victuals, and go about your business." [Lowell's note.]

Walk side by side with ghosts of martyred pigs,
Geese,—stop! humanity the list gives o'er,
For Graham nerves such thoughts can bear no more!
What constitutions those men must have had!
It well-nigh drives Benevolence stark mad,
To think how long they might have stretched their span
Had they but lived on chips or even bran;
For as it was they often reached fourscore,
Nay, sometimes even lingered on still more,
In spite of all the meat and drink and mirth,
Which had been preying on them from their birth,
Slow poisons, it is true, but sure to send
Their victims to the graveyard in the end.
Now the philanthropists have changed all that,
No heresy's so damnable as fat,
And soon they trust no mortal will be seen
Whom decency or bran have not made lean.
Nor is the day far distant when mankind
Shall brush time's gathering cobwebs from the mind,
And, rising far above base nature's thrall,
Become too wise to eat or drink at all.
Full many men grow thin from year to year
On sawdust puddings and imagined beer,
And one great hero, (so his brethren say,)
Lessened his useless dinner day by day,
Until at length, as every wise man ought,
He tried the plan of living upon nought.
As grew the spirit strong the flesh grew weak,
And in eight days the patriot scarce could speak,
Two more rolled on and put him in his bed,
Another,—and he scarce could raise his head.
His thin disciples thronged to see and hear
The lessening progress of a man so dear,
When, just as the attempt had met success,
And proved man thrived on nullity or less,
The skeleton turned slowly on its side,
Muttered, "I live, you see, on nought!" and—died!
The bones of this improver of our race
Were *thinly* followed to their resting place,
By *crowds* of worshippers from far and near,
Who keep the anniversary every year,
And on that day convene a general meeting
"For the Suppression of superfluous eating."

(N. B. The worms, not finding aught to eat,
Voted the man a "most notorious cheat.")

.　　.　　.　　.　　.

XXXIV

Shade of the past! recall that golden age,
The brightest line on Alma Mater's page,
When Massachusetts and her sisters young
Stood fair as Helen from her eggshell sprung,
Their red cheeks blushing on the passer by
In all the glow of maiden modesty!
Blest days! when Freshmen in the college yard[24]
Trembled if Seniors did but eye them hard;
Compelled by law to walk uncovered there,
Their wigs grew restive with each breath of air,
And sometimes did, with all their weight of curls,
Perform with grace a few aerial twirls.
They dug Greek roots, nor joined in deep debate
On equal rights and great affairs of state.
Enough for them to carry down their bowls
Each morn and eve for Commons' milk and rolls,
At noon to gather round the frugal table
And get the lion's share if they were able;
They never shed a sympathetic tear
For Afric's sufferings o'er their daily beer,[25]
Nor as they mixed the sugar in their cup
Groaned for slave-labor ere they drank it up.
No brighter light upon their brains had beamed,
Of other diet they had never dreamed;
They little thought that in their beef or roll,
They swallowed parts of "Universal *Soul*,"
(Unless indeed they thought of some such stuff,
And scraped to show it, when their meat was tough,)
Nor knew (poor ignoramuses!) how good
A knotty formula might be for food.
Those days are past; oh change thou rulest all,
From lofty Sophomore to Freshman small!

[24] "And at all times the *Freshmen* were to keep their hats off in the yard, unless when it rained. The resident graduates and all the senior classes were allowed to send the Freshmen on errands as they saw fit."—See PEIRCE'S *History*, p. 309. [Lowell's note.]

[25] "The breakfast was two sizings of bread and a *cue of beer*."—PEIRCE, p. 219. [Lowell's note.]

Poor Alma Mater feels thy withering blight
And even PROCTORS bow before thy might!

Where is that band,—Bellona tell me where,—
Whose banner once so proudly wooed the air,
And thrice a year on Exhibition days
Flung out its folds to bask in beauty's gaze?
Alas that banner, rent in many a fight,
No more shall greet the blushing ensign's sight,
No more shall kindle valor's fading eye
And lead the marshalled ranks to victory!
No more the braying trump and rattling drum
Tell the glad town-boy that the warriors come,
No more shall Freshman wipe his streaming eyes,
Swelling to reach the regulated size,
And hearts, for their small casings all too large,
Throb for the honor of the bloodless charge!
Brave band! how ardent was the serried line
When led to battle with good Kirkland's wine,
And how each manly bosom mocked at fear
In the fierce onset upon Quincy's cheer!
All this is gone, and graduates as they pass,
Can only shake their heads and sigh "Alas!"
The flag neglected darkly gathers dust,
The sword's bright eye grows dim with gathering rust,
Mars o'er the relics hangs with drooping head,—
The flower of Harvard's chivalry is dead!

But though old Harvard's gallant soldiers sleep,
Her navy still is queen upon the deep,
And still each year she spreads her swelling sail[26]
To court the dalliance of the summer gale;
And still all those who do not take a part
In college honors, learn the seaman's art,
And when one qualm of sorrow gives them pain,
Cast all their burdens on the azure main.
Gently sweet Westernwind unfurl thy pinion,
To waft them through old Neptune's blue dominion,
Softly as calmest slumber rustle o'er
The wave that bears them from the lessening shore,
And bring in safety landward through the foam
These floating bulwarks of their country home!

[26] Alas! she didn't *this* year! [Lowell's note.]

Shades of Hippocrates and Galen! tell
Where are the youths who loved your art so well?
Gone,—like the snow before the Southwind's breath,
Gone,—like a patient to expectant Death,
Who wisely hopes to 'scape all human ills,
Not by a rope, but,—Doctor Brandreth's pills!
Weep Esculapius! weep above the tomb,
Where lie thy sons cut off in manhood's bloom!
None knew so well as they to trace the woes
Of sickly students, and prescribe repose,
None could administer with so much skill
A dose from Willard's, or an oyster pill;
For, unlike most practitioners who try
On some poor dog their skill in pharmacy,
These youthful heroes nobly dared the worst,
And boldly tried their own prescriptions first.
They brought the cold bath to its *highest* glory,
Testing its value from some upper story,
In all complaints of spirit or of flesh,
Particularly when the case was *Fresh*.

XXXV

Classmates, I've nearly done, and yet to day,
Our last together,—there is much to say,—
The strength of ties that twine around the heart
Is but half known till they are torn apart.
Four years we've been here making friends and foes,
With passable success, as this world goes,
And this perhaps is our last earthly chance,
To give a friendly or a chilling glance.
Four years, four long and seeming snailpaced years
Of revels, quarrels, friendships, smiles, and tears,
Have passed,—and do we gather here
As when the bell first smote our Freshman ear?
Has no sharp pang of common sorrow wrung us?
Has not Death's icy hand been stretched among us?
Has no loved voice become forever still?
No merry heart grown heavy, cold, and chill?
Has no bright eye waxed dim, no red cheek pale
At the dread horrors of the "shadowy vale"?
Ay! one there was,[27]—alas for me that mine

[27] Edward Charles Mussey—drowned while bathing in Charles River in July, 1835. [Continued, p. 245.]

Should be the task to trace this mournful line!—
Whose seat stands empty, whose brief journey's o'er,
The place that knew him knows him now no more.
Alas! too soon he left our saddened band,
An earlier pilgrim to a better land!
Yes! while our sojourn here hath lingered on,
One bright, pure spirit to his home hath gone,
Whose sunny smile, whose mind serenely gay,
Once cheered the dulness of our weary way,—
A heart more warm, more manly, and sincere,
More pure and gentle is not beating here.
That heart, when first we gathered here for prayer,
With youthful hope was dancing light as air,
And Alma Mater, were he with us now,
Had twined her wreath to grace his manly brow.

Classmate! while yet our trembling voices swell
The mournful melody of this farewell,
Oh, from thy spirit-home above descend,
And in the strain thy voice of music blend!
Brother! if pall and hearse and mourners' tread
Are all of death,—then thou indeed art dead;
But if thy sainted image deep imprest
Within the shrine of every Classmate's breast,
Entwined with evergreen,—if Memory's tear
Of tempered anguish o'er thine early bier,—
If to be cherished still with fond regret
Have aught of living,—here thou livest yet!
Pace Quiescas! may the wild flowers bloom
With fresher verdure round thy hallowed tomb,
Nurtured by dews, tears such as Heaven weeps
O'er the green pillow where her servant sleeps!

Watch o'er him Nature! truest friend of earth,
Who smilest on us ever from our birth,
And after death, when friends have all forgot,
Or scarce remember, still forgettest not!
Who, when affection's flowers have ceased to bloom,

"If friendship's smile, the better part of fame,
Should lend my song the only wreath I claim,
Whose voice would greet me with a sweeter tone,
Whose living hand more kindly press my own,
Than *thine?*" [Lowell's note.]

Twinest thy yearly wreath around our tomb
Of blue-eyed violets and that flower pale,
That claims a parent in the summer gale.
Oh! mildly cherish him,—for he was mild,
And like a mother,—for he was thy child,
And wantonly ne'er crushed the meanest thing
That nestled 'neath thy all-protecting wing!

XXXVI

Brothers! we part upon the sounding shore
    That curbs the waters of life's heaving sea,
We part perchance to meet again no more
    This side the haven of Eternity—
Then nerve to breast the billows' angry roar
    Alone!—this moment breaks our company,
And though we shrink to hear the waters moan,
We now must sink or struggle on—alone!

XXXVII

Alone! Alone! oh what a mournful spell
    One simple word may work upon the heart!
How many a tale one word—one look may tell
    Of pathos far beyond the reach of art!
How much of untold agony may dwell
    In those two little syllables—"We part!"
They touch a thrilling string within the breast,
No time—no sorrow e'er can put at rest.

XXXVIII

Each word of friendship lightly spoke to day
    May be a resting-place for Memory—
Each silly jokelet, scattered by the way,
    May call the woman to some graybeard's eye,
As Fancy wanders back in idle play
    To these bright hours when boyish hopes were high.
Poor withered buds, nipt by the world's cold blast,
To deck the bosom of the mournful past!

XXXIX

Nay, e'en this silly, half-forgotten song
    May win a smile upon some wrinkled cheek,
As some gray classmate slowly spells along,
    Aloud (as old men will, whose wits grow weak)

With spectacles on nose, and voice half strong,
   Half blending with an aged treble squeak—
Shaking his drowsy head as it recalls
Some long-lost dream of Alma Mater's halls.

XL

Those last lines make me think of Time and Fate,
   Who, think you, will outlive the rest o' the class—
Perchance himself—and die at last too late?
   Who shall sleep soundly 'neath next summer's grass?
Nay, smile not, Reader! that may be *thy* date—
   For e'en these very moments, as they pass,
Carry some mother's son, with youthful form
As dear as thine, to pillow with the worm!

XLI

Enough of this—whate'er may be our lot,
   We'll look with love upon our sojourn here,
And memory still shall hover round the spot,
   Nor check the tender tribute of a tear,—
A Classmate—Brother—ne'er shall be forgot,
   While one poor leaf makes glad life's waning year—
And though old Time in his provoking way
May change our locks—our hearts shall ne'er grow gray!

XLII

Now onward! single, and yet not alone,
   But in the hollow of His mighty hand
Who yoked the planets in their boundless zone,
   Who set the ocean and the steadfast land,
And yet who calls the meanest thing his own—
   Launch out then boldly from the idle strand,
Where'er we wander on the pathless deep
His arm is nigh to guide us and to keep!

XLIII

Youth's morn shines clear, hurrah! the wave is bright,
   The gleaming ripples dance right joyously,
And through the foam our barks shall bound as light
   As floats yon vapor in its upper sea—
Hoist sail! we'll dare Misfortune's fellest spite,
   And buffet stoutly with old Destiny,
Until we reach some pleasant sunny isle
In life's long voyage where to rest awhile!

XLIV

And now farewell! again—again farewell!
 That word, though mournful, has a soothing tone,
Like the sad music of a passing bell,
 Which, swelling from some hamlet far and lone,
Hath travelled long o'er forest, hill, and dell,
 To warn us that some brother soul hath flown—
God bless you all! farewell yet once agen!
Plunge in the strife and quit yourselves like men!

Lady! whom I have dared to call my muse,
 With thee my lay began, with thee shall end—
Thou can'st not such a poor request refuse
 To let thine image with its closing blend!
As turn the flowers to the quiet dews,
 Fairest, so turns my yearning heart to thee,
For thee it pineth—as the homesick shell
 Mourns to be once again beneath the sea—
Oh let thine eyes upon this tribute dwell,
 And think—one moment kindly think of me!
 Alone—my spirit seeks thy company,
And in all beautiful communes with thine,
 In crowds—it ever seeks alone to be
To dream of gazing in thy gentle eyne!

Concord, August 21, 1838.

NOTES ON THE POEMS

Page 3: "Ye Yankees of the Bay State." *Boston Morning Post,* February 26, 1839. p. 1. Lowell's prefatory note was dated *"Boston, Feb.* 20, 1839" and read: *"Mr. Greene*—I have heard that Governor Everett has sent a message to the Legislature, saying that we have nothing to do with the troubles in Maine; I confess, that though I agree with him in politics, (as far as I have any) I could not keep down my indignation on hearing this, but boiled over into the following verses, which you may print if you will." Governor Everett was a Whig. The poem relates to the Maine border dispute between the United States and Canada which led in 1839 to the so-called "Aroostook War" in which armed engagements occurred.

Page 4: "The Lover's Drink-Song." *Southern Literary Messenger,* VI, no. 6 (June, 1840), 469. A MS of this poem appears on pp. 14, 15 of the MS, now in the Pierpont Morgan Library, of the volume *A Year's Life.* This MS must have been going to press within a few months after the poem appeared in the *Southern Literary Messenger,* but for some reason Lowell decided not to reproduce it and crossed it out in the MS. The Pierpont Morgan MS is identical with the version in the *Southern Literary Messenger* except for minor variations in punctuation. An earlier MS appears in a letter to Loring, May 17, 1840 (Harvard Library). A sentence in the letter associates the poem with Lowell's affection for Maria White whom he had met the previous autumn. Differences between the printed version and the Loring MS are indicated in the footnotes.

Page 5: "Agatha." *Boston Miscellany of Literature,* I, no. 1 (January, 1842), 9-10. The text is dated "September, 1840." Ascribed conjecturally to Lowell by Scudder, II, Appendix C, 423; listed in Cooke.

Page 8: "The Two." *Boston Miscellany of Literature,* I, no. 5 (May, 1842), 213-14. "By James R. Lowell." The text is dated "Nov. 1840."

Page 9: "Callirhöe." *Graham's Magazine,* XVIII, no. 3 (March, 1841), 100-101. "By H. Perceval." The text is dated "Cambridge, Mass., 1841." This poem is mentioned in two letters to Loring: March 29, 1840, and June 29, 1840 (Harvard Library). These letters indicate that the poem was submitted to *Burton's Magazine* in competition for a prize of $100. for a "poem of over 200 lines." In the second letter, Lowell wrote that he meant to send the poem to Margaret Fuller for publication in the *Dial*.

Page 14: "Sonnet—To Keats." *Boston Miscellany of Literature*, I, no. 1 (January, 1842) 3. "By James Russell Lowell." The text is dated "March, 1841." A MS of this poem will be found on p. 1 of the MS of the volume, *A Year's Life* in the Pierpont Morgan Library. The poem, dated "March 28, 1841," did not appear in the printed volume which went to press toward the end of 1840. Since the page concerning this MS poem is laid in before the dedicatory poem of the volume, it seems unlikely that it was part of the copy sent to press by Lowell for his volume.

Page 14: "Merry England." *Graham's Magazine*, XIX, no. 5 (November, 1841) 238-39. "By J. R. Lowell." This is one of the most extraordinary of the poet's early humanitarian expressions of his interest in social reform. In it he makes reference to his disapproval of England in the "Opium War" which was ended in the next year, 1842, by the Treaty of Nanking. At the same time he refers with wry approval to the emancipation of slaves in the British Colonies which had occurred in 1833. The bulk of his poem, however, is a satire against British privileged classes centering upon his sympathy for the oppressed classes then engaged in the long struggle known as the Chartist movement. Ever since the unsatisfactory Reform Bill of 1832 there had been continuous agitation leading to the "People's Charter," so-called, a declaration on popular objectives in 1838. In the same year, of course, the Anti-Corn League was formed through the activities of John Bright and Richard Cobden. It was less than 3 years after these events that Lowell was writing the present poem, so that his references are in the nature of contemporary protest. Indeed, it was not until the next year, 1842, that the first reasonably liberal Factory Act was passed. The other element of satire in this poem is directed toward the situation in Ireland, which had been aggravated since the Catholic Relief Act of 1829 liberalized the laws permitting Catholics to hold certain offices, while at the same time imposing property qualifications which excluded the poor even from the franchise. The poem shows his contemporary and immediate interest in economic and social reform at the very moment when the conditions stimulated by the Industrial Revolution and by British discrimination against the less privileged classes were most severe. The copy of this poem addressed to "Charles J.

Peterson, Esq., Philadelphia, Penn." and dated within, "April 17. 1841," is in the Berg Collection, New York Public Library. The variants are from this MS.

Page 18: "I love those poets, of whatever creed." *Arcturus,* III, no. XVIII (May, 1842), 407-8. "By James Russell Lowell." The text is dated *"April* 20, 1841." This poem is number III of the group of three "Sonnets." The first will be found on p. 23. The second, beginning "The hope of truth grows stronger day by day," will be found in the *Collected Edition.*

Page 19: Sonnet. "To die is gain." *Dial,* II, no. I (July, 1841), 129. By "Hugh Peters." A letter from Emerson to Lowell dated December 10, 1840 (Harvard Library) reads in part as follows: "I heartily thank you for trusting me with your gay verses. If they have not a high poetical merit, they have broad good nature and good breeding. I sent them, without any name, to Miss Fuller, who will gladly print the last one, in the next *Dial,* unless you forbid its separation; and will put the others in the vast editorial Drawer to take their chance for future insertion with the other sylphs and gnomes now imprisoned or hereafter to be imprisoned in that limbo." The "next Dial" to which Emerson referred was volume I, no. 3, January, 1841. It contained the sonnet "To a Voice Heard in Mt. Auburn, 1839," which was presumably that which Emerson promised Miss Fuller would print. This was printed by Lowell later in *A Year's Life.* The sonnet "To die is gain" is presumably one of the "gay verses," acknowledged by Emerson's letter, and held over for subsequent publication.

Page 19: Sonnet. "Whene'er I read in mournful history." *Boston Miscellany of Literature,* I, no. 5 (May, 1842), 200. "By James R. Lowell." The text is dated "Sept. 25, 1841."

Page 20: Sonnet. "Like some black mountain glooming huge aloof." *Boston Miscellany of Literature,* I, no. 2 (February, 1842), 54. "By James R. Lowell." The text is dated "Oct., 1841."

Page 20: "The Lesson—To Irene." By "J. R. Lowell." The only known copy of this poem, hitherto unlisted, is a clipping from a newspaper or magazine, bearing no date or indication of the title of the publication. Below the text of the poem, however, is printed the date "Oct. 11, 1841." This clipping is among the materials which Mrs. L. B. Rantoul, granddaughter of the poet, has deposited in the Harvard Library. The clipping bears a few slight amendments chiefly in typography or punctuation in what appears to be Lowell's hand. These have been followed in the text.

Page 21: "Ballad." *Graham's Magazine*, XIX, no. 4 (October, 1841), 171. "By J. R. Lowell."

Page 23: "My Father, since I love, thy presence cries." *Arcturus*, III, no. XVIII (May, 1842), 407-8. "By James Russell Lowell." The text is dated "Nov. 29, 1841." This poem is number I of the group of three "Sonnets." The third will be found on p. 18. The second beginning "The hope of truth grows stronger day by day" will be found in the *Collected Edition*.

Page 24: "Sonnet—Sunset and Moonshine." *Arcturus*, III, no. XIV (January, 1842), 141. "By J. R. Lowell." *Arcturus* printed two sonnets. The first of these is "To the Spirit of Keats" (*Collected Edition*). The second, "Sonnet—Sunset and Moonshine," was reprinted in *Bulletin of the New York Public Library*, II, no. 12 (December, 1898), 445, together with the letter to Duyckinck offering the poems for publication in *Arcturus*. Lowell's letter to Duyckinck and his MS of the two poems are in the N. Y. Public Library. The variants are from this MS. Duyckinck's reply to Lowell, December 17, 1841, accepting the poems is in Harvard Library.

Page 24: "The Loved One." *National Anti-Slavery Standard*, II, no. 28 (December 16, 1841), 112. "By James Russell Lowell."

Page 25: "The Ballad of the Stranger." *The Token and Atlantic Souvenir* (Boston: D. H. Williams, 1842), 133-37. "By J. R. Lowell." This was Lowell's first contribution to an annual. (See letters to Loring, February 18 and March 14, 1841 in the Harvard Library.)

Page 28: Sonnet. "Only as thou herein canst not see me." *Dial*, II, no. 3 (January, 1842), 357. By "J. R. L." This poem was sent by Lowell to Emerson in a letter of November 27, 1841, reprinted in *New Letters*, pp. 7-8. The variants are from the MS of this letter which is in the possession of Mrs. Stanley Cunningham, the poet's granddaughter.

Page 28: Sonnet. "When in a book I find a pleasant thought." *Dial*, II, no. 3 (January, 1842), 357. By "J. R. L." The text is dated "April, 1819." This poem was reprinted in *New Letters*, pp. 6-7, with one change in capitalization. The text in the *Dial* bore the obviously erroneous date, "April, 1819." Cooke conjectured that the date should be April, 1839. But Howe printed his version from a letter sent by Lowell to Emerson, November 18, 1841 in which the poet dated his poem "April, 1841."

Page 29: "To an Æolian Harp at Night." *Boston Miscellany of Literature*, II, no. 6 (December, 1842), 267-69. The text is dated

"February, 1842." Ascribed to Lowell conjecturally in Scudder, II, Appendix C, 425; listed in Cooke.

Page 31: Sonnet. "If some small savor creep into my rhyme." *Graham's Magazine*, XX, no. 2 (February, 1842), 90. By "J. R. L."

Page 31: Sonnet. "Thou art a woman, and therein thou art." *National Anti-Slavery Standard*, II, no. 35 (February 3, 1842), 140. "By James Russell Lowell."

Page 32: "Fancies about a Rosebud." *Graham's Magazine*, XX, no. 3 (March, 1842), 173. "By James Russell Lowell."

Page 34: "Farewell." *Graham's Magazine*, XX, no. 6 (June, 1842), 305-6. "By James Russell Lowell." A passage consisting of stanza 2 and the first six lines of stanza 4 was reprinted in *The Ladies' Casket* (Lowell and Boston: J. Wesley Hansen, 1847). In this book of gems and sentiments Lowell's poem appeared under "Sapphire."

Page 37: "The True Radical." *Boston Miscellany of Literature*, II, no. 2 (August, 1842), 77. Ascribed conjecturally to Lowell by Scudder, II, Appendix C, 424; listed in Cooke.

Page 37: "Hymn." *Order of Services; at the Dedication of the New Church: Erected by the Congregational Society in Watertown: August 3, 1842.* The fourth item is "4. Original Hymn, by James R. Lowell, Esq." Facsimile reprint in Chamberlain and Livingston, p. 8. In a letter to Loring, May 10, 1839 (Harvard Library), Lowell wrote:

> What is Religion? 'tis to go
> To church one day in seven,
> And think that *we*, of all men, know
> The only way to heaven.

Page 38: Sonnet. "Poet, if men from wisdom turn away." *National Anti-Slavery Standard*, III, no. 13, whole no. 117 (September 1, 1842), 52. "By James Russell Lowell."

Page 39: "Voltaire." *The Pioneer*, I, no. 1 (January, 1843), 5. Ascribed to Lowell conjecturally by Scudder, II, Appendix C, 425; listed by Cooke.

Page 39: "The Follower." *The Pioneer*, I, no. 1 (January, 1843), 11. Ascribed conjecturally to Lowell by Scudder, II, Appendix C, 425.

Page 39: "The Poet and Apollo." *The Pioneer*, I, no. 1 (January, 1843), 31-32. By "H. P." Listed by Joyce, H. E., *Modern Language Notes*, XXXV, no. 4, 250.

Page 40: "A Love Thought." *The Pioneer*, I, no. 3 (March, 1843), 119.

Page 40: "Wordsworth." *Graham's Magazine*, XXVI, no. 3 (March,

1843), 190. Ascribed conjecturally to Lowell by Scudder, II, Appendix C, 425.

Page 41: "Winter." *The Present,* I, nos. IX and X (March 1, 1844), 300-1. "By J. R. Lowell."

Page 42: "A Rallying-Cry for New-England, Against the Annexation of Texas." *Boston Courier,* March 19, 1844. "By a Yankee." Reprinted in *The Liberty Minstrel,* George W. Clark, ed., (New York: Leavitt and Alden, 1844), pp. 70-72. This version shows very slight variations of punctuation and spelling. It omits stanzas 7, 10, 11, and 12. This poem was later reprinted in an article by Anna D. Hallowell entitled "An Episode in the Life of James Russell Lowell," *Harper's Weekly,* XXXVI, no. 1844 (April 23, 1892), 393-95. This article was based upon letters (Harvard Library) from Lowell to Edward M. Davis, Anna Hallowell's father. They concern the friendship of Lowell for the Davis family of Philadelphia whom he met as a result of Maria White's visit in 1843. Upon her return to Watertown, Maria White sent to her hostess, Mrs. Edward M. Davis, the only known manuscript of this poem, dated May 26, 1844 (Harvard Library). This MS, in the poet's hand, is identical with the text reproduced from the *Boston Courier* in this volume except for minor variations in punctuation and capitalization. At two points the poet has apparently attempted to improve his poem by a change of word, and then upon reconsideration, has restored the original reading. This poem was published two years and three months before the first of the *Biglow Papers,* which reflected Lowell's opposition to the Mexican War. The violent opposition to the annexation of Texas expressed in "A Rallying-Cry" is therefore the more interesting. Lowell signed the poem simply "By a Yankee" instead of using his own name because he recognized its more than usual intensity as indicated by the following excerpt from his aforementioned letter of May 26, 1844 in presenting his MS to the Davises. "Had I entirely approved either the spirit or the execution of these verses, I had put my name to them. But they were written in great haste and for a particular object, and I used therefore such arguments as I thought would influence the mass of my readers, viz: a swinging ballad metre, some sectional prejudice and vanity, some denunciation, some scriptural allusions, and no cant. I wished *it* to be violent, because I thought the occasion demanded violence, but I had no wish to be violent myself, and therefore, I let it go anonymously. Had I written aught in my own

name, it would have been entirely different." Stanzas 7, 8, 9
of this poem were inserted after stanza 10 of "Another Rally-
ing Cry. By a Yankee," *Boston Courier,* January 30, 1845
when Lowell collected it in *Poems* (1848) under the title
"Anti-Texas." (See p. 44 and the following note.)

Page 44: "Anti-Texas." Printed in *Boston Courier,* January 30, 1845,
under the title "Another Rallying Cry. By a Yankee." This
poem is here printed for its relationship with "A Rallying-
Cry" (see preceding note) although it does not fall precisely
within the definition of this volume. "Another Rallying Cry"
was prefaced: "The following verses were intended for our
paper of yesterday, [see sub-title] but did not reach us in
season. It will be perceived that they were written before
the news of the passage of the Texas Resolutions had been re-
ceived. But verses so good are at no time inappropriate." The
variants are from the newspaper text. Stanzas 11, 12, 13 of the
present text were not in the *Courier* version. When reprinting
the poem in *Poems* (1848), Lowell inserted (after stanza 10)
stanzas 7, 8, 9 from the earlier poem, "A Rallying-Cry."

Page 46: "A Mystical Ballad." *Graham's Magazine,* XXIV, no. 5 (May,
1844), 214. "By James Russell Lowell."

Page 49: "New Year's Eve, 1844." *Graham's Magazine,* XXV, no. 1
(July, 1844), 15-16. "By James Russell Lowell."

Page 52: "The Happy Martyrdom." *The Liberty Bell,* by Friends of
Freedom (Boston: Massachusetts Anti-Slavery Fair, 1845),
pp. 147-50. "By James Russell Lowell."

Page 54: "An Epigram, on Certain Conservatives." *Broadway Journal,*
January 25, 1845, p. 58.

Page 54: "Now is Always Best." *Broadway Journal,* January 25, 1845,
p. 58. By "James Russell Lowell."

Page 56: "Orpheus." *American Review,* II, no. 2 (August, 1845), 131-32.
"By J. R. Lowell."

Page 58: "An Extract." *The Liberty Bell,* by Friends of Freedom (Bos-
ton: National Anti-Slavery Bazaar, 1848), pp. 180-83. "By
James Russell Lowell." The variants are from a rough draft
in one of Lowell's notebooks in the Harvard Library.

Page 60: "The Ex-Mayor's Crumbs of Consolation: A Pathetic Ballad."
National Anti-Slavery Standard, IX, no. 22, whole no. 438
(October 26, 1848), 86. Unsigned but following a column
signed "J. R. L." This poem was inspired by the same incident
that caused Lowell to write his vigorous tribute "To W. L.
Garrison" to be found in the *Collected Edition.* According to
Scudder, I, 258-59: "In the fall of 1848, Harrison Gray Otis,

writing in advocacy of the election of Zachary Taylor, referred
to an incident in 1831, when, as Mayor of Boston, he answered
an application from the Governors of Virginia and Georgia for
information respecting the persons responsible for *The Lib-
erator.* 'Some time afterward,' he says, 'it was reported to me
by the city officers that they had ferreted out the paper and its
editor: that his office was an obscure hole, his only visible
auxiliary a negro boy, and his supporters a very few insig-
nificant persons of all colors.' " It will be remembered that
Lowell opposed the candidacy of Zachary Taylor not only
for his exploits in the Mexican War but also because Lowell
considered him a slave-holder. Lowell at once clipped Otis'
sentence as above from a contemporary newspaper and wrote
beneath it the poem "To W. L. Garrison" which was published
in the *National Anti-Slavery Standard,* October 19, 1848. Still
not satisfied he wrote the second poem, "The Ex-Mayor's
Crumbs of Consolation" reproduced in this volume, and it
appeared a week later, October 26, in the *Standard.* Hearing
of Otis' death, which occurred two days after the publication
of this satire upon him, Lowell wrote to Gay: "I would not
have squibbed him if I had known he was sick, but I never
hear anything." (Scudder, I, footnote, p. 259.) This poem
was reproduced in connection with the Scudder passage just
quoted. The Latin line in the second stanza read *Taustissimis
votis,* an obvious error, which Scudder corrected.

Page 62: "The Burial of Theobald." *The Liberty Bell,* by Friends of
Freedom (Boston: National Anti-Slavery Bazaar, 1849), pp.
269-74. "By James Russell Lowell." A rough draft of the first
5 stanzas of this poem will be found in one of Lowell's note-
books in the Harvard Library. The variants are from this MS.
A letter to Sydney H. Gay, December 20, 1848 (*Letters,* I, p.
197) reads: ". . . . I have sent you some poems of which
neither you nor I need be ashamed. I am afraid to think of
what I gave them for the "Liberty Bell." I half-parodied it to
myself as I went along, of which the following is a sufficient
specimen, and will make you laugh when you see the original:

> "By God's just judgment I am damned!"
> With a loud voice he cried,
> And then his coffin-lid he slammed,
> And bolted it inside."

Page 65: "King Retro." *National Anti-Slavery Standard,* IX, no. 50,
whole no. 466 (May 10, 1849), 199. By "J. R. L." The rather

carelessly edited text in the *National Anti-Slavery Standard* has been followed in this edition except for the correction of certain obvious errors: Stanza IX, line 1, "wroth" for "wrath"; Stanza XXV, line 2, "Apostles" for "Apostler"; Stanza XXV, line 3, "can'st" for "can't." The numbering of stanza XXIII as XXII in the *Standard* has also been corrected.

Page 72: "Lady Bird, lady bird, fly away home!" *Holden's Dollar Magazine*, III, no. 6 (June, 1849), 382. This poem is part of a letter to Charles F. Briggs, then editor of this magazine. Briggs printed the entire letter without permission in his column "Topics of the Month" under the sub-heading "A Pepysian Letter." Since this delightful letter was filled with intimate comment intended only for Briggs' eye, it caused the poet a great deal of embarrassment even though the editor had attempted to disguise the personal references by printing only initials instead of full names. For example, the reference to the unhappy impression made by Emerson in a recent lecture at the Cambridge Lyceum was unmistakable. In an unpublished portion of a letter to Briggs, November 25, 1849 (Harvard Library), Lowell scolds his friend vigorously for having caused him so much discomfort by the unauthorized publication. Higginson in *Old Cambridge*, pp. 160-72 reprinted the entire letter from *Holden's Dollar Magazine* with the interpolated verses. Before the poem, Lowell wrote: "I copy below one of my latest poems. I have attempted to complete a fine old ballad-fragment, how successfully you must judge. It has been very popular with the small public for whom it was specially intended." Between the two sections of the poem, Lowell wrote: "Thus far, you perceive, the material instinct gets the upper hand, but now the Lady Bird arrives at the scene of desolation, and the house-keeping qualities of mind are electrified into morbid activity. The word 'hopple' is finely local, being in the Mab [Mabel Lowell] dialect. It means to scramble down confusedly." At the end of the poem, Lowell wrote: "This, you observe, teaches children not to value themselves too highly, to respect crockery and varnish, and to cultivate self-reliance."

Page 72: "Out of Doors." *Graham's Magazine*, XXXVI, no. 4 (April, 1850), 257. "By James Russell Lowell."

Page 74: "The Northern Sancho Panza and His Vicarious Cork Tree." *National Anti-Slavery Standard*, XI, no. 8, whole no. 528 (July 18, 1850), 30. By "J. R. L." The variants are from a rough

draft of part of this poem which is in one of Lowell's note-
books in Harvard Library.

Page 76:   "A Dream I Had." *National Anti-Slavery Standard,* XI, no. 27,
whole no. 247 (November 28, 1850), 106. By "J. R. L." For
the connection of this poem with Lowell's attitude toward the
Compromise of 1850 and toward Daniel Webster's career in
this period see Introduction p. xviii.

Page 79:   "On Receiving a Piece of Flax-Cotton." *National Anti-Slavery
Standard,* XI, no. 49, whole no. 569 (May 1, 1851), 194. By
"J. R. L." A typed copy of this poem exists in the Harvard
Library bearing, in Lowell's hand, the memorandum *"Nat'l
A. S. Standard* May, 1851." It shows a few changes in punctua-
tion and the following changes in phraseology: Stanza 6, line
4, "churning sea" instead of "spurning sea"; Stanza 8, line 2,
"Is sickly ripeness" instead of "In sickly ripeness."

Page 80:   "Our Own, His Wanderings and Personal Adventures." *Put-
nam's Monthly,* I (1853), no. 4 (April), 403-8; no. 5 (May)
533-35; no. 6 (June) 687-90. This poem resulted from Lowell's
proposal, made to his friends, Briggs and George W. Curtis,
the editors of *Putnam's,* for a long, humorous poem which
would be continued for an indefinite number of issues of
the magazine. Briggs was never very enthusiastic about the
poem, and, convinced that it was not meeting with the
approval of his readers, discouraged Lowell from proceeding
beyond the third installment. The poet's plan was to imper-
sonate a travelling correspondent who would satirize men
and things, make humorous comments on foreign lands, and
flavor the whole with Yankee wit. The history of this matter
is discussed in Greenslet, p. 102, and in Scudder, I, 351-53.
See also the letters of Lowell: In Howe, *New Letters,* p. 42, to
Edmund Quincy, June 7, 1853; and the partly unpublished
letters to Briggs in the Harvard Collection—February 17,
1853; March 24, 1853; March, 1853 (as dated in pencil beside
Lowell's heading "Wednesday again"); June 10, 1853; Sep-
tember, 1853 (passage omitted by Norton in *Letters,* I, 270);
February 8, 1854; and February 25, 1854. Nearly fifteen years
later when Lowell was planning the volume *Under the Wil-
lows,* he decided to preserve of "Our Own" the two stanzas
now called "Aladdin." ("Progression F" in this edition.) It
was not until 1890 when he was preparing the Riverside Edi-
tion that Lowell decided to rescue from oblivion the lines
which he entitled "Fragments of an Unfinished Poem." These
fragments are identified as the following passages in the

present text: "Progression B Leading to Digression C" (pp. 83-85); "Digression D" lines 93-125 (pp. 88-89); "Progression F" the last 64 lines of the poem (pp. 98-100). The variants are from a typescript indicated as MS I and from a more primitive version for Progression E labelled MS II, both at Harvard Library.

Page 80: The Greek sub-heading is a quotation from the speech of Aeneas addressed to Achates as they first looked at the paintings in the Temple of Juno at Carthage. (Virgil, *Aeneid*, I, 460.) The subject of the painting was the siege of Troy: "What section of the earth is not full of our labor (hardships)?"

Page 81: Sir John Franklin (1786-1847) arctic explorer credited with the discovery of the "Northwest Passage." On his last exploration, begun in 1845, he disappeared. Thirty-nine relief expeditions were sent to find him in the decade from 1847 to 1857. Five such expeditions were sent in 1853, the year Lowell wrote this poem, and nine had been sent the year before.

Page 82: "Howadji" refers to George William Curtis, one of the editors of *Putnam's*, whose *Nile Notes of a Howadji* and *The Howadji in Syria*, books concerning his travels in Egypt and Syria, had been published the two previous years. (See Introduction p. xxii.)

Page 83: "Harry Franco" was the pen name of Charles F. Briggs, the other editor of *Putnam's*. (See Introduction p. xxii.)

Page 83: Charles Fourier (1772-1837). The Fourierist movement was then at its height. Promoted by Albert Brisbane, 41 phalanges had been founded in the United States between 1840 and 1850.

Page 83: "Brook Farm." (See note on Fourier above.) Founded in 1841, became a Fourierist Phalanx in 1843 and for two years published *The Phalanx*. Note Lowell's reference to the "phalansterian beets." The line "Time should wander Ripleying along" refers obviously to George Ripley, the president of the Brook Farm Institute.

Page 87: "Pernoctent nobis," i.e. "Let them (our studies) spend the night with us." Cicero was here speaking of a liberal education (or literature). Oration—*Pro Archia*, VII, 16.

Page 87: "Recensuit et praefationem addidit Gelasmus:" i.e. "Gelamus has gone over it and added a preface." Probably Gelasmus is a made-up name from "gelaō" (γελάω) meaning "laugh."

Page 87: The Latin footnote translated literally means: "To write nothings is as easy as drinking; but to write intelligently what is unintelligible; to speak insanely quite frequently, properly, and freely; to turn to the laughable that which is openly impossible so that it might amuse the lowliest heart,—that is the height of intellect."

Page 88: "rari nantes," i.e., "rare swimmers." Virgil, *Aeneid*, I, 118.

Page 88: "With *mediums* and prophetic chairs." In 1855 it was claimed that nearly two million people in the United States were believers in spiritualism. In 1847 Margaret and Kate Fox, with Horace Greeley, presented to Congress a petition, bearing 15,000 names, asking for a Federal investigation of the spiritualists.

Page 100: Rejected portion of "Our Own." From its relationship to the surviving fragments of MS, and because it begins with a quatrain almost identical with that which introduces Progression D, these passages may have been excluded either from the beginning or the end of that Progression. The subject matter in this rejected passage could be related to the published text of Progression D at either of these suggested points. This portion of the poem is printed from a MS in Harvard Library found in a notebook entitled "J. R. L. 1850 Notes and Rough-drafts."

Page 103: "Menenius, thou who fain wouldst know how calmly men can pass." *Collected Edition*, I, 46-47, "Cambridge Thirty Years Ago: A Memoir Addressed to the Edelmann Storg in Rome." These 15 lines are in the same meter and tone as "Our Own." Proof that these lines were part of the rejected portion of "Our Own" is found on the pages of Lowell's notebook at Harvard Library (see preceding note) where two versions of these lines are written following the rejected portion which is printed in this text, pp. 100-103. In "Cambridge Thirty Years Ago," Lowell was describing Harvard Commencement in the old days when side shows were a part of the celebration. He wrote: "Were Commencement what it used to be, I should be tempted to take a booth myself, and try an experiment recommended by a satirist of some merit, whose works were long ago dead and (I fear) deedeed to boot." Following the stanzas, Lowell questioned; "My dear Storg, would you come to my show, and, instead of looking in my glass, insist on taking your money's worth in staring at the exhibitor?" The two versions in MS of these lines with their variants are given in addition to the printed version from the essay.

Page 104: "Peschiera." *Putnam's Monthly*, III, no. 17 (May, 1854), 522. Peschiera sul Garda, in the province of Verona, was one of the four fortified towns known as the Quadrilateral, in north

Italy. By controlling them Austria maintained a firm hold on Lombardy. Peschiera had been recaptured by the Piedmontese in 1848.

Page 105: "Without and Within, No. II, The Restaurant." *Putnam's Monthly*, III, no. 17 (May, 1854), 559. Ascribed conjecturally to Lowell by Scudder, II, Appendix C, 434; listed by Cooke. This poem is related to one in *Collected Edition*, called "Without and Within," published in *Putnam's Monthly* in April, 1854, the month preceding the publication of the text in the present volume. As will be seen by comparison, the poems present similar situations, but the spirit of the present text is highly vernacular in contrast to the poem which Lowell collected. In Stanza 9, line 2, the Latin phrase recalls Horace, *Sermons*, I, 4, line 34 "Faenum habet in cornu, longe fuge" where the reference is to the custom of binding with hay the horns of a dangerous bull.

Page 107: "In-doors and Out." *Putnam's Monthly*, V, no. 27 (March, 1855), 287-88. Campbell suggested that this poem resembled "The Forlorn" *(Collected Edition)* PMLA, XXXVIII, 936.

Page 108: "Hymn." *The Boston Mob of "Gentlemen of Property and Standing." Proceedings of the Anti-Slavery Meeting Held in Stacy Hall, Boston on the Twentieth Anniversary of the Mob of October 21, 1835.* Phonographic report by J. M. W. Yerrinton. Boston: Published by R. F. Wallcut, 1855, p. 31. Pamphlet in the University of Pennsylvania Library. Chamberlain and Livingston (pp. 45-46) say the poem was reprinted as a broadside in 1856, headed *Anti-Slavery Festival in Faneuil Hall. A Welcome to Parker Pillsbury.* According to the pamphlet the meeting was called to order by William Lloyd Garrison and Francis Jackson was called upon to take the chair. After several short addresses, scripture reading, and a prayer, a poem by Whittier was read. A speech by William Lloyd Garrison was the principle item on the program, after which: "The following hymn, by JAMES RUSSELL LOWELL, was then sung, to the tune of 'Scots wha hae' . . ." The hymn is then printed entire without a title.

Page 109: "Verses." *Atlantic Monthly*, C, no. 5 (November, 1907), 577-78. Charles E. Norton dated the poem "September or October, 1857." The letter which Lowell wrote to Norton enclosing the poem (Harvard Library) says: "I enclose the autograph I half-promised you once. In reading them you must not forget the date at which they are supposed to have been written—though I have only succeeded in hitting the

style here and there." The variants are from a rough draft of
this poem to be found in one of Lowell's notebooks (Harvard
Library). The MS shows 4 stanzas, in pencil, which corre-
spond to stanzas 1, 3, 4, 5 of the present text. Across the side
of the page, in ink, is written stanza 2.

Page 110:   *The Power of Sound: A Rhymed Lecture by James Russell
Lowell.* Privately Printed. N. Y., 1896. Copyright 1896, by
C. E. Norton, 75 copies, of which 25 are on Japanese paper
and 50 on handmade. Gilliss Press. Introductory note by
Charles Eliot Norton, pp. ix-x. Hale refers to this poem, p. 13
and pp. 121-23. Apparently, however, Hale thought he re-
ferred to two separated works, for in the first instance he
called it "The Power of Music," and in the second, properly,
"The Power of Sound." In the first instance he quoted 12 lines
of the poem, and in the second, 58 lines. Scudder, I, 20-21
mentions the poem and quotes 20 lines. The introductory note
in the volume of 1896 is reprinted entire below, together with
the annotations written by Norton which appeared at the end
of that volume.

Introductory Note: "Mr. Lowell did not esteem this rhymed
lecture of sufficient worth to include it in his published Poems.
It was too hasty a piece of improvisation to deserve his *Im-
primatur.* But though his judgment of it as a whole be ac-
cepted as correct, it yet contains passages of such excellence,
alike of humor and of sentiment, and it affords such illustra-
tion of his convictions in regard to public affairs in the period
just before our Civil War, that, I believe, there can be no
question as to the propriety of preserving it in print, and I
have therefore acceded with pleasure to Mr. Holden's proposal
to print an edition of it for private circulation.

"I have been unable to ascertain the precise date either of
the writing or the delivery of the lecture; nor do I know how
often, or, except in a single instance, where it was read in
public. An approximate date for its original composition, how-
ever, and for additions subsequently made to it, may be fixed
by internal evidence. There are several references in it to
incidents which occurred during the summer of 1857, from
which it may be concluded that it was written in the autumn
or early winter of that year; while other references in the addi-
tions show that the latest of them belong to the spring of 1862.

"The only existing copy of the poem is in print on galley
slips, cut-up so as to make twenty-three pages. The margins

of many of these pages and the back of one of them are full of corrections and additions written in ink or pencil. It was put into type and cut up into its present form for convenience of reading in public.

"Mr. Lowell gave the pages to me shortly after the first delivery of the poem, and I had them bound." C. E. Norton, June, 1896.

Page 110: 1. The lines enclosed in brackets, beginning,

I come no stranger, . . .

to,

Whate'er its pangs, . . .

do not appear in the lecture as first delivered. They were inserted at the time of its later delivery at Newburyport, Mass., in the spring of 1862-3. The four generations of his kindred to whom Mr. Lowell refers were:

1st. Percival, the first New England Lowell. He was of Somersetshire, England. He came to America in 1639, and was one of the early settlers of the town of Newbury. He died in Newbury on the 8th of January, 1665.

2nd. John, son of Percival, who came from England with his father, and died in Newbury in 1647.

John, son of the preceding John, was born in England, and came with his father and grandfather to America. He lived mainly in Boston, and died there in 1694. His son Ebenezer was born in Boston in 1675 and died there in 1711.

3d. John, son of Ebenezer and Elizabeth (Shaler) Lowell, was born in Boston March 14th, 1703/4. In 1726 he was ordained pastor of the Third Parish in Newbury, which became the First Parish of Newburyport. He died there in 1767, the last of the lineal ancestors of the poet who slept in its graveyard.

4th. John, son of the Rev. John, born at Newbury in 1735, and died there in 1736.

The second son of the Rev. John, also named John, was born in 1743. He was appointed by Washington in 1789 judge of the district court, and in 1801 he was appointed chief judge of the first circuit. He died in 1802. His son, the Rev. Charles Lowell, born 1782, died 1861, was the father of James Russell Lowell.

Page 115: 2. In January, 1862, when Lowell was writing that masterpiece, one of the finest of his Biglow Papers, *"Mason and*

Slidell: A Yankee Idyll," he introduced into it a portion of the
passage beginning:—

O strange New World that yet wast never young,

changing and improving it as follows:—

> *I feel my sperit swellin' with a cry*
> *Thet seems to say, "Break forth an' prophesy!"*
> *O strange New World, thet yit wast never young,*
> *Whose youth from thee by gripin' need was wrung,*
> *Brown foundlin' o' the woods, whose baby-bed*
> *Was prowled roun' by the Injun's cracklin' tread,*
> *An' who grew'st strong thru shifts an' wants an' pains,*
> *Nussed by stern men with empires in their brains,*
> *Who saw in vision their young Ishmel strain*
> *With each hard hand a vassal ocean's mane,*
> *Thou, skilled by Freedom an' by gret events*
> *To pitch new States ez Old-World men pitch tents,*
> *Thou, taught by Fate to know Jehovah's plan*
> *Thet man's devices can't unmake a man,*
> *An' whose free latch-string never was drawed in*
> *Against the poorest child of Adam's kin,—*
> *The grave's not dug where traitor hands shall lay*
> *In fearful haste thy murdered corse away!*

Page 116:   3. In the later delivery of the poem, after the war had begun,
the verse,

> *If for her* [sic] *children there should come a time*

was changed to,

> *When for her children there shall come a time*

and the verse

> *Let Kansas answer from her reddened fields,*

to,

> *Make this proud answer, from thy reddened fields,*

The struggle in Kansas was at its height in 1856-7.

Page 119:   4. Béranger died on July 16, 1857.

Page 119:   5. This fine verse was inserted in "Mason and Slidell":

> *I recollect how sailors' rights was won,*
> *Yard locked in yard, hot gun-lip kissing gun;*

Page 119: 6. This verse was changed in manuscript to read:

> *Another Cumberland, her thunders spent*

It was on March 8, 1862, that the Cumberland was sunk, and, probably soon after this memorable event, this lecture was read in public for the last time. The passage in which this verse occurs had already found place, with invigorating changes, in "Mason and Slidell," published in the Atlantic Monthly for February, 1862, where as part of one of the speeches of "The Bridge," it reads:

> Better that all our ships an' all their crews
> Should sink to rot in ocean's dreamless ooze,
> Each torn flag wavin' challenge as it went,
> An' each dumb gun a brave man's moniment,
> Than seek sech peace as only cowards crave:
> Give me the peace of dead men or of brave!

Page 120: 7. Lowell's fortieth birthday was the twenty-second of February, 1859.

Page 121: 8. The siege and relief of Lucknow were in the summer and autumn of 1857.

Page 126: "Epigram on J. M." *Atlantic Monthly*, I, no. 7 (May, 1858), 846. "J. M." appears to refer to John Mitchel.

Page 126: "The Trustee's Lament." *Atlantic Monthly*, II, no. 10 (August, 1858), 370-73. The poem refers to the Dudley Observatory, Albany, N. Y., erected 1851-56, by subscription. Scudder, I, 424-25, quotes an unidentified letter from Lowell which refers to the popular controversy treated in this poem: "I am urged to take ground in the Albany controversy, but do not feel that there is any *ought* in the matter, but am sure the Trustees will beat in the end. I think it would be unwise to let the magazine *Atlantic Monthly* take a losing side unless clear justice required it. Am I not right?" It will be remembered that the *Atlantic* was less than a year old and that Lowell was serving as its first editor when he printed this anonymous poem.

Page 130: "The Fatal Curiosity." *The Victoria Regia*, Adelaide A. Proctor, ed. (London: Victoria Press, 1861), pp. 83-84. By "J. R. Lowell." The volume in which this poem appeared had a curious history, connected with the insurgent feminism of the time. According to the preface of *The Victoria Regia*, a committee appointed by the Council of the National Association for the Promotion of Social Science (London) in 1859 surveyed the possibility of promoting the employment of women in various industries thought suitable for their capacity. One of these was the printing industry. The Victoria Press which proposed to employ only women was inaugurated on the 25th of March, 1860, and published *The Victoria Regia* as a volume the next year, "as a choice specimen of the skill attained by" the lady compositors. It contained contributions from approximately 20 women and 30 men, among whom, beside Lowell, were Tennyson, Owen Meredith, Harriet Martineau, Thackeray, Mary Howitt, Coventry Patmore, Mathew Arnold, Anthony Trollope, and Leigh Hunt.

Page 131: "Before the Embers." *Only Once.* Original Papers, by various contributors. Published for the Benefit of the New York Infirmary for Women and Children, 1862. "By James Russell Lowell." The poem, "My Portrait Gallery," in Lowell's *Collected Edition*, consists of 15 lines from this poem and one additional line written apparently for the new poem. The lines which Lowell used for "Before the Embers" were as follows: Stanza 3, the first 6 lines; Stanza 4, the last 9 lines. Lowell's new line in "My Portrait Gallery" was introduced as the second line of the passage from Stanza 4.

Page 133: *Il Pesceballo.* Opera Seria: in un Atto. Musica del Maestro Rossibelli-Donimozarti. Cambridge, 1862. Reprinted by the Caxton Club, Chicago, 1899 (210 copies). Prefaced by a letter to the President, Charles L. Hutchinson, from Charles E. Norton, June 29, 1899. This letter gives an account of the circumstances of the writing and producing of the operetta. In this reprint is also given what Norton says is the genuine ballad, "The Lay of the One Fishball," written a few years before by George M. Lane, published anonymously in New York in 1855, and still popular with college glee clubs. The operetta is also reprinted in *The Bibelot*, XVII, no. 11 (November, 1911), 373-409. Again reprinted (50 copies) by Thomas B. Mosher, Portland, Maine, October, 1912, with an interesting account of the history of the operetta, a facsimile of a program, and the musical score of "The One Fishball." This operetta was composed in Italian by Francis James Child while he was engaged in writing and compiling *War Songs for Free Men*. The theme was suggested by Lane's ballad which was based upon an adventure of his own. When Child got his Italian verse into shape he asked Lowell to revise it. In addition to possibly revising the Italian text, Lowell wrote the amusing English version printed in the present text. The brief interludes of recitative were arranged by Child's friend,

Professor Paine, according to Norton. However, in a copy of the 1862 text (Harvard Library) which belonged to Mrs. Gustavus Hay there is the following note: "The recatifs were written by Mr. J. C. D. Parker." According to Norton, Child composed his operetta to raise money for the United States Sanitary Commission. Mrs. Hay's note says that the rehearsals were held in her home in Garden Street in 1862. A copy of the operetta (Harvard Library) which belonged to William S. Thayer notes: "Sung in Cambridge for the benefit of the United States Sanitary Commission May 1862–." A letter from Child to Samuel Tuckerman, possibly written in 1887 (see Mosher's reprint, pp. 49-50) says: "There were performances two successive years. . . . In the second case . . . we gave the money which we made (1500 dollars) to Edward Everett for his East Tennessee Fund. The performance was in Horticultural Hall." A letter from Dr. S. W. Langmaid, December 19, 1887 (Mosher, p. 49) says: "I think the date of the performance was 1862 but of this I am not sure. The place was Chickering's Hall, Washington Street, where Jordan and Marsh's store now is and I believe the cause was that of the loyal Tennessee people who were impoverished by the War." The facsimile of the program for the second performance reads: "Grand Opera, For the Benefit of the People of East Tennessee. On Tuesday, Thursday, and Saturday Evenings, May 10th, 12th, and 14th." This must, from the calendar, be ascribed to the year 1863. The cast (Mosher, pp. 48-49) was as follows:

"La Padrona, Signora Fiorrancio, Mrs. Mary Quincy Gould.
La Serva, Signora Lavalletta, Mrs. Dr. Slade.
Lo Straniero, Signor Lungoprato, Dr. S. W. Langmaid.
Il Cameriere, Signor Sottobosco, Francis Underwood.
Il Corriere, Signor Silesiano, Sebastian Schlesinger.
Leader of the Chorus, Signor Toccamano, Samuel Tuckerman.
Conductor and Leader of the Orchestra, Signor Parchero,
    J. D. C. Parker assisted by Signor Gugligalli, Wilcox.
Amateurs in society and Harvard supplied the Chorus."

The names of the actors of the three principal roles are corroborated by annotations in William S. Thayer's copy and Bessie Parsons' copy (dated "May 8th, 1862") both in the Harvard Library. Norton's copy of *Il Pesceballo* has this note: "Names of airs written in by F. J. Child." The songs sung by the characters in the operetta are adapted to the following familiar melodies:

Scene   I.   Chorus to air of *La dolce aurora,* from "Moses in Egypt."

Scene   II.   Song of the Stranger adapted to the Serenade in "The Barber of Seville."

Scene   IV.   Song of the Padrona to the *Non più mesta* of *La Cenerentola.*

Scene   V.   Duet to *La dove prende Amor recetto* of the "Magic Flute."

Scene   VI.   Cavatina to the *Di pescator* of "Lucrezia Borgia."

Scene VII.   Aria to the *Madamina* of "Don Giovanni."

Scene VIII.   Chorus to the *Guerra, Guerra,* of "Norma."

Scene   IX.   Duet to the *O sole più ratto* of "Lucia."

Scene   X.   Cavatina to the *Meco all'altar* of "Norma," chorus of same to the *Bando, Bando,* of "Lucrezia Borgia," and trio which follows to *Guai se tu sfuggi* of the same opera.

Scene   XI.   The piece concludes with the aria *Vieni!* of "La Favorita."

Page 142:   "A Worthy Ditty." *The Nation,* II, no. 30 (January 25, 1866), 106-7. By "J. R. L." This poem reflects the divided opinion of the country as to the measure of severity which it was necessary to apply in restoring order in the south. It will be remembered that this condition was aggravated by the recent assassination of Lincoln and the accession of Johnson to the Presidency.

Page 144:   "Mr. Worsley's Nightmare." *The Nation,* II, no. 40 (April 5, 1866), 426-28. By "J. R. L." A typed copy of this poem exists in the Harvard Library. On the back of the MS is a memorandum in what looks like Norton's hand identifying it as having been published in *The Nation.* This typescript shows three negligible corrections in Lowell's hand. In the fourth speech of the Frogs, line 2, "in your ocean" is changed to "in all your ocean." The first speech of Bacchus, line 12, corrects "Erebus's" to read "Erebus'." The speech of Worsley, which is the fourth speech from the end of the poem, contains a correction of line 4 from "treading on one's toe" to "stumbling over..."

Page 151:   "Hob Gobbling's Song." *Our Young Folks,* III, no. 1 (January, 1867), 23-24. By "James Russell Lowell." Lowell wrote to

Fields in the fall of 1866: "I have a jolly little poem that would do for a Christmas number, called 'Hob Gobbling's Song,' written years ago for my nephews, now all dead. Just think of it! and three of the four in battle. Who could have dreamed it twenty years ago?" (Scudder, II, 106-7.) The three nephews who died in the Civil War were Charles Russell Lowell, who rose to the rank of Brigadier General and died in October, 1864, from wounds received at the battle of Cedar Creek; James Jackson Lowell, Lieutenant, who was mortally wounded at Glendale, Va., in June, 1862; and William Lowell Putnam, Lieutenant, who was killed in the front of battle at Ball's Bluff in October, 1861. In one of Lowell's notebooks in the Harvard Library are 2 drafts of this poem, here referred to as MS I and MS II. MS I was apparently written throughout with few corrections. MS II, judging from the change in Lowell's hand, was written at a later time and consists of amendments upon MS I, placed on the margins. When Lowell published this poem he made a selection of lines from both MSS and rearranged them in new stanzas. The source of the lines in the present text is indicated in outline below:

Stanza 1, entire: MS I; 11. 7 and 8 also in MS II.

2, entire: MS II.

3, 11. 1-4: MS I; 11. 5-8: MS II.

4, 11. 1-4: MS I; 11. 5 and 6: MS II; 11. 7 and 8: a new interpolation for the printed version.

5, 11. 1-4: MS II; 11. 5-8: MS I.

6, entire: MS I; 1. 8 also in MS II.

7, 11. 1 and 2: identical in both MSS; 11. 3-8: MS II.

8, 11. 1 and 2: a new interpolation for the printed version; 11. 3-8: MS I.

Page 154: "Poseidon Fields, who dost the Atlantic sway." This poem was not published except in the *Letters* and therefore hardly falls within the definition of this volume. It has been included, however, simply because it is a particularly pleasant illustration of Lowell's scholarly high spirits. In a letter to James T. Fields, March 23, 1869 (Huntington Library) Lowell wrote: "I have hammered out fourteen lines to you. . . . Your name does not consent so kindly to an invocation as Stoddard or Taylor or Boker or Richard or Bayard, which, albeit trochees, may well displace an iambus in the first foot.

'Richard, thy verse that like molasses runs,' launches your sonnet without a hitch. I tried at first to evade the difficulty by beginning boldly

'James T., the year in its revolving round
Hath brought once more the tributary pig—' but it wants that classical turn which lends grace to your true sonnet as shaped by the great masters in this kind of writing. So I have hit on another expedient which I think will serve the turn. As I find some of my critics blame me as too scholarly and obscure because I use such words as *microcosm*—which send even *well-read* men to their dictionaries—I have added a few notes." The text is from the original.

Page 155: "Charles Dickens." *Appleton's Journal*, IV, no. 85 (November 12, 1870), 591. By "J. R. Lowell." Not listed in Cooke; noted by Killis Campbell, *Modern Language Notes*, XXXVIII, 121. A MS of this poem exists in the Harvard Library as part of the letter from Lowell to Fields, July 17, 1870. It shows that Lowell was distressed by the current disparagement of Dickens who had died on June 9, a little more than a month before. Lowell was offering the poem to James T. Fields, for publication in either the *Atlantic Monthly* or *Every Saturday*. Lowell wrote: "Instead of going to church today . . . I have written a sermon. It is not a proper sermon, but a cross between that and an epigram—a kind of bull-terrier, in short with the size of the one and the prick-ears and docked tail of the other nor without his special talent for rats . . . my sonnet . . . hit me like a stray shot from nowhere that I could divine, and five minutes saw it finished. So why may it not be good?" For some reason Fields did not use the poem. Robert Carter, who had been co-editor with Lowell in their youthful adventure with the *Pioneer*, was now editing *Appleton's Journal*. In March he had written Lowell requesting contributions. (Scudder, II, 144.) Lowell's reply indicated he was then too busy but apparently Field's rejection gave him opportunity to satisfy his friend's request.

Page 155: "To Madame du Chatelet." *The Poets and Poetry of Europe*, Henry W. Longfellow, ed. (Philadelphia: Porter and Coates, 1871) p. 841. Signed "J. R. Lowell" in the Table of Contents. There is a MS of this poem in the Pierpont Morgan Library dated "14th Feb^y, 1871—" The letter which accompanies the poem is addressed to Miss Alger: "I send you a translation from a little poem of Voltaire, I have hardly done justice (not to say shown mercy to) the charm of the original. But it will serve the purpose for which you want it, I hope."

Page 157: "An Epitaph." *The Nation*, XIX, no. 483 (October 1, 1874), 216. The text is dated "1872." Fifty copies of this were re-

printed as a pamphlet but not published. *James Fisk, Jr.,
An Epitaph,* Worthington C. Ford, Boston: The Merrymount
Press. (Copy in The Historical Society of Pennsylvania.)
This reprint is identical with the present text but for a comma
following the word "wine" in line 2. The pamphlet, however,
contains also a second version of the poem which Lowell pre-
pared tentatively for his volume, *Heartsease and Rue* (1888),
but decided not to include in that work. These circumstances
are explained by Worthington C. Ford in a prefatory note to
the pamphlet, as follows: "The sonnet printed on the next
leaf was written by James Russell Lowell on James Fisk, Jr.,
shot by Edward S. Stokes in the first week of January, 1872.
It was printed in *The Nation,* New York, October 1, 1874.
Thirteen years later a volume of Mr. Lowell's verse was in
preparation, and he intended to include a much altered form
of the Fisk "Epitaph"; but a lawyer advised against it, and his
advice was accepted. "I think you must leave it out," Mr.
Lowell wrote, December 30, 1887. "It will keep." An un-
published letter from George Putnam to Norton, January 16,
1893 (Harvard Library), refers to this matter: "The epigram
(*sic*) on Fiske (*sic*) . . . can now be republished . . . without
risk. I advised them to strike it out of the proofs at the time
because it was clearly libellous on Gould, and although it was
extremely unlikely that he would take any notice of it, he
might make it very uncomfortable for them if he should.

Page 157: "The World's Fair, 1876." *The Nation,* XXI, no. 527 (August
5, 1875), 82. By "J. R. L." Reprinted in Scudder, II, 192, and
last 16 lines reprinted in a footnote, *Letters,* II, 373-74.
Lowell's concern over the apparent breakdown of democratic
processes and justice in the gilded age is concretely exempli-
fied by several references in this poem:

1. "Show 'em your Civil Service:" Senator Boutwell of
   Massachusetts had been, as Lowell said in his letter to
   Joel Benton (January 19, 1876): "a chief obstacle to
   Civil-Service reform (our main hope) . . .
2. "By paying quarters for collecting cents:" Note the
   "Sanborn contracts" in Massachusetts.
3. "By making paper-collars current bills:" obviously a
   reference to monetary inflation by fiat money.
4. The "latest style in martyrs—Tweed"; William M. Tweed
   was almost synonymous with the corrupt political
   "Rings" in city politics to which Lowell refers in the
   last 8 lines. Tweed's martyrdom, to which Lowell sar-

castically refers, consisted of a luxurious existence in the
Ludlow Street jail. Upon his first indictment, four years
earlier, he had been able to offer bond of a million
dollars guaranteed by such men as Jay Gould.

Scudder (II, 190-96) relates this poem with two others of the
same period, "Tempora Mutantur" and "Agassiz" both col-
lected in *Heartsease and Rue*. Scudder made use of the letter
to Joel Benton acknowledging Benton's article, "Mr. Lowell's
Recent Political Verse" (*The Christian Union*, December 10,
1875). Benton's defense was the result of wide-spread criti-
cism of Lowell occasioned by the poet's publication of these
three satiric poems soon after his return from Europe in 1874.
In his letter to Benton, Lowell explains that his satire was not
the result, as his detractors suggested, of any weakening of
his faith in democracy. On the contrary: "I put my sarcasm
into the mouth of Brother Jonathan, thereby implying and
meaning to imply that the common-sense of my countrymen
was awakening to the facts, and that *therefore* things were
not so desperate as they seemed." The corruption of American
political life, Lowell continued, was being used as an argu-
ment in England to foster aristocratic attitudes in that country
and in France. "I came home, and instead of wrath at such
abominations, I found banter."

Page 158: "Campaign Epigrams," *Nation*, XXIII, no. 585 (September 14,
1876), 163; and no. 589 (October 12, 1876), 224. Three "Cam-
paign Epigrams" were published in no. 585 and two in
no. 589. One of these entitled "Defrauding Nature" was re-
printed in the volume *Heartsease and Rue* with the title "The
Boss." It was included in the *Collected Edition*. The remain-
ing four are reproduced here. Of these "The Widow's Mite"
appeared in Scudder, II, 206. These "Campaign Epigrams"
represent the national election of 1876, the disputed election
in which Governor Hayes of Ohio, Republican, ran against
Governor Tilden of New York, the Democrat. Lowell was
deeply interested in this election as a result of his concern for
the reform of political and economic abuses as shown in his
satiric poems of the previous year (see note on "The World's
Fair" above). He took a leading part in the pre-convention
activities of the Republicans of Cambridge, declined to run
for election to the House of Representatives, and accepted
appointment as presidential elector. (Scudder, II, 200-20.)
Some of the references in these "Campaign Epigrams" may
be explained:

1. "A Coincidence": "Banks." Nathaniel Prentiss Banks was then a representative from Massachusetts, having been elected on the Democratic ticket in 1874. As the election of 1876 approached, however, Banks supported the Republican, Hayes. The poem suggests that Lowell did not welcome the support of the political turn-coat Banks.

2. "The Widow's Mite." The MS of this poem is found in the letter to Godkin, September 10, 1876, Harvard Library. The word "Widow" probably referred to General B. F. Butler (see note on "Moieties" below). Butler had been active in Massachusetts politics and was disparagingly mentioned in Lowell's letter to Joel Benton which was referred to in the note on "The World's Fair." Lowell's opposition to Butler was no doubt sharpened by the latter's advocacy of greenback inflation as a means of paying off the Civil War debt, and also by Butler's proven collusion with the Sanborn Contracts to which Lowell also referred in "The World's Fair." (*c.v.*)

3. "Moieties." Among the letters in the Harvard Library there is an anonymous copy of the "Campaign Epigrams." In pencil beside "Moieties" there is this explanation for the word "Widow"; "cant name for General Butler." See note on "The Widow's Mite" above. This poem contains another reference to the Sanborn contracts.

4. "The Astronomer Misplaced." George S. Boutwell, former Governor of Massachusetts, Representative in Congress from 1863-1869, and Secretary of the Treasury under Grant was now United States Senator from Massachusetts. Lowell's irritation at Boutwell's opposition to Civil Service reform has been noted. (See "The World's Fair" above.) The first line of this poem refers to a remark made by Boutwell in a speech during President Johnson's impeachment trial of which he had been appointed one of the Managers in the House of Representatives.

Page 158: "Three Scenes in the Life of a Portrait." In "Mr. Lowell and His Spanish Friends" by Doña Emilia Gayangos de Riaño, who presumably added the footnotes. *Century*, XXXVIII, n. s. (LX), no. 2 (June, 1900), 293. This poem was written by Lowell in reference to a portrait of himself which was in the possession of Doña de Riaño of Madrid. This Spanish friend had been intimate with the Lowells during the mission to Spain. Lowell sent her the poem in January, 1879.

Page 161: "Cuiviscunque." *Specimens of Printing Types in Use at the Marion Press,* Jamaica, Queensborough, New York, 1899. p. 9. This specimen page, "10-point and 8-point Caslon Old-style," prints a letter by Lowell, London, March 18, 1881, addressed to "Lord C." The poem follows the letter. Lowell signed his verses "Quivis" and then added: "At the old stand in Grub-st., where all orders for autographs are supplied at the shortest notice. No connection with any other firm."

Page 161: "Verses." *Atlantic Monthly,* LXXXVI, no. 518 (December, 1900). Three poems are found here: "To P. G. S. Written in a Gift Copy of Mr. Lowell's Poems" (p. 177), "Written in a Copy of 'Among My Books' for P. G. S." (p. 178), and "Written in a Copy of 'Fireside Travels' for P. G. S." These poems were addressed to Phoebe Garnaut Smalley, adopted daughter of Wendell Phillips and wife of George W. Smalley. In the Berg Collection of the New York Public Library will be found the 1881 *Fireside Travels* in which Lowell inscribed this poem. It is addressed "To Mrs. G. W. Smalley with affectionate regards of J. R. L., viii April, 1882." Smalley was the London correspondent (and in charge of the European correspondence) for the New York *Tribune.* The Smalleys summered at Whitby, England and introduced Lowell to this village where he delighted in spending his vacations. Evelyn Smalley (see following note) was one of the daughters.

Page 162: "Verses Written in a copy of Shakspeare." *Century,* LIX, no. 1 (November, 1899), 49. The poem is printed with an introduction by Evelyn G. Smalley (see preceding note). In her childhood Lowell had given her a set of Shakespeare for a birthday present. The poem is dated April 29, 1884.

Page 163: "Street Doors." The only copy of this poem seen by the editor was found in the Harvard Library. It is a newspaper clipping and written along the margin in an unknown hand is found: "St Paul Pioneer—Press, Dec. 31, 1885." The text prints the title, then the following comments: "A Poem. By James Russell Lowell. Now published for the first time. [Copyrighted by Backeller & Co.]"

Page 164: "His Ship." *Harper's Magazine,* LXXXIV, no. 499 (December, 1891), 141-42. There are two MSS of this poem. MS I is in ink in Lowell's hand. It is a part of the material deposited in the Harvard Library by Mrs. L. B. Rantoul. It bears a date, in pencil, possibly in Lowell's hand, "Dec. 1889." Variants between this MS and the magazine text have been indicated in the footnotes 1-29 in the present edition. Since the poem was posthumously published, it is interesting to note that all of these changes in MS are clearly Lowell's except possibly those indicated by notes 3 and 23. MS II dated "December 1889" is not in Lowell's hand. It bears a few minor changes in punctuation. It gives evidence of being later than MS I since it follows the corrections of that MS. There are apparently two errors of transcription: in stanza 3, 1. 4, the word "of" is omitted; in stanza 6, 1. 3, "fruitless" is copied as "faithless." However, there is a fundamental change in the last line of the poem which is indicated in note 30 on the present text.

Page 167: "The Infant Prodigy." *The Nation*, L, no. 1296 (May 1, 1890), 347-48. By "F de T." A MS entitled "The New Septimus Felton" is in the Harvard Library but it lacks stanzas 11, 12, and 13. Scudder, II, 397 quotes the letter from Lowell to Godkin, editor of *The Nation* dated April 29, 1890, offering the poem for publication. The present writer has no explanation for the fact that there would be only two days between the date given by Scudder for Lowell's letter to Godkin and the appearance of the poem under the title "The Infant Prodigy." Lowell's title in the MS refers of course to Hawthorne's posthumous novel *Septimus Felton: or the Elixir of Life.* (1871.) The poem was written at the height of the controversy over the McKinley Tariff Act which McKinley, then Senator, drafted in favor of the "infant industries" represented by the Industrial League, the Iron and Steel Association, and the National Association of Wool Manufacturers.

Page 168: "My Brook." *New York Ledger* Sunday Supplement, December 13, 1890. pp. 20-21. "By James Russell Lowell." Illustrated by Wilson de Meza. This poem was reprinted in Hale, *James Russell Lowell and His Friends,* pp. 285-86, where it follows the *Ledger* text except for minor variations in punctuation, capitalization, and spelling. As illustrative material, Hale also published a facsimile, facing p. 274, of the first 2 and last 2 stanzas of this poem from a signed MS in Lowell's hand, dated "14th Sept.: 1889." Hale lists the MS as "in the possession of the Rev. Minot J. Savage" who was minister at the Church of the Unity in Boston. Lowell sent his friend Savage a copy of the poem before its publication. This MS is now in the Berg Collection at the New York Public Library and is referred to in the variant readings as MS II. An earlier MS of

the poem is in the possession of Mrs. Lois Cunningham and
in the variant readings is MS I.

Page 171:   "In a Volume of Sir Thomas Browne." *Atlantic Monthly,*
LXVI, no. 393 (July, 1890), 63. By "James Russell Lowell."
This poem was reprinted "from the *Atlantic Monthly*" in
Critic, XVII, no. 343 (July 26, 1890), 49.

Page 172:   "Inscription for a Memorial Bust of Fielding." *Atlantic
Monthly,* LXVI, no. 395 (September, 1890), 322. By "James
Russell Lowell." Reprinted "from the *Atlantic Monthly*" in
Critic, XVII, no. 348 (August 30, 1890), 108 and in *Literary
News,* n.s. XII, no. 2 (February, 1891), 59. Greenslet, p. 234,
quotes a letter from Lowell to Aldrich, May 8, 1890, which
enclosed a group of poems for the *Atlantic:* "The Fielding I
had forgotten and found written on the back of a letter.
I wrote it when I unveiled the bust of F. at Taunton, but
never offered it to the burghers of that town." In the Harvard
Library among the materials deposited by Mrs. L. B. Rantoul
is a MS of this poem. On one side in Lowell's hand are these
lines:

> Sad Fielding looked (or Hogarth saw him so)
> From hand to foot a man of English build,
> Truth's too frank friend

(Originally "Truth's too outspoken friend") On the other side
of the MS, the poet began again and composed what is prob-
ably the first draft of the poem as it appears in the *Atlantic.*
The variant readings are shown in the notes to the text in this
edition.

Page 172:   "For a Birthday." *Cosmopolitan,* XIII, no. 2 (June, 1892), 162.
There is a MS version of this poem in the Harvard Library
among the materials deposited by Mrs. L. B. Rantoul.

Page 173:   "I am driven by my longing." *Century,* XLVIII, n.s. XXVI,
no. 1 (May, 1894), 26-27. This translation is illustrative mate-
rial in a prose selection, perhaps from Lowell's lecture notes.
Lowell wrote: "Let me read you a few passages from a poem
which grew up under the true conditions of natural and primi-
tive literature—remoteness, primitiveness of manners, and de-
pendence on native traditions. I mean the epic of Finland—
Kalevala." Lowell's translation is of the first 82 and the last
99 lines of the poem. Norton footnotes the poem: "This trans-
lation is Mr. Lowell's, and, so far as I know, has not been
printed."

Page 177:   "Verses." *Atlantic Monthly,* LXXXVI, no. 518 (December,

1900), 721-22. The first of these three separate poems bears the heading: "To P. G. S. Written in a Gift Copy of Mr. Lowell's Poems." The second poem is headed: "Written in a Copy of 'Among My Books' for P. G. S." The third poem was "Written in a Copy of 'Fireside Travels' for P. G. S." (See pp. 178 and 161.)

Page 178:   "Verses." See preceding note.

COLLEGE VERSE

Harvardiana. (See Introduction, p. xii.) The following six-
teen poems are from this undergraduate magazine the winter
of 1837-38. As one of the five editors, Lowell sent the follow-
ing poem to William H. Shackford, August 24, 1837. The text
is from the original in the Harvard Library.

Dear Shack a circular I send ye
The whilk I hope will not offend ye;
If sae, 'twad tak' Auld Nick to mend ye
 O' sic an ill
But, gin ye are as when I kenn'd ye
 It never will!

Gin ye could get ae body's name
'Twad add forever to his fame
To help to kindle up the flame
 O' sic a journal
Whose reputation though quite lame
 Will be eternal.

Now gif ye do your vera best
In this maist glorious behest
By gettin' names and a' the rest
 I need na tell
Yese thus fulfil the airn'st request
 O'

 J. R. L.

Page 181: "Homer's neu Heldengedicht." IV, no. I (September, 1837),
18-25. By "R." This poem and the fifteen that follow it
all appeared unsigned, except as indicated, in *Harvardiana*,
September, 1837 to July, 1838. Cambridge: Published by
John Owen.

Page 187: "In Imitation of Burns." IV, no. I (September, 1837), 31.

Page 188: "Dramatic Sketch." IV, no. I (September, 1837), 39-40.

Page 191: "The Serenade." IV, no. II (October, 1837), 65.

Page 192: "What Is It?" IV, no. II (October, 1837), 57. By "S."

Page 193: "Saratoga Lake." IV, no. III (November, 1837), 111-13.

Page 195: "Scenes from an Unpublished Drama." IV, no. IV (January,
1838), 143-49.

Page 202: "Skillygoliana. No. II." IV, no. IV (January, 1838), 157-59.

The "Skillygoliana" was a series of four papers whose purpose
was expressed by Lowell in the first paper: "For a long time
a dim shadow of an idea has been floating in our brain, that
it would be a good plan, (instead of committing to the devour-
ing element the "rejected addresses" of our correspondents,) to
select from them such passages as possessed merit in any way,
and string them together, thus saving ourselves some brain-
harrowing productions, and the printer's devil some sole
leather." The materials in prose and verse which composed
"Skillygoliana" seem to be from various hands. Certain pas-
sages have been identified as Lowell's by his bibliographers.
Of these only the verse has been reproduced, except for one
related prose passage. As for the name, Hale (pp. 37-38) says:
"The choice of the title 'Skillygoliana,' was, without doubt,
Lowell's own. 'Skillygolee' is defined in the Century Diction-
ary in words which give the point to his use of it: 'A poor,
thin, watery kind of broth or soup . . . served out to prisoners
in the hulks, paupers in workhouses, and the like; a drink
made of oatmeal, sugar, and water, formerly served out to
sailors in the British navy.'"

Page 205: "Skillygoliana. No. III." IV, no. V (February, 1838), 196-97.
This poem was published in part in Hale, p. 38.

Page 206: "Uhland's 'Des Knaben Berglied.'" IV, no. VII (April, 1838),
277-78.

Page 207: "A Dead Letter." IV, no. VIII (May, 1838), 317.

Page 208: "Extracts from a 'Hasty Pudding Poem.'" IV, no. IX (June,
1838), 343-45. A portion of this poem was printed in Hale,
p. 39. This poem is an extract from the minutes of the Hasty
Pudding Club, of which Lowell was secretary from January
11, 1837 to April 28, 1837 and from July 7, 1837 to January 12,
1838.

Page 211: "Translations from Uhland: 'Das Ständchen.'" IV, no. IX
(June, 1838), 352. By "A.B."

Page 211: "Translations from Uhland: 'Der Weisse Hirsch.'" IV, no. IX
(June, 1838), 353. By "A.B."

Page 212: "To Mount Washington." IV, no. X (July, 1838), 387-88.
A MS of this poem forms part of a letter to George B. Loring,
July 25, 1838. (Harvard Library.) This MS contains the mar-
ginal glosses shown in the notes to the text. Lowell wrote
Loring: "Some of it satisfies me. I have some idea of sending
it to the Courier, or to Nat. Hale to publish in the Respectable
Daily."

Page 214: "Song." IV, no. X (July, 1838), 389-90. A MS version in a letter to George B. Loring, August 17, 1838 exists (Harvard Library). Part of the letter and the poem were printed in Scudder, I, 54-55, with changes in punctuation. Lowell, in printing the poem in *Harvardiana,* made certain changes which are shown in the footnotes to the text. The "Miss B." referred to in the MS version was Caroline Brooks then betrothed to E. R. Hoar. As Lowell admitted to Loring, "she runs in my head and heart more than she has any right to." Following the poem, the author wrote with boyish enthusiasm, "By Jove I like that better than anything I have written for this 2 years! . . . it ran off the end of my pen so that it must be better than I can make it, why, I *like* it. I do." .

Page 216:   "To the Class of '38, By their Ostracized Poet, (so called,) J.R.L." This was printed as a broadside, evidently for distribution to the members of the Class of 1838 and their friends. A copy of the broadside, addressed in Lowell's hand to G. B. Loring, North Andover, is in the Harvard Library. A photograph of this broadside was published in Hale, opposite p. 50.

Page 217:   *Class Poem.* Cambridge Press: Metcalf, Torry, and Ballou, 1838. Completed under protest during Lowell's rustication at Concord. See letters to George B. Loring July 1, 8, 25, and August 9, 1838, and letter from Loring August 19, 1838 (Harvard Library). Letters from Eben Wright July 3, 20, 1838 and letter from Nathan Hale, Jr. August 20, 1838 (Harvard Library). The suppressed dedication to which Lowell refers in his note (1) was evidently a disparagement of Francis Bowen, a tutor from 1835-39 at Harvard who was partly responsible for Lowell's rustication and who was unpopular with the Harvard students. In Dr. Francis Burnett's MSS is a letter, July 3, 1838, from Mrs. Charles R. Lowell, Lowell's sister-in-law, who joins her husband in advising against the publication of the poem. It recommends some interesting changes in certain lines. Evidently Lowell had sent her the poem with a request for criticism. Small portions of this poem have been printed in Scudder and Hale and various later critics have referred to and quoted from the poem.

See Introduction, p. xvii.

BIBLIOGRAPHY

BIBLIOGRAPHY

Bibliography

Campbell, Killis. "Bibliographical Notes on Lowell." *Studies in English,* no. 4, University of Texas Bulletin, no. 2411 (March 15, 1924), pp. 115-19.

——, "Lowell's Uncollected Poems." *Publications of the Modern Language Association,* XXXVIII, no. 4 (December, 1923), 933-37.

——, "Three Notes on Lowell." *Modern Language Notes,* XXXVIII, no. 2 (February, 1923), 121-22.

Chamberlain, Jacob Chester and Livingston, Luther Samuel. *A Bibliography of the First Editions in Book Form of the Writings of James Russell Lowell.* New York: Privately printed, The De Vinne Press, 1914.

Cooke, George Willis. *A Bibliography of James Russell Lowell.* Boston: Houghton, Mifflin and Company, 1906.

Joyce, Hewette Elwell. "A Bibliographical Note on James Russell Lowell." *Modern Language Notes,* XXXV, no. 4 (April, 1920), 249-50.

Lowell's Writings

Manuscripts: Harvard University Library, Pierpont Morgan Library, New York Public Library, Huntington Library.

The Complete Writings of James Russell Lowell. Elmwood Edition. 16 volumes. XIV, XV, XVI, *Letters of James Russell Lowell.* Charles E. Norton, ed. Boston: Houghton, Mifflin and Company, 1904.

New Letters of James Russell Lowell. M. A. De Wolfe Howe, ed. New York: Harper and Brothers, 1932.

The Anti-Slavery Papers of James Russell Lowell. William Belmont Parker, ed., 2 volumes. Boston: Houghton, Mifflin and Company, 1902.

Class Poem. Cambridge Press: Privately printed, Metcalf, Torry and Ballou, 1838.

A Year's Life. Boston: C. C. Little and J. Brown, 1841.

Poems. Cambridge: John Owen, 1844.

Poems. Second Series. Cambridge: George Nichols. Boston: B. B. Mussey and Company, 1848.

A Fable for Critics. New York: G. P. Putnam, 1848.

The Biglow Papers. Cambridge: George Nichols. New York: G. P. Putnam, 1848.

The Vision of Sir Launfal. Cambridge: George Nichols, 1848.

Poems. 2 volumes. Boston: Ticknor, Reed, and Fields, 1849.

Il Pesceballo. Words by F. J. Child, English text by Lowell. Cambridge: Privately printed, 1862.

The Biglow Papers. Second Series. Boston: James R. Osgood and Company, 1867.

Under the Willows. Boston: Fields, Osgood and Company, 1869.

The Cathedral. Boston: Fields, Osgood and Company, 1870.

Heartsease and Rue. Boston: Houghton, Mifflin and Company, 1888.

Last Poems of James Russell Lowell. Boston: Houghton, Mifflin and Company, 1895.

The Power of Sound: A Rhymed Lecture. New York: Privately printed, The Gilliss Press, 1896.

INDEX OF TITLES

286 *Index of Titles*

INDEX OF FIRST LINES

289